DIMENSIONS OF RURAL DEVELOPMENT IN NORTH-EAST INDIA

DIMENSIONS OF RURAL DEVELOPMENT IN NORTH-EAST INDIA

EDITED BY
B. Datta Ray
Gurudas Das

AKANSHA PUBLISHING HOUSE
NEW DELHI-110 059 (INDIA)

AKANSHA PUBLISHING HOUSE
R 37-B, Vani Vihar, Uttam Nagar
New Delhi-110059
Email: ektabooks@yahoo.com
Ph. : 25640621

DIMENSIONS OF RURAL DEVELOPMENT IN NORTH-EAST INDIA

First Edition 2004
ISBN 81–87606–23-1

[The responsibility for the facts stated, conclusions reached etc. is entirely that of the Authors. The publisher and Editors are not responsible for them, whatsoever.]

PRINTED IN INDIA

Published by M.P. Misra for Akansha Publishing House, New Delhi and Printed at Mehra Offset Press, Delhi.

PREFACE

Rural development in most of the developing countries has remained an illusive agenda. The urban bias inherent in the process of market-led growth calls for state activism in order to counter the market imperfections and failures to boost up the rural economies. The enclave nature of growth in the developing countries including India has significantly widened the rural-urban disparity in terms of economic opportunities and basic minimum services that people value in their life. In fact, the urban civilization is outpacing its rural counterparts at lightening speed. Besides economic opportunities, the image of urban culture is also increasingly pushing the age old rural heritage out of the cultural consciousness of the nations.

Since independence India has evolved an elaborate institutional framework to look after the developmental needs of the rural sector. This institutional structure, through which the programmes designed specifically for rural development are executed, has also undergone changes over time. From Community Development Block approach, emphasized during the 1950s and 60s, to Panchayati Raj since the 1990s. Besides the shifts in implementing institutional units, more and more content has also been added to the programmes of rural development over time in order to tackle the widening urban rural disparity.

The heterogeneous impact of the rural development programmes upon the spatio-temporal plain calls for their area specific evaluation. This book, the outcome of a seminar on "Rural Development, Small Industries and Peoples' Participation in North East India", held on December 10-11, 2001, organised by The North eastern Council for Social Science Rese arch (NE IC S S R), at Shillong, attempts to assess the state of sectoral development of the rural economies, impact of the rural development programmes, functioning of the implementing agencies and peoples' participation in them in the North Eastern Region.

B. Datta Ray
Gurudas Das

CONTENTS

INDUSTRY, ENTREPRENEURSHIP AND MARKET

TECHNOLOGY, TOURISM AND COOPERATION

EDUCATION, GENDER AND POVERTY

CONTRIBUTORS

Agarwal, A.K., Department of Economics, Mizoram University, Aizawl-796007.

Alam, K., 7 Mile, Jalukbari, Guwahati-780014.

Alam, Sazzad, 7 Mile, Jalukbari, Guwahati-780014.

Baishya, Prabin, Manik Kutir, P. Kakati Road, Sualkuchi, Kamrup, Assam.

Banerjee, Amalesh, 100 B, Netaji Subhash Chandra Bose Road, Regent Park, Kolkatta-700044.

Bhattacharya, Prasanta, Department of Geography, Gauhati University, Guwahati.

Bhattacharyya, T.N., Department of Geography, Gauhati University, Guwahati.

Chakraborty, Gorky, Department of Economics, Doom Dooma College, Dibrugarh, Assam.

Das, Gurudas, Department of Economics, North Eastern Hill University, Shillong793014.

Das, Susmita, Department of Geography, St. Mary's College, Shollong, Meghalaya.

De, Utpal Kumar, Department of Economics, North Eastern Hill University, Shillong793014.

Ghosh, Anjali, Psychology Research Unit, Indian Statistical Institute, Kolkatta.

Ghosh, Bhola Nath, Sociological Research Unit, Indian Statistical Institute, Kolkatta.

Goswami, Chayanika, FORE School of Management, Kutub Institutional Area, New Delhi-110016.

Hazarika, Bolin, Department of Political Science, Gauhati University, Guwahati.

Khonglah, M.P., State Resource Centre, Shillong.

Lahiri, Tarun Bikas, 5/40, ID Dum Dum Road, Kolkatta-700030.

Lyndem, B., State Resource Centre, Shillong.

Panda, B., Department of Economics, I.G. Govt. College, Tezu, Arunachal Pradesh.

Phukon, Girin, Department of Political Science, Dibrugarh University, Dibrugarh, Assam.

Prasain, G.P., Department of Commerce, Manipur University, Imphal-795003.

Rajput, Kishore S., Department of Economics, St. Anthony's College, Shillong-793001.

Sarma, Nripendra N., Assam Institute of Management, Guwahati.

Sarma, Suranjan, Department of Economics, Demoria College, Khetri, Kamrup, Assam.

Satapathy, K.K., Division of Agricultural Engineering, ICAR, Barapani-793103, Meghalaya.

Sengupta, Sutapa, Department of Geography, St. Mary's College, Shillong-793003.

Singh, Chandrika, Department of Political Science, Nagaland University, Nagaland.

Singh, Rajmoni, Department of Commerce, Manipur University, Imphal-795003.

Singh, R.K.P., Division of Agricultural Engineering, ICAR, Barapani-793103, Meghalaya.

APPROACHES TO RURAL DEVELOPMENT

1

RURAL DEVELOPMENT: Need for Agricultural and Small Scale Industrial Development in North-east India

A. K. Agarwal

Almost all underdeveloped countries are characterised by lack of employment opportunities, especially in the rural areas and India is no exception. As in most developing countries the trend rate of growth in India has been higher in the modern industrial and service sectors both of which are urban based - than in the agricultural sector (Chenery and Syrquin, 1986). There has been much debate about how much India's poor have shared in the country's economic growth. The optimism of many of Indian post independence planners, who believed that the country's (largely urban based) industrialisation would bring lasting long term gains to both the urban and rural poor, has not been shared by many critics. Revallion and Datt (1996) noted that growth in both primary and tertiary sectors was poverty reducing, the tertiary sector generating a larger impact; though the difference between the two sectors is not significant. By contrast secondary sector growth had no significant impact on the rate of poverty reduction in either urban or rural areas. Fostering the conditions in the rural economy in both primary and tertiary sectors must thus be considered central to an effective strategy for development and poverty reduction in India. Growth and diversification of production through new technology and managerial skill has had big impact.

Development in backward countries, necessarily implies rural development which is by and large a comprehensive issue to be conceived and attempted, considering the complexities and vastness of rural scenario special efforts are necessary to tackle the problem, especially of the rural poor (Agarwal, 1996). Such development encompasses growth, improvement in equity, health care, nutrition, education and ecological balance. Thus rural development includes an overall development of the rural population.

Agriculture and Rural Development

Agriculture plays a unique role as a supplier of food and its importance lies to the welfare of the farmers and others in the rural population, and its role in the economic development. As economies develop the share of agricultural labour to total labour falls to 2 to 3 percent. In that way off-farm migration helps the development of the rest of the economy. As more people leave agriculture, the economic base on non-agriculture increases, boosting migration rates. But as labour leaves agriculture, labour productivity in agriculture increases, income differentials falls and migration declines. So off-farm migration leads simultaneously to an increase of income in the rural sector and to development of non-agriculture. This process takes a long time to complete, however (Larson and Mundlak: 1995).

About 70 percent of the area of North-East is hilly and mountainous accommodating about 30 per cent of the regional population. The rural population of North-East is essentially of peasant farmers. Farming system in the hills is dominated by age-old primitive method of shifting cultivation or slash and burn method. The average annual operational area under *jhum* cultivation is between 1 to 1. 5 hectare per family (Maithani, 1995). With rapid increase in population over the years, fallow period has been reduced from 10 years and more to 3 to 4 years, in most hill areas. As a result of high population density in the valley (the main producing areas of the region) the land holding size has been reduced to uneconomic levels, e.g., more than 80 per cent of farmers in Assam are small farmers and above 60 per cent of holding is of less than 1 hectare size. The galloping population has increased pressure on the land resources resulting in widening of disparities both between and within communities as clans who traditionally had less access to land are most under pressure. The region is net importer of foodgrains from neighbouring states estimated at 1.5 million tons annually, huge quantity of animal protein and other consumer goods.

Natural vegetation represents an important factor of production in the context of shifting cultivation. Over-exploitation of this factor may cause significant loss of income among rural communities. The long fallow period plays important role of replenishing the fertility of the land by allowing natural vegetation to grow which is incorporated into the soil as natural fertility (Usually as ashes after burning) at the time of cultivation. The short fallow period due to population pressure leads to insufficient growth of natural vegetation and consequently to low soil fertility, soil instability, flooding and sliding. Thus the rich vegetation during a long fallow period is a form of capital that accumulates and is eventually used at the time of cultivation. The closed forest areas (undisturbed by cultivation) also play important protection against soil erosion, watershed destruction and flooding.

The growing pressure of population requires expansion of the cultivated land either by diminishing forest land or by reducing the length of the fallow periods. Both the phenomenon are present in the north-east. An increase in land size under cultivation has a direct output-increasing effect at the cost of reducing the natural capital, thus reducing agricultural productivity. An optimal fraction of the land should be cultivated in order to maximise social income. If the level of land cultivated is above or below the optimum, income is reduced. Since the biomass is an important factor of production, the large losses of forest and the considerable reduction in fallow periods over the past few decades have implied a considerable loss of productive natural capital that is likely to have reduced by productivity of labour and other resources.

The village ownership or community ownership of land provides the farmers exclusive rights on the land usually for as long as they cultivate it. Individual cultivators act as if the biomass resource has no social costs beyond the purely private costs clearing the land. They try to over exploit the natural resources by cultivating too much. In deciding how much land to cultivate, farmers in this case are likely to consider only the private costs, ignoring contemporary and inter-temporal effects on other cultivators.

In case of adequate community controls, individuals would behave as if they fully accounted for both the private and social costs of clearing land. This part is well taken care by the villagers while going for allotment of jhum land for cultivation to the individuals but still some scope of clearing forest land can not be ruled out causing diminishing of the forest lands. Further; the individual cultivators are not prone to use usually expensive substitute inputs, i.e., chemical fertilisers, for natural vegetation (and thus increase land productivity) as long as forest or fallow communal lands are available for clearing. The communities often fail to develop adequate controls on the use of communal resources because of population growth and rapid westernisation of traditional values.

It is possible that an efficient allocation of common resources requires certain specific conditions to facilitate collective action and that such conditions are not always present in most poor countries. In general, it appears that efficiency of the commons tends to be present in communities with low density of population where the transaction and monitoring costs are low (Baland and Platteau, 1996). The paradox is that it is precisely in case of high and rapid increasing population density that collective action is most needed to achieve an efficient use of common resources (Lopez, 1998).

Poorer countries with lower ratio of wages to rents, rely more on labour than on machines. The advanced techniques are more capital (human and physical) intensive, the capital scarcity determines the pace at which new techniques along with decisions on input demand are implemented. Speedy and effective efforts should be made for developing location specific production technologies and to carry them quickly to the farms. Availability of inputs at reasonable rates and the desired quantity should be assured. The focus of the agricultural policy should be the small and marginal farmers, therefore, radical changes are required in our subsidy policy and in the structure of subsidies as well as of other policies.

The north-east is encountered with a serious threat as to how to match fast growing labour force with employment. For this purpose new job opportunities in non-farm sector should be created. The non-farm activities of rural workforce are found to be casual in nature but yield larger income comparing what the traditional occupations would have done. It has been noticed that the industrialised and urbanised centres do have influence on the adjoining rural areas to diversify the occupational pattern of rural households. Iyyampillai and Jayakumar (1997) suggest that the degree of urbanisation and literacy rate appear to be the two major factors that influence the levels of non-farm employment. Most of the rural workforce engaged in non-farm activities belong to the category of less educated and traditionally skilled and thereby are forced to work under poor working and wage conditions. Emphasis has to be laid on training in various non-farm activities to these persons for gainful employment.

The jhumias support their family income and supplement consumption from livestock, a grove of bamboo, coconut, arecanut, backyard fishpond, traditional loom, handicraft skill and the cropping pattern on jhum land, which represents a complex mix of inter-crops including paddy, maize, beans, tapioca, ginger, chillies and a range of vegetables. All these constituents make a viable asset base for a self-reliant and sustainable economy. The approach to develop the hilly areas should be to build up this asset base rather than distributing inputs and doling out assistance which are rarely used and adopted properly. This however calls for adoption of radically different methods and approaches to development involving active participation of the people at all stages of decision making.

Industrial Setting

As on March 1994, the region had 166 large and medium scale industries. Out of these industries, more than 70 percent were in Assam. Some of them have been declared sick. Practically speaking there is hardly any large or medium private industry outside Assam. Gross output per employee as well as fixed capital per employee is less in the region compare to all India average. This indicates either low fixed capital or over-employment. Net value added is high in states having oil, and gas or mining industries like Assam, Meghalaya and Tripura. But it is negative in Manipur (Sachdeva, 1998 : 32).

Sachdeva has further noted that the major contribution of value of output by manufacturing industries in the region are in food sector, wood and wood products, nonmetallic mineral products, rubber plastic and petroleum and in paper products. In Assam and Tripura about half of the units are in the food sector. In Nagaland 71 percent of them are in wood products. In Meghalaya 64 percent are based on mineral products. Outside these four or five areas, there is hardly any industry. Overall, the region contributes little over 1 percent to the value of output of manufacturing factory sector of India (Sachdeva: 1998:34).

It must be understood that private capital is a critical component for industrial progress in the region. Higher levels of private investments are essential to generate productive employment, to raise productivity and improve work culture. Despite announcements and appointing many commissions, the centre is less likely (or less able) to increase public expenditure to remove infrastructural bottlenecks, Therefore, the bulk of capital that will be required to improve supply responses in the region will ultimately have to come from private rather than government sources. Under the given circumstances attracting private capital should be given highest priority compared to what has been so far. At least as much effort should be devoted to this task as is devoted to securing aid from the centre.

Nearly three-fourth of territorial spread of the region covers hill terrain intersected with innumerable streams and rivers. For this reason development of transport and communication network are seriously handicapped. Under this situation, industrialization programme need to be structurally decentralised by setting up of small scale and household industries based on locally available resources using labour intensive technology producing goods and service for meeting local and regional demand. It is the small industries and household industries which should occupy the core position in rural development programmes.

Rural Industrialization and People's Participation

It has boon asserted since long that for balanced development of the country suitable industries have to be developed in rural areas which would help gradually in upgrading the simple production techniques used by village artisans, weavers, blacksmiths and a host of other functionaries. Rural industrialisation would transform a stagnant rural economy into dynamic industrialised economy. Besides it would develop local entrepreneurship. For example, the establishment of agro-processing units on co-operative basis in Maharashtra is encouraging agriculturists to become entrepreneurs too.

Rural industrialisation (Jain, 1974) has to be differentiated from the approaches followed so far. It involves full participation of the local factors and agents in the establishment of industries. The villages will be the growth centres, and agriculture will be the kingpin on the base. The mode of rural industrialisation depend upon the nature of industrial activity, access to resources and availability of marketing opportunities to individual enterprise as well as the level of skill and enterprise. When production is to be carried on a large scale or the nature of processing is such that large scale production could be viable and which is justified as well from the point of view of productivity and growth, large units in the cooperative sector should be encouraged. If production can be carried out conveniently on a small scale basis in family households, individuals may be encouraged to set up such units fitted with modified technology.

Any judgement on new technology should be arrived at by looking interrelated aspects of costs, scale and employment. Research in evolving suitable technology supported with training facilities to use the technology must receive a high priority. The rural industrial units facing no competition from urban organised industries should be promoted by strengthening the marketing arrangement, easy credit supply, and adequate supply of inputs at reasonable prices. The emergence of new industries also depends on network of science and technology, availability of basic infrastructure like power, communication and transport (Agarwal,1993).

We should link the agro-industries witl the needs of rural people and produce the major part of their forward and backward linkages within the village economy. The backward linkages in the farm and allied activities are most effectively produced by agro-industries, but the surplus that these activities produce gets mostly appropriated outside the area because their product have a demand which is mostly urban. On the other hand, industries producing inputs for agricultural and allied production would produce forward linkages but the material required for their output mostly comes from urban areas. Local skills and technology can very well be used in these industries, but the modernisation of agriculture itself leads to the change in the nature and quality of inputs required.

It has been noted that both in respect of articles of consumption as well as inputs used in agriculture, the relative price movements show a gain for the agriculturists in the post-reform period. Parikh *et al.*, (1995) while supporting the reforms in favour of the agricultural growth point out that measures for liberalisation of trade and industry already introduced are likely to have a beneficial impact on agriculture in the long run by turning the terms of trade in its favour, which may attract greater investment into this sector. However, it may be noted that a mere favourable price environment by itself may not be sufficient to evoke adequate supply response by attracting private investment unless public investment in infrastructure and human resource development is stepped up in the less developed areas for ensuring a broad-based and employment-oriented growth. Hanumantha Rao (1996) observed that the development policy has to be more inclusive, concerned not merely with 'structural adjustment' with a view to simultaneously making friendly to the poor basically by strengthening their socio-economic position. In tribal belts and the hills of country where the impact of green revolution had not been noticed, the rural development strategy should comprise of extension of cultivable area under settled cultivation in place of shifting cultivation, shifting of jhumias in some other fruitful occupation under TRYSEM programme, creation of gainful employment opportunities by using available agricultural, horticultural and forest potential. It calls for vigorous approach for creating suitable industrial climate for exploiting such vast potential. Some of the industries emphasising on value added include livestock feed, processed food industry, rice mills, and rice husk-based units, soyabean - based edible, oil mills, production of starch and sago from tapioca roots, ginger-based oleoresin and ayurvedic drug units, rubber, tea, coffee plantation and their produce-based processing units, citronella oil-based industries producing numerous cosmetics, perfumery and pharmaceutical products of common use, fruit processing units based on abundantly grown horticultural products like pineapple, banana, apple, orange, guava and papaya, etc.

Cash crops successfully grown in the north-east region of the country needs attention including cashew, coconut, and saffron cultivation on commercial scale. Experimental plantation of black pepper, cinnamon and coffee have given promising results. The cultivation of these crops will contribute a lot in the economy of this region.

Animal husbandry is an age-old activity in the hills and tribal areas but there is hardly any industry based on dairy products and animal wastes like hides, skins, bones and other by products of slaughter houses. Other units include piggery with ancillary bacon processing, broiler and other poultry farms units for polishing and egg grading in main production centres and livestock feed units.

Conclusion

Rural industrialisation should form an integral part of the overall strategy of hill area development and should be accompanied by and well integrated with the development of agriculture. Finally any strategy for the development of hilly and tribal areas should cautiously take care of the traditional skills, crafts, occupation of the people, their needs, aspirations, constraints, limitations and inherent capabilities. In most cases, it may be more necessary to evolve appropriate technology depending upon its local conditions than to transfer already existing technologies. Above all strenuous efforts towards generating awareness about the utilities and usefulness of the newly developed technologies need to be mobilised as a prerequisite for their introduction in the area. Training in relevant areas should be another priority item.

REFERENCES

Agarwal, A.K., (1993), "Rural Development in Tribal Areas Through Agro-Industries", in V.S Mahajan, (ed), *Employment Through Rural Development: Towards Sustainability*, Deep & Deep Publications, New Delhi, p.296.

Agarwal, A. K., (1996), Prospects of Rural and Agricultural Development", in V.S. Mahajan, (ed), *Agriculture, Rural Development and Panchayati Raj*, Vol. 1, Deep & Deep Publications, New Delhi, pp. 195-205.

Baland, J.M and J.P Platteau, (1996), *Halting Degradation of Natural Resources*, Oxford, FAO and Clarendon Press.

Chenery, H.B., and Moshe Syrquin, (1986), "Typical Patterns of Transformation", in H.B. Chenery, S. Robinson and Moshe Syrquin, (eds), *Industrialisation and Growth*, Oxford University Press, New York.

Hanumantha Rao, C.H., (1996), "Economic Reforms, Agricultural Growth and Rural Poverty: Some Reflections on the Relevance of East and South-East Asian Experience for India", The Indian Economic Journal, Vol. 43. No. 4 April-June, pp. 1-11.

Iyyampillai. S. and N. Jayakumar, (1997), "Non-Farm Employment and Income in Rural Tamil Nadu : An Analysis of Macro and micro Level Data, Political Economy Journal of India, Vol. 6 No. 3 & 4, July-December, pp. 136-39.

Jain, O.P., (1974), *Rural Industrialisation*, Commercial Publication Bureau, New Delhi. p. 13.

Larson, Donald and Yair Mundlak., (1995), "On the International Migration of Agricultural Labour", Policy Research Working Paper, 1425, World Bank International Economics Department, Washington, D.C. quoted in World Bank Policy and Research Bulletin, January–March, 1997. p. 2.

Lopez, Ramon, (1998), "The Tragedy of the Commons in the Cognitive Agriculture: Empirical Evidence and Implications for Evaluating Trade Policies", The World Bank Economic Review, Vol. 12. No.1 January, pp.103-31.

Maithani, B.P., (1995), "Subsistence is Sustainable: Thoughts on Rural Development in North East India and the 21st century", *Journal of the NEC*, Vol. 15 No.1, January-March, p.2.

Parikh, K., *et. al.*, (1995), "Strategies for Agricultural Liberalisation, Consequences for Growth", Welfare and Distribution, Indira Gandhi *Institute of Development Research*, Mumbai, (Mimeo).

Revallion, Martin, and Gaurav Datt, (1996), "How important to India's poor is the Sectoral Composition of Economic Growth", The *World Bank Economic Review*, Vol 10. No.1, January, pp.1-25.

Sachdeva, Gulshan, (1998), "Economic Situation in North-East (Draft Report), Centre for Policy Research", Dharma Marg, Chanakyapuri, New Delhi, pp.32-34.

2

RURAL DEVELOPMENT IN NORTH-EAST : An overview

Tarun Bikas Lahiri

M.S. Swaminathan, the celebrated agricultural scientist told in course of a speech on Rural Poor, 'Famines in India are not famines of food, but of work. There are 9 crore jobless in India right now with more than 70 lakh additional people entering into the job market every year. The industries can absorb barely 5 lakh of these new entrants leaving more than 65 lakh which yearly add to the enormous pool of unemployed'. Though the remark was made in 1981, there has been no significant change of situation. What Swaminathan underlined is absolutely true. Currently there are 60 million tones of surplus food grains languishing in FCI godowns (2002) yet a substantial percentage of rural poor cannot secure two full meals a day due to lack of purchasing power. This situation can only be reversed if sustainable employment could be created in rural areas. Increase of employment will come only through a change which requires prevention of natural degradation, rise in productivity, starting of new enterprises which demands proper planning and organization. In order to develop strategies for change, a quick look at the present state may be helpful.

As more than 70% (72.22 % in 2001) of India's population is rural, overwhelming proportion of people below poverty line live in villages of India. Such rural-urban difference is expected to be same in North-East states also. Because, except Mizoram, all the N-E states are much less urbanized than Indian average. So, by and large, due to dominance of rural habitat, N-E is poorer than other regions.

Percentage of population living below poverty line

	1987-88	*1989-90*
Rural	33.4	28.4
Urban	20.1	19.3
Total	29.9	25.8

Source : Indian Economy, Vol. 1, Sept 1991, CMIE, Mumbai.

OVERVIEW OF RURAL SITUATION

N-E Rural Population and its Distribution

By 2001 census, seven N-E states of Arunachal Pradesh, Assam, Manipur, Meghalaya, Mizoram, Nagaland and Tripura have a combined rural population of 32,523,012 persons. Assam, the most populous state in the region has highest percentage of rural population of N-E (71.5 %). Tripura, the second most populous state in N-E., is way behind Assam holding about 8% of N.E's rural population.

In the N-E region nearly 40,000 villages bear the load of 32.5 million people. Average population size of a village is less than 1000. Average village size is highest in Tripura (3093) and lowest in Arunachal Pradesh (238). Rural population distribution pattern provides direction for framing development strategies.

Table 1 shows rural population, number of villages and average size of the villages by states of the North-East as in 2001(however number of villages by states are of 1991).

N-E : Overall demographic features

Table 2 presents overall demographic features of N-E states, levels of literacy, urbanization etc. Total area of 7 N-E states is 255,028 sq. km, habitat of about 38.5 million persons in 2001 and support 3.74% of India's population. However, as the N-E. States are dominantly rural, so, out of India's total rural population of 741,660,293 in 2001. N-E states cover 8% of India's population. N-E states share of rural population is 4.38%. In all the N-E. states except Assam, density of population is less than national average. In case of urbanization, all N-E states except Mizoram are behind national average. Assam is most populous with least urbanization, Mizoram is the least populous with highest urbanisation. By literacy rate, N-E states are more or less same as that of national average. But Mizoram outshines with nearly 91% male and 86% female literacy, followed by Tripura. However literacy rate has little impact on decadal (1991-2001) population growth rate which is higher than national rate except Triupura and Assam which showed a lower growth rate. Nagaland recorded the highest growth rate in 1991-2001, i.e., 64.41%.

Overall Levels of Development

Centre for Monitoring Indian Economy, on the basis of selected indicators, ascertained levels of development of all states and districts of India. As a whole all criteria taken together India is given the value of 100, rest of the states relate to national average of 100. Developed states exceeded 100 mark, less developed states falls below 100. The N-E. states show remarkable uniformity, values range between 54 and 55 only. Only Arunachal has a little higher value of 66, perhaps because of sparse population which gives it highest per capita food grains production in N-E.

Respective RDIs of states of N-E. together with their status related to development indicators are given in Table 3 which includes participation ratio and shows dominance of agricultural workers.

Land Use Characteristics

Latest available land use statistics of 1995-96 and 1998-99 are presented in Table 4. The difference between total cultivated area and total cultivable area indicate scope for further expansion of agriculture. Specially Assam, Meghalaya, Mizoram and Nagaland appear to have considerable scope, whereas in rest of the states in the N-E scope is marginal.

Rice is the principal crop in all the states except in the district of West Kameng of Arunachal where Maize takes the pride of place (Table 6). Maize is also an important crop in Arunachal as a whole also in Meghalaya, Mizoram and Nagaland. Tea commands considerable coverage in Cachar, Darrang, Dibrugarh and Sibsagar Districts of Assam.

Though Rice is the main crop, productivity is quite low specially in Arunachal and Assam. Manipur with 2290 kg/ha tops in rice productivity. However, all the N-E. States stand far behind when compared with Tamil Nadu 3443kg/ha, Punjab 3152 kg and A.P. 2781 kg (see Table 4)

Though it may not apply to Assam to that extent, the reason for low productivity may be related to widespread Jhum cultivation.

Jhum or shifting cultivation covers considerable larger area than settled cultivated land in Arunachal, Nagaland, Manipur, Mizoram and Meghalaya (Table 5).

Level of Agricultural Modernisation

Table 7 indicates per Ha consumption of fertilizers (N+P+K), percentage share of electricity consumption in agriculture vis-a-vis total electricity consumption, percentage of villages electrified and percentage of irrigated area of total crop area.

It appears that Manipur is outstanding with highest per Ha consumption of inorganic fertilizers and area coverage by irrigation. Surprisingly, Nagaland has the highest percentage of area under irrigation though its per Ha consumption of fertilizers (N+P+K) is very low in the region alongside Arunachal. As irrigated area has greater ability to digest fertilizers, perhaps it may be presumed that Nagaland uses more organic fertilizers.

However, by standard of per Ha consumption of fertilisers, N-E ranks lowest in India with an average of 29.16 kg per Ha. All India average is 87.45 kg, its North Zone 129.59 kg followed by South Zone with 113.66 kg.

Electric consumption for agriculture is lowest in N-E with average of 3.43% whereas southern region is at the top with 35.93%.

N-E : Land Use: Forests Coverage

N-E region holds the top position in the country for widespread forest coverage. Even in populous Assam, where density of population is higher than national average, forests cover 30.20% (1999) of its geographical area against All-India average of 19.39%. Mizoram, Nagaland and Arunachal have very high forests coverage. But in every state open forests cover larger area than Arunachal and Assam (See Table 8). The forests yield a large number of major and minor forest products including food.

In the N-E, bamboo which is grown very widely is an important raw material for pulp and paper industry. For instance, nearly 40% of geographical area of Mizoram is covered by bamboo. Projected demand of bamboo for pulp and paper is as given below:

Demand of Bamboos for Pulp and Paper

(000 tonnes)

	Bamboo Demand	
	1985	*2000*
High Estimate (Paper & Pulp)	3,123	3,546
Law Estimate (")	2352	1,936
Other Non-industrial uses	2,960	3,459

Source : Shah S.A.: *Forestry for People*, ICAR, New Delhi, 1996

Apart from industrial and other commercial uses, forests also provide food. Shimongs of Arunachal consume abundant supply of roots, fruits and leaves as well as meat of wild animals. Starvation is unknown to them. The diet of Abhors that is largely based on forest produce has been considered as superior to the average Indian diet.

But the forest wealth of N-E has been endangered due to large-scale clearance of forests for extensive Jhum cultivation which has different names in different localities such as *Jhum, Kumri, Podu.* This practice is mostly associated with tribals. Deforestation is robbing the country of its natural defense against environmental degradation and its impact is seen in accelerated soil erosion, silting of dams and rivers and change in micro climates besides loss of green gold.

It is seen from the Forest Survey by GOI that there had been a net loss of 633 sq. km. of forest area in N-E from 1991 to 1993. However, Jhuming is not the sole reason for deforestation in every state of N-E For example, in Assam, loss due to extensive lumbering is causing deforestation more than by Jhuming. However, thanks to afforestation programmes, there has been some gains in Nagaland and Tripura (See Table 9). But losses elsewhere is quite large, in Mizoram alone 437 sq. km. of forest was lost between 1994-98.

The vital need for protecting forests has been ably summarized by Gunner Paulsen : forests "are useful to man in two different ways: as producers of a wide variety of goods called 'forest produce and as custodian of favourable environmental conditions. Both are indisputably essential to the well being indeed for survival of man".

STRATEGY FOR RURAL DEVELOPMENT IN N-E

Response to Two All India Programmes

A general review has been made of certain socio-economic conditions, pattern of use of agriculture and allied resources as prevailing in the N-E Region. Inputs from it may help in framing strategy for bringing a change towards better living in rural areas of N-E

Before commenting upon possible areas of attention for rural change, it may be useful to look into the response of N-E States to all India Rural Development Programmes, viz., IRDP and JRY.

As it is known, IRDP is mainly family oriented and aims at assisting the families living below poverty line to cross the line in a way that is sustainable. JRY funds are mainly for landless wage-earners which are meant for public works though assistance for individual household is also a component of it.

It is surprising that in case of IRDP, percentage of achievement to target was much short of All- India figure except in case of Manipur and Tripura which stand much above than national average (see Table -10)

In contrast, JRY had been largely successful. Except Arunachal and Meghalaya, rest of the states showed higher percentage of utilisation than All India average (see Table 11).

Manipur and Tripura's achievement in IRDP is commendable. In JRY, Nagaland and Mizoram occupy first and second place. Position of Arunachal is weak both in IRDP and JRY. Performance of Arunachal and Meghalaya is much weaker in respect of JRY.

Does the relative success of JRY point to preference for wage earning than endeavouring for sustainable self sufficiency in the N-E

ENVIRONMENTAL OPPORTUNITIES : ITS UTILIZATION

Hydro Power

The alliance of terrain, climate (moderate to heavy rainfall) and torrents provide ample opportunity for harnessing hydro power. The scope is particularly noteworthy all along the flanks of the Brahmaputra Valley. Examples of such harnessing is found at Umtu Project near Guwahati and Barapani Dam on way to Shillong. Such opportunities exist elsewhere in N-E States. Examples: Ranganadi Project in Lower Subansiri District of Arunachal, Gumti Dam in Tripura etc. But these developments also create environmental problems which will be discussed later.

Forest Wealth, The Task of Preservation : It has been seen that very valuable forest wealth of the N-E is being depleted. Ways are to be considered not only for arresting it but to find ways to have more trees in the region. Agro Forestry is one answer. Under it, fast growing native trees under different situations are identified and incorporated into the cropping system. It meets fuel and fodder needs of local community

Revival of Woodlots which are also known as 'sacred groves' will be useful. Under this system, part of the land used to be set aside for protection of biological communities as well as for regulated harvests. In Mizoram, specially in remote areas, this system still survives. However, for arrest of deforestation regulation of jhum or shifting cultivation is most vital. To point out the gravity of problem, extensive incidence of jhuming in Mizoram may be cited. It is estimated that as many as 50,000 families in Mizoram depend upon jhuming. As a result nearly 40,000 Ha of forests are being destroyed annually. Such extensive practice of shifting cultivation is also seen in Arunachal, Nagaland, Manipur and Meghalaya (See Table 5).

Lately, jhum cultivation has been increasingly damaging because previous favourable 20 year cycle, due to population pressure, has been reduced to 5 year cycle. This has affected yield from the farm besides causing environmental damage. Mizoram government has adopted a policy whereby cultivators are given incentives and financial assistance to pick up alternative profession giving up shifting cultivation.

In Nagaland, redevelopment of shifting cultivation is widely practiced now. Fast growing plant species like alder are grown in intervening 5 year cycle which give a good harvest. This system is in use by tribal farmers in the Angami, Chakesang, Yim, Chunger and Konyak areas.

Indian Council of Agricultural Research (ICAR) unit at Shillong recommended a model of 3 tier land use for hill regions which proposed that upper 1/3rd of slope be allotted for forestry, the middle part of the slope be used for plantation / horticultural crops and the lower 1/3rd for terraced cultivation. This system was not in conformity with social structure of tribal communities. So the proposal found little acceptance.

A good example of terraced cultivation on slopes with least soil erosion is found in the villages of Buddhist Monpas in the western part of Arunachal. Monpas are well organised, live in good houses. But Abhors and Tagins of Arunachal present a different picture of unskilled agricultural practices.

Raising Agricultural Productivity and Diversification

Much larger quantity of inorganic fertilizers are consumed by tea gardens in the N-E In cultivated areas, per Ha consumption of fertilizers is lowest in India (Table 7). Electricity consumption by agricultural sector is either nil or very low. Productivity of rice, main crop of this region, due to the factors noted is far behind other states (see Table -4). Crops other than rice command much lower coverage except in few districts (see Table 6).

So raising agricultural productivity, using cultivable fallow, crop diversification and introduction of some cash crops wherever possible should get priority in N-E as its population is overwhelmingly dependent on agriculture.

Pineapple as Cash Crop and Input to Fruit Preservation Industry

There could be various ways of crop diversification. Pineapples provides a good possibility. In 1992-93, by area and production, Assam ranked first, Karnataka stood second by production. Meghalaya, Manipur, Tripura and Nagaland have sizeable land coverage by pineapple. However, productivity is quite low in N-E Tamil Nadu produces 41.00 tonnes per Ha, Karnataka 34.90 tones /Ha, whereas Assam, the leading producer in N-E, produces only 13.30 tonnes /Ha (see Table -12) If proper care is taken, 53,000 to 59,000 plants are planted per ha, the cost benefit ratio could be quite attractive as 1: 4.2 found out by the Kerala Agricultural University. The main problem is marketing, weak accessibility of N-E. States is the greatest constraint. Fruits when need to be transported for long distances requiring several days, refrigerated transport is necessary to slow down ripening process.

Whereas 97% of world production of pineapple is used by canning industry, elsewhere, in India the proportion is less than 10%. Development of Canning Industry at nodal locations commanding pineapple growing cluster of villages seems to be a distinct potential for higher income and increment in rural employment.

An Idea about export market for Indian pineapple is given below:

Export of Fresh Pineapple from India: 1995-96

Country	*Quantity (tonnes)*
Nepal	102,335
Russia	76,000
All India	239,220 (Steadily increasing from 1993-94

Source : Pineapple: ICAR

India : Export of Pineapple Juice, 1995 - 96

Russia	302,376 (tonnes)
All India	320,736

Note : In previous year, Ukraine was the leading importer. For pineapple squash, Russia largest importer , followed by Ukraine. Germany was an important importer of processed Pineapple.

It appears that Nepal is a good market for fresh Indian pineapple. Till processing and canning industry remain undeveloped, N-E may target Nepal market for export of its fresh fruits.

Industry

In spite of its good natural resources like petroleum, gas and coal, N-E region is very undeveloped industrially. In all the states of N-E less than 5% of workers are engaged in manufacturing including household industries (1993). However, Tea Industry of N-E because of its export market is quite important.

Assam Tea Industry

At The 26th annual general meeting of the Assam Branch of the Indian Tea Association (Abita) in November 2001 at Jorhat, the picture presented was quite grim. Assam's tea gardens are located on high terraces of the plains/hill margins produce nearly half of India's output (400 m kg annually). Nearly 12-15% of Assam's population is dependent on tea. Tea industry's demand for plywood, coal and fertilizers promote production of these goods. The industry also provides casual and permanent employment to about 6 lakh workers. Though maximum employment is required in picking season. The demand for skilled labor throughout the year is rather limited. Migrant labour specially in picking season has the dominant role.

Crisis of the tea industry as viewed by ABITA CHAIRMAN Bharat Singh is related to

(a) Sluggish growth

(b) Higher cost of production

(c) Declining prices

(d) Deterioration of quality

The other factors contributing to the decline in quality related to government's issuing factory licenses to people without their own plantations. They secure leaves from various sources that have adversely affected quality. Further, small tea gardens, presently major players, rarely seek advice from Toklai Research Station. Technical advice from Toklai station could improve quality of Tea.

Due to these reasons, Abita chairman noted that hundreds of gardens are incurring losses because of slow down as huge stocks of tea remain unsold for long periods (*The Telegraph*, Dec 1, 2001, p. 8).

Cottage and Household Industry

Every state in the N-E has formulated industrial policies to provide incentives for small scale industries. The nature of incentives provided by each state is more or less same which include allotment of land, shed, helping manpower development, capital investment subsidy, transport subsidy, subsidies for technical know-how, subsidy of interest, on power lines, preparation of project report single window assistance and likewise. Such package is found in Arunachal Industrial policy, 1994, Assam's Policy of 1991, Manipur in 1990, Meghalaya in 1988, Mizoram 1989, and Tripura 1992.

However, in spite of such policies of the States, much headway has not yet been made as reflected in very low percentage of workers engaged by industries including household industries.

Assam has nearly 1/7th of India's handlooms. There is also good promise in the N-E for fostering cottage silk industry. Production of raw silk was sizeable in the states of Assam, Manipur, Meghalaya and Nagaland.

For promoting rural household industries, the experience of Sri Lanka may be noteworthy. Sri Lanka, a very small island country, is also predominantly rural, 78% of its population live in villages (1992), but Sri Lanka's quality of life is better than India. In Human Development Index (UNDP report) Sri Lanka ranks 90 aga nst India's position of 135. One reason is widespread rural household industrial employment. Large international companies, using cheap Lanka labour particularly women, get garments prepared as per the designs given by those companies. Supply of raw materials and marketing responsibility of those good are taken care of by controlling companies. If such network for utilizing skills of N-E states could be organised, then household industries may expand manifold. Commendable artistic skills exist in these states:

Sates	*Production* (tonnes)
Assam	534
Manipur	217
Meghalaya	196
Nagaland	23

Note : Karnataka was the highest producer with 8327 tonnes followed by A.P. with 2447 tonnes

Source: Indian Agriculture in Brief, 2000

Some other Areas of Promise

Fruit preservation and canning industry has possibilities in view of sizeable quantity of fruit productions like pineapple, oranges etc.

N-E States have marvellous natural beauty with mountains, forests, lakes and valleys which could attract a large number of tourists. But very few tourists visit the region for lack of accessibility, insecurity, want of basic facilities and amenities. Attitudinal change of local people towards visitors would promote tourism. Presently the bulk of visitors from all over the country come to Kamakshya in Guwahati as pilgrims. Kaziranga games sanctuary, Shillong with its natural beauty, Manipur with its rich cultural heritage and such other places could draw lot more visitors if suitable programmes backed by facilities for movement and stay could be organised. This would boost the economy of the region and could be a source of employment.

Checking of Environmental Degradation: Should be of Primary Concern

Floods occur every year in one part or other of the great Brahmaputra Valley which is about 650 km long and 100 km wide. Nalbari subregion is worst affected. It is surprising that in spite of tremendous technological progress, no effective flood control programme could yet be drawn and implemented.

Control of Soil Erosion

The problem of soil erosion related to deforestation, cultivation of slopes without adequate care has been dealt earlier. Now few other facets of environmental degradation may by considered. The Loktak lake of Manipur, biggest in eastern India is facing continuous decay. The Keibul Lamajo National Park, country's only floating sanctuary, located in this lake is in danger. Fishes of the lake used to support thousands of villagers living on all sides of the lake. However, unchecked denudation leading to soil creep in the lake is causing rapid decay. All rivers of Manipur discharge in this lake. If effective afforestation is not taken up, together with dredging, survival of the lake will continue to be threatened. Moreover, 150 MW power project drawing water from the lake through tunnel without recycling has led to loss of water and affecting life of the lake.

The Gumti Dam of Tripura, because of the lack of proper advance planning, has led to environmental degradation. It was built to generate 10 MW of Hydel Power.

For construction of this Dam, some 46 sq. km of land with rich rice fields and forests have been lost. Nearly 5000 tribal families have been uprooted. Bulk of those displaced migrated to upper catchment areas of the Gumti and practicing jhum cultivation which led to environmental degradation. So, proper prior planning is essential.

Deforestation is the greatest threat to environment in the N-E Region. Its effect is seen in two ways, decreasing rainfall specially in upper Assam and increasing incidence of floods.

There has been several efforts for replacing jhum by terrace cultivation. Subsidies and inputs used to be given as incentives. It worked so long as subsidies continue but farmers revert back to jhum when subsidies are withdrawn.

Conclusion

Prospects and problems of rural development in N-E have been discussed in brief. Those are to be considered location specific. In the tribal areas of the N-E ecological conditions change drastically over short distances. So development strategies are to be adopted accordingly. In other words, micro-level planning should be the approach.

Cultural heterogeneity of the N-E should be given due consideration. There are about 55 tribes living in N-E The major groups are divided into subgroups. Studies in sociology of kinship throw light on tribal organizations and their behavioural pattern. While the cooperative spirit is the tribal way of life, he is also conscious about independence of family as unit. For emotional participation of the people these factors should be given due consideration in the process of developmental planning.

This implies that development planning for tribal and other rural groups should be in tune with the value system that people can understand, appreciate and identify themselves with it.

Rural development or any form of development is bound to suffer if unrest and violence continue to disintegrate the society. For the N-E, specially for hill states, dearth of central assistance prima facie does not seem to be a great limitation. For example, in Mizoram, 5th plan had an outlay of Rs. 46.56 crores, 6th plan Rs. 130 crores, 7th Plan (1985-90) 260 crores. Certainly more assistance will bring more reconstruction specially because development in this region was initially slow. But in the present socio-economic conditions of the country, limitation of resources going to remain a constraint for long time to come. Therefore, best utilization of available resources are to be ensured. A uniform plan for whole of the North-East will not be practical, micro level plans meeting area wise needs are to be prepared. However, this mosaic should have interlinks as development is not possible in isolation.

REFERENCES

Centre for Monitoring of Indian Economy (CMIE): *Indian Economy*, Vol 1, Sept 1991.

Census of India, 2001 : Paper 2 of Series 9, *Rural Urban Distribution of Population.*

Government of India, Ministry of Agriculture, Agriculture Statistics Division : *Indian Agriculture in Brief*, 2000.

Government of India, National Remote sensing Agency, Hyderabad: Land Use, Satellite based data, 1990.

Government of India, Ministry of Environment & Forests: *State of Forest Report*,2000.

Government of India, Ministry of Environment & Forests, *Forest Survey of India*. 1993, Dehradun.

National Institute of Rural Development (NIRD), Hyderabad : *Rural Development Statistics*, 1992.

Chadha, Reddy and Sikhmany: *Pineapple*, ICAR, Directorate of Information and Publication of Agriculture, New Delhi, January 1998.

Sarvekshana: 52 nd Issue July-September 1992, NSSO.

Report of Central Electricity Authority, 1990.

Govt. of India, Publication Division, Ministry of Information and Broadcasting :Small Scale Industries, Incentives & Facilities for Development, January 1995.

Lahiri, T.B., 'North East States : Considerations for Determining Priorities in Social Sciences Research.

Lalnithaganga, P., *Mizoram*, Publication Division, June 1997.

Shah, S.A. : *Forestry For People*, ICAR, Pusa, NewDelhi, December 1996.

Table 1 : Rural Population, Number of Village and Average Village Size, 2001

States	*Rural Population (1991)*	*No. of Village Size*	*Average*
Arunachal Pradesh	8,68,429 (2.67)	3,649	238
Assam	2,32,48,994 (71.50)	25,590	909
Manipur	18,18,224 (5.59)	2,212	822
Meghalaya	18,53,457 (5.69)	5,629	329
Mizoram	4,50,018 (1.38)	785	573
Nagaland	16,35,816 (5.02)	1225	1335
Tripura	26,48,074 (8.15)	856	3094
Total :	3,25,23,012 (100.00)	39,946	814

Source: Census of India, 2001

Note: Figures within bracket indicate states percentage share of Total Rural of N. E. Region. India's Total Rural Population in 2001 is 74,16,60,293. N. E. States' share: 4.38%

Table 2 : Population Distribution, Decadal Percentage Growth, Sex-Ratio, Population Density, Literacy Rate, Urban Percentage in NE States, 2001

State/India	Persons 2001	%tage decadal growth rate		No. of females per '000 males		Population density per sq km		Literacy rate 2001		State's share of population amomg NE state total 2001	Urban population %tage to total population
		1981-91	1991-01	1991	2201	1991	2001	Male	Female		
INDIA	**1027015247**	**23.86**	**21.34**	**927**	**933**	**267**	**324**	**75.85**	**54.16**		
1. Arunachal Pradesh	10,91,117	36.83	26.21	859	901	10	13	64.07	44.24	2.83	20.41 (12.80)
2. Assam	2,66,38,407	24.24	18.85	923	932	286	340	71.93	56.03	69.22	12.72 (11.10)
3. Manipur	23,88,634	29.29	30.02	958	978	82	107	77.87	59.70	6.20	23.88 (27.52)
4. Meghalaya	23,06,069	32.86	29.94	955	975	79	103	66.14	60.41	5.99	19.63 (18.60)
5. Mizoram	8,91,058	39.70	29.18	921	938	33	42	90.69	86.13	2.31	49.50 (46.10)
6. Nagaland	19,88,636	56.08	64.41	886	909	73	120	71.77	61.92	5.16	17.74 (17.21)
7. Tripura	31,91,168	34.30	15.74	945	950	263	304	81.47	65.41	8.29	17.02 (15.30)

Total Popu. 3,84,95,089
of N.E. States, 2001

Note: Total population of N. E. States account for 3.74% of India's total in 2001 overall Popu. Density is 150.94 persons sq.krn. against India's 324 in 2001.

Figures within brackets show 1991 percentage

Total Area of 7 N. E. States : 2,55,028 sq. km. = about 8% of India's area sq. km.

Total Popu. in 1991 was : 3,13,86,911 = nearly 4% of India's Population

Average density o f Popu. in NE was 123 per sq. km. in 1991 against India's 267

Source: Census of India, 1991 & 2001.

TABLE 3: Relative Development Index of N.E.

(Figure within bracket indicate All-India average)

	Relative Dev. Index	Population Growth Rate Per Year	Urbanisation %	Literacy %	Female Literacy %	Workers as % of Total Population	Agri & allied workers as % of main workers	Per capital Foodgrains Production Kgs.	Road Length Per 100 sq. km	Per Capital Bank Credit Rs.
1. Arunachal Pradesh	66 (100)	3.11 (2.14)	12.80 (25.73)	41.59 (52.21)	29.69 (39.29)	46.24 (37.46)	67.26 (66.92)	210 (173)	8.51 (60.14)	320 (1978)
2. Assam	54 (100)	2.13 (2.14)	11.10 (25.73)	52.89 (52.21)	43.03 (39.29)	36.09 (37.46)	73.50 (66.92	119 (173)	81.98 (60.14)	581 (1978)
3. Manipur	55 (100)	2.54 (2.14)	27.52 (25.73)	59.89 (52.21)	47.60 (39.29)	42.18 (37.46)	69.97 (66.92)	151 (173)	29.43 (60.14)	483 (1978)
4. Meghalaya	54 (100)	2.80 (2.14)	18.60 (25.73)	49.10 (52.21)	44.85 (39.29)	42.67 37.46	(74.21) (66.92)	75 (173)	28.59 (60.14)	435 (1978)
5. Mizoram	54 (100)	3.35 (2.14)	46.10 (25.73)	82.27 (52.21)	78.60 (39.29)	48.91 (37.46)	65.77 (66.92)	82 (173)	15.50 (60.14)	343 (1978)
6. Nagaland	55 (100)	4.60 (2.14)	17.21 (25.73)	61.65 (52.21)	54.75 (39.29)	42.68 (37.46)	75.20 (66.92)	93 (173)	47.59 (60.14)	807 (1978)
7. Tripura	55 (100)	2.95 (2.14)	15.30 (25.73)	60.44 (52.21)	49.65 (39.29)	31.14 (37.46)	63.79 (66.92)	156 (173)	106.47 (60.14)	714 (1978)

Source: Profile of District, November 1993, Published by Centre for Monitoring Indian Economy, Bombay.

Table 4 : Land use Characteristics, Average Farm Size, Principal Crop & yield rate in NE States

State	*Reporting for land use (1995-96) (000 Ha)*	*Forest (1995-96) (000 Ha)*	*Total Cultivated Area (1995-96) (000 Ha)*	*Total Cultivable Area (1995-96) (000 Ha)*	*Percentage share of Rice to Total Cropped Area (1995-96)*	*Average size of operations Holdings (1990-91) (Ha)*	*Yield of Rice Kg/Ha 1998-99*
1. Arunachal Pradesh	5495	5154	213	293	48.6	3.72	988
2. Assam	7850	2012	2854.	3229	63.6	1.27 .	1345
3. Manipur	2211	602	140	164	84.6	1.23	2290
4. Meghalaya	2241	937	272	1074	42.1	1.77	1420
5. Mizoram	2088	1598	109	445	59.6	1.38	1649
6. Nagaland	1546	863	325	626	61.4	6.82	1445
7. Tripura	1049	606	281	310	54.2	0.97	1939
All India	299875	68479	156024	183626	23.0	1.55	1928

Note : (a) Maize is an important crop in Arunachal (13.5%), Meghalaya (6.9%) Mizoram (7.3%), Nagaland (12.3%)
(b) Highest yield of Rice (Kg. per Ha) is found in Tamil Nadu 3443 Kg., Punjab 3152 Kg. & A.P. 2781 Kg.

Source : Indian Agriculture in Brief, 2000, Agriculture Statistics Division, Ministry of Agriculture, Govt. of India

TABLE 5 : Land use Pattern in N.E. States 1990 (Satellite based data)

State	*Agricultural Land % of total area*			*Plantation (%)*	*Forest (%)*	*Wasteland (%)*
	Kharif	*Rabi*	*Double Cropped*			
1. Arunachal Pradesh	a. 4.55% b. 2.46%	–	–	–	82.81	–
2. Assam	37.61%	22.22%	18.93%	12.34%	21.90	13.50
3. Nagaland	a. 28.58% b. 2.35%	–	–	–	68.09	–
4. Manipur	a. 25.91% b. 7.58%	–	–	–	63.33	–
5. Mizoram	a. 4.06% b. 3.26%	–	–	–	92.81	–
6. Meghalaya	a. 32.56%	–	–	–	63.80	–
7. Tripura	a. 4.81% b. 14.76%	–	– 4.84%	–	36.90	–

Note : (a) Under Shifting cultivation
(b) Under settled agriculture

Source : National Remote Sensing Agency, Hyderabad

Table 6 : Some Important Crop-Coverage in N.E.States (Other than Rice), 1993

States	*District*	*Crop*	*Area as Percentage of District Total*
Arunachal Pradesh	Changlang	Maize	9.23
	Dibang Valley	Maize	29.66
	East Kameng	Maize	14.84
	East Siang	Maize	20.43
	Lohit	Maize	33.27
	Lower Subansiri	Maize	17.28
	Tawang	Potato	32.50
	Do	Wheat	31.98
	Tirap	Maize	30.88
	Upper Subansiri	Maize	15.22
	West Kameng	Maize	58.47
	West Siang	Maize	15.11
Assam	Cachar	Tea	18.48
	Darrang	Tea	14.13
	Dibrugarh	Tea	25.84
	Sibsagar	Tea	34.75
Meghalaya	East Garo Hills	Ginger	13.32
	East Khasi Hills	Potato	32.10
	Jaintia Hills	Maize	20.72
	West Khasi Hills	Potato	33.03

Note : Table reflects where crop coverage exceeds nearly 10% of cultivated area. However, Rapeseed command such share in several districts of Assam.

Source : Centre for Monitoring Indian Economy, Bombay, November 1993.

Table 7 : Modernisation Status Of Agricultural Activities : Certain Indicators

States	*Per Ha Consumption of Fertilisers (kg) (N+P+K)*		*Percentage Share of Electricity Consumption in agriculture vis-a-vis Total Consumption 1995-96*	*Percentage of village Electrified as on 31-3-98*	*Percentage of irrigated area of Total crop area 1995-96*
	1996-97	*1997-98*			
Assam	14.59	21.93	2.46	77.0	15
Manipur	48.64	49.68	0.53	88.9	27.7
Meghalaya	14.43	15.00	0.57	45.5	18.9
Nagaland	3.89	4.28	-	94.8	31.6
Tripura	18.80	29.28	16.00 (1994-95)	93.9	13.1
Arunachal Pradesh	2.16	2.19	-	59.2	14.7
Mizoram	3.37	10.18	-	98.0	8.3

Note: (a) Tea Board of N.E. consume substantial Quantity of Fertilisers which was 32014 in 1996-97 and 42780 tonnes in 1997-98.
(b) By per Ha consumption of Fertiliser in 1997-98, North Zone with 129.59 kg. tops the list followed by South Zone 113.66 and West Zone 60.15. N.E. Zone ranks lowest with average of 29.16 kg. All India average is 87.45 kg.
(c)In 1995-96 percentage share of electricity consumption by agri sector is highest in Southern Region (35.93), followed by Western Region (33.57), Northern Region (32.30), Eastern Region (9.93), N.E. India ranks lowest with 3.43, All India average is 30.95.
(d) All India average of villages electrification in 1998 was 85.45

Source: Indian Agriculture in Brief, 2000.

Table 8 : Extent of Dense Forest, Open Forest, Mangrove

States	*Dense Forest Sq. Km.*	*Open Forest Sq. Km.*	*Mangrove*	*Total Forest Cover Sq. Km.*	*Percentage of Geographical Area*
Arunachal Pradesh	57,756	11,091	0	68,847	82.21
Assam	14,517	9171	0	23,688	30.20
Manipur	5,936	11,448	0	17,384	77.86
Meghalaya	5,925	9,708	0	15,633	69.70
Mizoram	3,786	14,552	0	18,338	86.99
Nagaland	5,137	9,027	0	14,164	85.43
Tripura	2,228	3,517	0	5,745	54.79

Source : Forest Survey of India, Ministry of Environment and Forest: State of Forest Report, 1999

Table 9 : N.E. States : Change in Forest Area from 1991 to 1993 (Sq.Km.)

State	*Loss Due to Jhuming*	*Other Reason*	*Total Loss*	*Gain Due to Afforestation*	*Net Loss /Gain*
Arunachal Pradesh	70	28	98	-	-98
Assam	165	190	355	112	-243.
Manipur	28	36	64	-	-64
Meghalaya	110	2	112	6	-106
Mizoram	256	-	256	100	-156
Nagaland	63	-	63	90	+27
Tripura	10	27	37	40	+3
Total	702	281	983	348	-633

Source : Forest Survey, Ministry of Environment & Forest, GOI, Dehradun 1993

Table 10: IRDP : Physical Progress for 1990-91 and 1991-92

State	Percentage of Achievement to Target*	
	1990-91	1991-92
Arunachal Pradesh	27.11	12.83
Assam	74.09	40.40
Manipur	358.79	212.21
Meghalaya	59.87	47.43
Mizoram	54.14	15.80
Nagaland	63.04	37.78
Tripura	249.73	36.12
All India	122.56	66.58

* Upto December 1991

Source: NIRD : Rural Development Statistics, 1992

Table 11 : JRY: Percentage of Fund Utilisation, 1990-91

State	*Percentage of Utilization*
Arunachal Pradesh	42.15
Assam	85.54
Manipur	88.95
Meghalaya	39.13
Mizoram	99.17
Nagaland	100.00
Tripura	86.20
All India	78.41

Source: NIRD : Rural Development Statistics 1992

Table 12 : Pineapple Area and Production, 1992-93

State	*Area (Ha)*	*Production (Tonnes)*	*Productivity (Tonnes/Ha)*
Assam	13,906	184,485	13.30
Manipur	6,450	60,500	9.38
Meghalaya	8,450	72,500	8.58
Mizoram	810	4,189	5.17
Nagaland	1,017	2,415	2.37
Tripura	3,706	32,000	8.63
India's Total	59,436	858,978	14.45

Note : By Area & Total Production, Assam ranked First, Karnataka stood second by production. By Productivity Tamil Nadu is first 41.00, Karnataka is second with 34.90 tonnes/Ha

Source: Chadha, Reddy & Sikhamany : Pineapple, ICAR, Directorate of Information and publication of Agriculture, New Delhi, Jan 1998

Table 13 : Rural Households, Primary Sources of Energy 1987-88

Per Thousand

State	*PRIMARY SOURCES OF ENERGY FOR LIGHTING*		
	Kerosine	*Electricity*	*Others*
Arunachal Pradesh	373	390	217
Assam	923	70	7
Manipur	678	297	25
Meghalaya	755	239	6
Mizoram	777	208	15
Nagaland	NA	NA	NA
Tripura	799	214	7
All India	746	238	16

Source : Sarvekshana, 52nd Issue, July-Sept 1992, NSSO

Table 14 : Electrification of Tribal Villages, 1989-90

State	*No. Tribal Villages*	*No. of Tribal Villages Electrified as on 31-3-90*
Arunachal Pradesh	3257	1354
Assam	6496	4339
Manipur	1384	683
Meghalaya	4902	2170
Mizoram	721	402
Nagaland	1112	1099
Tripura	2655	1130
All India	111,886	69,877

Source : Central Electricity Authority

3

DYNAMICS OF RURAL DEVELOPMENT: A Note

Amalesh Banerjee

Rural development and Urban development are the facets of development economics. Development theories mostly enunciated in terms of capital intensity and capital-output ratio are broadly concerned with urban development and urbanisation. Celebrated development theories of Harris Todaro, Lewis, Renisfei are engaged in this exercise of output measurement index and trickle down process. However, development experience of third world countries over decades brought out the grim experience of backwash affect of such big push programme. Question arose as to how these neoclassical framework of development theories is able to answer the needs of development of the common people who are in the vicious circles of various sorts. Sen has raised the question as to which way the development economics is making progress. Subsequent research of Sen, Mahabub Haque and the World Bank and others have brought to the fore the genuine question of human development both urban and rural as the prime objective of development. In that way neither urban nor rural development are mutually exclusive. Development process must strike a balance between these two dimensions in order to reach the peak of human development and welfare. Much of the present day maladies of developing countries lies in their almost exclusive concentration on capitalist development to the neglect of broad based rural development with peoples' participation. Biggest irony of the development economics is that development effort failed to address poverty and unemployment in the third world countries particularly in the rural areas.

I. Two approaches

There are two approaches to this problem of development in general and the rural development in particular. The first is the market approach and the second is asset approach. While the former prescribes that market adjustment will resolve the poverty problem and the price mechanism is the important tool for adjustments the second mechanism emphasizes on the peoples' participation and income generation in the process of development. Income generation and redistribution take place simultaneously along the process of development. In this approach the people earn income and acquire the ability to overcome the adversity. The structural approach emphasises on the economic and institutional framework first and then assumes to exploit the market mechanism with better entitlement of the individuals. Development economics of neo-classical genre seeks to overcome the lapses of institutional, structural and individual limitations by hypothetical measurement of utility gain and loss while the structuralist first proposes improvement of welfare of the economic system and then improve the welfare of individuals. Sen and others proceeded on this line and brought about global awareness of human development and eradication of poverty. The World Bank, after so many years of neo-classical practices, now discovered the virtues of the latter approach and proposes the new path for development economics. Keynesian economics had strongly laid foundation of this process of development although in a short term cyclical perspective.

In contemporary interpretation of World Bank support for poverty eradication and economic development of the third World countries, the activist programme is emphasised the World Bank's market approach to poverty eradication and economic development in the third world countries, primarily based on 'Washington Consensus' has floundered in many ways. It has lamented that contemporary economic reform based on this grand formula of 'consensus' has failed and by-passed the poor and vulnerable section of population. It has therefore come out with the modified programme comprising the activist agenda and liberalisation principle. This new package of World Bank poverty ameliorative programme emphasises on agricultural reforms, empowerment of people, asset formation, health improvement and removing social barriers. As such it is admitted that poverty is the result of economic, politi al and social process that interact with and reinforce each other in ways that exacrebate the deprivation of the poor people. Hence economic development in general and the development of the rural sector in particular in which most of the poor people live must be directed for creation of assets for have nots, empowerment of them with political and social organisation and rights so that they become capable to undertake positive action for production and distribution. In the third world countries most of the poor people live in the rural sector. In our country successive five year economic plans could not eliminate poverty problem in spite of several rural development programmes undertaken over last five decades. Therefore approach to rural development has to be re-examined without being obsessed with the market mechanism or command principle.

II. Rural Development in China

With this theoretical perspective in view we like to have a look at the Chinese experience before we go for study of rural development in our country in particular. In spite of rapid economic growth experienced over decades, China has to face the problem of relative poverty throughout the country and in the rural sector in particular. Growth process has left a large section of population particularly aged. During the Five Year Plan 1986-90, the poverty alleviation programme mainly targeted the Western region which is backward.

China has taken massive programme for rural development in two parts. First is the rural industrialisation with the expansion of town and village enterprises which supply about 50 percent of China's industrial product for export and provide employment. Secondly, the supporting programme comprises extension of health education and welfare services to the poor regions. The community - based such welfare programmes substantially help in reducing poverty. This two pronged programme reduced the rural-urban gap to some extent and ushered in the bottom-up process of development.

In India we launched massive programme for development in successive five year plans. The success of these programmes had been substantial. The average per capita income, industrial production and agricultural output have also increased. However, compared to the growth of population these growth rates have been sluggish and benefits of progress has not trickled down to the grass root level in rural areas. The result has been the persistence of poverty and backwardness in different regions of the country.

III. Index of Rural Development

The major single index of rural development is the reduction of poverty. It signifies the stage of development of the rural economic, political and social structures. The index of rural development and the action programme for eradication of poverty is delineated by the World Bank in this description: "Poor people live without fundamental freedoms of action and choice that the better-off take for granted. They often lack adequate food, shelter, education and health deprivations that keep them from leading the kind of life that everyone value They also face extreme vulnerability to ill health, economic dislocation and natural disasters. And they are often exposed to ill treatment by institutions of the state and society and are powerless to influence key decisions affecting their lives". Thus the poverty problem is multidimensional and rural and urban development has to be designed in such way as to address these multiple deprivation. Rural development process therefore have to be directed (i) quantitatively, to larger production in agriculture and industry, (ii) to improvement of welfare services and (iii) to built up structure for participation of the poor. The interaction of these facts together provide the foundation of rural development and eradication of rural poverty. How much we have done during the five year plans over decades to address these complex issues ?

Rural Development under Five years Plans

In our macro-planning a large segment of resources have been spent in the rural sector comprising agriculture, irrigation and power projects. In every plan rural sector was allocated a major share or fund. Besides these, every grand multipurpose projects, special rural development project like Community Development Projects, National Extension Services were being implemented since 1952. In fact much of the rural development programmes during the first two decades took place under the Community Development Projects. Later, this programme was modified and fitted in Panchayati Raj structure on the basis of Balwantrai Mehta Committee's recommendations in 1956. During the sixth-five year plan in 1978-79, the massive programme of IRDP was launched which was aimed at target group of poor people. Besides, some other special programme such as Training of Rural Youth for Self-Employment (TRYSEM), Development of Women and Children in Rural Areas (DWCRA), Jawahar Rozgar Yojna (JRY) or Nehru Rozgar Yojna (NRY), have been introduced in 1989-91. These schemes, mainly for employment of rural youth and women, have attained some success. Later, during nineties, a number of other programmes were launched for poverty alleviation, employment generation, literacy, health and social welfare. Special schemes have been launched for development of women and children which includes Indira Mahila Yojana (IMY), Balika Samridhi Yojana (BSY), Rural Women's Development and Employment Project (RWDEP), National Nutrition Policy (NNP) and Rashtriya Mahila Kosh (RMK). In 1999-2000 budget Central Government has made provision of Rs.1320 crores for implementation of these various elements for women and children. Separate schemes were also taken up for housing, sanitation and water supply. These efforts for improvement of the quality of life of the poor also made some impact on the reduction of poverty in overall estimate. In 1997- 98 and 1998-99 total programme for rural employment and poverty alleviation were to the tune of Rs.3867 and Rs.3966.6 crores.

There are certain inter-linkage in rural development and poverty eradication. It is assumed that accelerated economic growth with stable prices will reduce poverty and direct anti-poverty and employment schemes will be extensively addressed to the poor. The central overall major schemes of social sector and rural development was Rs.6575 crores in 1991-92 or 19.5 percent of total plan expenditure and 1.07 percent of GDP which increased to Rs.21563 crores or 28 per cent of plan expenditure and 1.12 percent of GDP in 1999-2000.

Against this macro-dimension of the progress in rural development, one has to analyze the causes of persistence of poverty and low level of living of the people in the rural sector in particular. These welfare support programmes will be successful only when the fundamental structure of production and asset ownership of the people are sufficiently strong. Also it is supposed that the existing social and administrative structure are favourably disposed towards the underprivileged and the growth of population will decline in the usual process. However, none of these assumptions were satisfied. While agricultural output has increased to some extent until nineties in different stages, in recent years agricultural growth declined. Growth of population, the recent census indicated, remained unabated. Asset holding of the rural people did not change much and around twenty percent people occupy seventy percent of rural asset. In respect of rural infrastructure comprising power, road communication and financial institution, the rural sector is still in a very backward condition. Rural development is therefore languishing as ever all over the country. Illiteracy, ill-health, social repression have combined with those poor physical condition to create the vicious circle of poverty and backwardness. In many areas in the rural sector, people are locked in the rocky terrain where all kinds of civilised conditions are totally absent. 'Life is further aggravated by occasional natural calamities like floods, drought and other kinds of disasters. When the 20 point programme of the old regime failed to eliminate many maladies of the age-old socio-economic structures we are to see how the new 14 point programme can meet those evils embedded in the socioeconomic structure.

These issues are very hardened in the North-Eastern states for various reasons. Besides the geographical condition, historical antecedents, segmented ethnic identities compounded with alien ideology have given rise to a very emotive and assertive situation in which rural sector remain largely unattended Alienation, deprivation and unrealised expectation have made the people of northeastern region very restive and aggressive. Rural unemployment has compounded along with rural stagnation and growth of population. It requires a radical action with massive investment in order to transform the rural socioeconomic formations of the North-Eastern states.

IV. Dynamics of Growth

Growth of an economy does not necessarily mean intensive capital investment all through . Dynamics of growth rests on two legs - skilled manpower and technological advance. Both these factors must be in balance otherwise there will be imperfection and inequality in the process of growth. Skilled work force working with capital makes it possible for the benefits of growth to be percolated down to the grassroot level. This process sustains the saving investment mutual balance via the institutional framework. This fundamental is equally applicable in urban as well as in the rural sector. In order to overcome the painful fallout of inequality and unemployment in the process of technological growth, modern growth economics emphasizes on the human resource development so that a skilled manpower can be employed and can earn income in the technologically advanced growth process. It is true in the case of rural development and in the u ban development as well. Growth process will be dragged if there is huge unemployment and the investment will be lagging behind the savings causing a paradox of thrift. Human resource development and their absorption (employment) in the production process that will ensure demand expansion and the dynamic process of growth. Equilibrium growth process will be achieved in a stable way in due course leaving behind the traverse of dualism and destabilising forces.

REFERENCES

Banerjee, Amalesh (1999) *Planning and Development Strategy.*

Bose, Ashish (2000) Reaching the unreached in Uttara Khand, Economic and Political Weekly, June 17.

Desai, M Bhupati (2001) *Organisation and Management of Rural Financial Sector.*

Ghosh, Alak (1994) Indian Economy, The New Book Stall, Kolkata.

Gupta, Anil K (2001) *Criteria and Indicators of Sustainability of Rural Development*, Oxford IBH Publishing Co. Pvt. Ltd., New Delhi.

Government of India, Planning Commission, Five year Plans.

Government of India, *Economic Survey* 2000-2001.

World Bank (2000) World Development Report, Oxford University Press, New York.

Suryanarayan M., (2000) How Real is the Secular Decline in Rural Poverty, Economic and Political weekly, June 17.

INSTITUTIONS AND PARTICIPATIONS

4

THE ROLE OF PANCHAYATI RAJ IN RURAL DEVELOPMENT

K. Alam
Sazzad Alam

Panchayati Raj, the ancient system of rural self-governance in India, has survived invasions, despotism, colonialism, and above all - time. This fact is aptly reflected in the statement made in 1930 by the British Viceroy of India, Charles Metcalf :

> *The Village Communities (i.e. the Panchayats) are little republics, having nearly everything they want within themselves. They seem to last where nothing else lasts. Dynasty after dynasty tumbles down, revolution succeeds to revolution, Hindu, Pathan, Moghal, Mahratta, Sikh, English, are masters in turn, but the Village Communities remain the same. The union of the Village Communities, each one forming a separated little state in itself, as I conceive, contributed more than any cause to the preservation of the people of India through all revolution and changes which they have suffered, and it is in a high degree, conducive to their happiness and to the enjoyment of great portion of freedom and independence.*

Therefore, the founding fathers of the post-independence modern Indian polity made it a point to mention Panchayati Raj in the original manuscript of the Indian Constitution, vide Article 40. And its statutory niche was secured by the 73rd Amendment by which it emerged as the 3rd tier of the Indian government. According to the provisions inserted by the amendment, democratically elected Panchayats are to be set up at the village, intermediate and district levels, with elections based on adult franchise held by independent State Election Commissions. Certain subjects have been earmarked for the exclusive jurisdiction of the Panchayats. Allocation of funds is to be made available by State Finance Commissions; and local tax collection can also be made. Besides, a great deal of autonomy has been provided to the Panchayats.

Mahatma Gandhi said *India lives in her villages.* Nearly three-fourths of the country's population live in the rural areas. But poverty, underdevelopment, illiteracy, ignorance, and lack of civic amenities characterise such areas. Hence, for the actual development of the country to take place, rural development is an essentiality. Since the onset of the 5-year plans, steps have been regularly taken in that direction. The Community Development Programme was launched in 1952. Successive plans, especially from the Sixth Plan onwards, have been looking upon rural development with benevolent eyes. A 20-point programme was announced in 1975, and another in 1982. Special programmes have started to alleviate poverty and engender rural development. Yet as far as the achievement of the cherished goals are concerned, certain basic problems have been faced, and the results cannot be regarded as satisfactory. The entire phenomenon has been more-or-less a spoon feeding exercise with inadequate association of the people.

Under such circumstances, it is quite apparent that Panchayati Raj can rectify many a shortcoming in the sphere of rural development. It can help in smoothening and accelerating the process in a number of ways. This was first pointed out by the Balwantrai G. Mehta Committee set up by the National Development Council in 1956. In its report submitted in 1957, the committee stressed on the necessity of grassroot-level self-government institutions to implement and supervise rural development. Reiterated by the Ashok Mehta committee in 1978, the fact was taken note of while formulating the 73rd Amendment and the consequent state legislations. The Eighth and the Ninth Five Year Plans have also taken strides in that direction. Panchayati Raj institutions thus have an important role to play in rural, development some of the major aspects of which have been discussed below.

Popular Participation

People's participation and rural development ought to go hand in hand. Involving the people in development programmes framed for their own development is essential, as this not only helps in making the people responsible and encouraging their initiative and self-reliance, but also in the mobilisation and effective utilisation of the local knowledge, skills, and resources. The traditional knowledge and skills of the local people have been acquired by the experience of several generations over a long period of time, and these result in more efficient use of resources, and help in minimizing waste and obtaining results with limited investments. People's participation may also ensure the local offer of labour, land, food, shelter or tools, for the running of a project. Together, these factors increase the flexibility of any development initiative and its responsiveness to local conditions, reduce the chances of mistakes, and often make up most of the difference between success and failure. As such, people's participation has of late perhaps become the standard mantra of rural development in India.

But till recently, the idea was that participation means getting people to co-operate in a project already designed for them from above. In other words, *"I manage you participate"* was the guiding principle. Institutional desires and the wishes of 'well-meaning' outsiders earned more weight than the felt needs and knowhow of the local people. Even when local participation in planning was actually pursued those consulted were usually local leaders and prominent people. This was known as the *top-down approach.* The approach failed almost in its totality, as many of the projects got entangled in delays, deviations, unforeseen constraints, unexpected outcomes and missed opportunities at the implementation stage. And, in many cases, wherein the projects were ultimately completed, the common man couldn't identify himself with the assets created (e.g. the hand pumps planted or fishery ponds dug) nor did he undertake the responsibility of their maintenance. To him, these were government property.

Actual people's participation in the process of rural development can be achieved only by the decentralisation of democracy. In other words, it is via the medium of Panchayati Raj that full local participation in the rural development process can be ensured. If the common rural people or their local-level representatives can discuss and decide what kind of development is required for the area, and can also supervise the work that is being done, most of the lacunae of the top-down approach of earlier programmes would be done away with.

Panchayati Raj in its present avatar is emancipated from many a major weakness. Oligarchy, patriarchy, absence of proper elections, along with negligible powers, responsibilities, resources, and autonomy, used to mark the entities that existed till now. But the 73 amendment and the consequent state legislations have removed these obstacles of popular participation. As a result, rural development is now being discussed and effected right from the lowest rung of the Panchayati Raj structure: the Gram Sabha, wherein even the general village folk have a say.

However, the mere activation of the Participatory Process via the medium of Panchayati Raj may not be sufficient. First, deep cynicism still exist among many people towards Panchayats. Even some of the elected members of the Panchayat bodies doubt whether attending PR meetings is really worth missing their daily wage. This is partly on account of the disorientation of the elite and erosion of self-confidence of the people in general caused by long colonial rule, partly on account of the poor track record of the Panchayats so far and partly on account of lack of trust in people, especially with regard to their capacity of being honest and efficient. Secondly, the complex rural reality has meant that being freed from bondage has not ipso facto resulted in the freedom as many expected it to. In the prevalent scenario in the villages, although people from the weaker sections may have got elected through the quota system, their feeble voices normally get drowned by the high decibels of those of the upper strata of the rural society Thirdly, the members of the Panchayat bodies generally do not have the abilities to participate in and run these institutions. This is mainly because the majority of people do not possess even the functional literacy and are normally bereft of the minimum threshold level of skills required of Panchayat members, to be able to participate in a meaningful manner.

The panacea is to develop intermediary voluntary organisations to act as bridges. As these non-government organisations (NGOs) work in the social sector, they have strong links at the grassroots. They can therefore not only remove the misgivings of the people about the Panchayat system, but also impart the requisite training to prospective members of the Panchayat bodies. Moreover, such organisations may cater to the interests of special disadvantaged groups viz. women, tribals, small farmers, *dalits*, landless labourers, and so on. Further, they may also ensure the development of a minimurn common package of human skills.

Such non-governmental organisations have sprung up all around the country providing an environment of optimism for the future. Most NGOs run training programmes for leadership development, capacity building, group dynamics management, etc., some of which have been organised specifically for PRI members, e.g., SEARCH and UMA in Karnataka, FRCH in Maharashtra, CINI in West Bengal and YIP in Andhra Pradesh. The NGOs catering to the disadvantaged sections of the rural society have been able to organise these sections of people into political entities and ensure that their interests are taken care of, besides creating proper representative leadership from them.

Making a retrospective analysis, we can definitely say that the Panchayati Raj system has encouraged popular participation in the rural development process in the states of West Bengal and Kerala, wherein the Panchayati Raj institutions are in an advanced state of development rural people have become really conscious of their rights, vis-a-vis development, and play an active part in the process.

Even in the state of Andhra Pradesh, the Janambhoomi programme could be a success because of the presence of the Panchayats. The Janambhoomi programme based on the *Saemaul or Undong* programme of South Korea, is one of the best examples available in the country to showcase the success of rural development by popular participation through Panchayats. Idealising the concept of self-help and service, the programme has made an effort to:

1. Involve people from all walks of life in decision-making and in the development process, through the Panchayats and allied voluntary organisations.
2. Effect social mobilisation and capacity building of the community especially the poor.
3. Take Government to the doorsteps of the people.
4. Get voluntary labour contribution *(shramdanam)* for the works.
5. Provide the right to information and social auditing.
6. Have participatory planning for the Basic Minimum Services such as primary and adult education, health, family welfare, drinking water, sanitation, etc.

Surveys conducted have revealed that the programme has been a grand success. People could understand their rights and duties as a result of the programme, and work together for their socio-economic development. But the requisite people's participation was possible only because of active Panchayat bodies in the state.

Women Empowerment

As noted by Ms. Nirmala Buch in her write-up on *Women's experience in New Panchayats: We are well aware about the pivotal role played by women in building a family, society and the world at large. No wonder the preeminent status of women in Panchayats is therefore the edifice for ushering in sustainable development from the grassroots in a bottom line approach.*

The Panchayats in their present form, have the provision for the reservation of not less than one-third of the seats and offices for the fairer sex. Even in the seats and posts already reserved for the disadvantaged groups like the Scheduled Castes and the Scheduled Tribes, not less than a third have been earmarked for the women folk of these groups. These features have been introduced as a culmination of a century long struggle for gender equity. Till recently there used to be token membership of women. Now we have over a third of them in every rural local body, providing what has been described as the *Critical Mass.* Naturally this has provided the requisite scope for the discussion of women-related issues in the Panchayats; and has created a space for women's needs within the structural framework of politics. Besides, the rural local bodies would now provide greater power and say to the women folk, especially with regard to the development of the area.

Thus, the process is going to reduce gender discrimination to a large extent, and result in a balanced growth in the rural areas. Greater awareness about government policies, their rights, and issues like family planning, reproductive rights, educational and health needs of the girl-child, among the common women-folk, that would ensure as a result, would in turn go a long way in taking the rural society forward.

But certain problems continue to linger on.

It has been observed that in many places, elected women members habitually remain absent in the PRI meetings. Even at places wherein the female attendance in the Panchayats is generally satisfactory, the women members are not given any opportunity to speak or to express themselves. The reasons are obvious. The rural society in those places has not yet emancipated itself from its patriarchal yoke and cannot accept women as equal partners for progress. And, a society that has fixed gender-based roles for the women-folk cannot be expected to change drastically by a wave of the constitutional amendment band.

The women member, who worry about crying babies and hungry husbands back home, would themselves think twice before going to attend the Panchayat meetings. Besides, their own nervousness , passivity, and lack of formal education stand in the way of their equal participation.

Table I : Number of Elected Women members by various States (as on August 1997)

Sl No.	State	In Gram Panchayats		In Anchalic Panchayats		In Zila Parishads	
		No.	%age	No.	% age	No.	%age
1.	Andhra Pradesh	78000	34	5420	37	363	33
2.	Arunachal Pradesh	86	2	39	3	–	0
3.	Assam	5469	18	669	26	–	0
4.	Bihar	–	0	–	0	–	0
5.	Goa	468	37	–	–	–	0
6.	Gujarat	21351	17	1275	33	254	33
7.	Haryana	17928	30	807	32	101	32
8.	Himachal Pradesh	1877	10	180	11	27	11
9.	Karnataka	35305	44	1343	40	33	4
10.	Kerala	-	0	-	0	0	0
11.	Madhya Pradesh	156181	33	3169	35	31	3
12.	Maharashtra	–	0	1435	41	–	0
13.	Orissa	27036	33	1754	33	284	33
14.	Punjab	23990	30	326	13	89	32
15.	Rajasthan	33566	30	1740	32	33	3
16.	Sikkim	27	2	–	–	1	1
17.	Tamil Nadu	31548	25	2295	35	22	3
18.	Tripura	1805	28	67	1	24	32
19.	Uttar Pradesh	120591	15	13865	23	634	24
20.	West Bengal	21742	35	3202	34	22	3
21.	Andaman & Nicobar Islands	229	34	–	–	10	33
22.	Dadra & Nagar Haveli	46	34	–	–	4	25
23.	Daman & Diu	25	40	–	–	5	33
24.	Pondicherry	–	0	–	–	–	0
	TOTAL	577270	21	37611	25	2516	16

Source : Website of National Institute of Rural Development (www.nird.org)

Women reservation in Panchayats has not fully benefited the common women-folk. Just giving women positions in the Panchayats is not good enough for addressing issues like gender justice. Rather, since most women have strong class and caste identities, they cannot be expected to align themselves with other women, going against their class, caste, or religious loyalties. Besides, it has been found that:

(a) the well-to-do upper strata women dominate the reserved seats. In Maharashtra, the women members are mainly from the Marathas and families owning more than 20 acres of land; and in Karnataka, from the upper caste Lingayats and Vokkaligas.

(b) the female kins of powerful politicians generally enter the Panchayats via the seats earmarked for women. The women's political connectivity is especially important in states like Bihar and Uttar Pradesh.

(c) the women members and office-holders are only leaders-by-proxy. They are like puppets in the hands of their male relatives. The family has been observed at times to be controlling and dictating actions and decisions of the women representatives.

Such women members definitely cannot be expected to discuss women-related issues in the Panchayats; nor can they be expected to have any sort of fellow feeling for the disadvantaged classes of women.

And in many states, even the women representation does not conform to the stipulation. This is quite apparent from Table 1 showing the number of elected women members in different states.

Yet there are clouds with silver linings. Exploding the myth of women's innate disability in shouldering responsibilities in the public life because of their illiteracy, lack of mobility, seclusion and dependency, lakhs of women have come forward to get elected to the Panchayats. Out of them, more than half a million have been positions of chairpersons. Such an entry itself is unprecedented. And many a woman, as chairperson of the Panchayat, is playing the role not only of chairing the meetings of the local body, but also of an executive authority entrusted with its successful working. Besides, an increasing number of women from the lower socio-economic groups with no previous political experience of their families, are entering the panchayats. Moreover, in states like Kerala and Andhra Pradesh, the women members, are actively participating in the proceedings. And last but not the least, after getting the necessary self-confidence on getting elected, many women members and office-holders have become independent enough to carry out quite an amount of good work. The example of Fatima Bi of Andhra Pradesh is apt in the case. This illiterate woman from the orthodox Muslim community became the President of the Gram Panchayat of her village Kalva. Overcoming her initial shyness, she got motivated enough to bring about large scale socio-economic development in her village. As a result, she received a U.N.O. award in 1998.

Much of the credit for the silver linings goes to non-governmental organisations. The NGOs have played a noteworthy role in organising women in whatever sector they have worked-health, self-help groups, housing, water and sanitation, education and watershed. The opportunities obtained by the women in the small groups dealing with the above issues have given them some sort of an empowered in the smaller arena, and have been a kind of 'testing ground' for them to enter a larger arena, As has been reported, involvement with NGOs and participation in larger people's movements have given the women concerned a more assertive stance. Such women, who have been supported and nurtured by NGOs, on entering the PRIs, have an edge over other women in the PRIs. The best examples of this phenomenon are the 'Right to Information' movement in Rajasthan and the 'Anti Arrach' movement in Andhra Pradesh.

On the whole, the provision for reservation of seats and offices for women, has in fact revolutionised the rural power structure in many a state where Panchayati Raj has taken strong roots. Nature resists change. Therefore there are initial hiccups in the process. But in the long run, the rural society is going to witness genuine gender equality and empowerment of women.

Socio-economic Development

Socio-economic condition in rural India is still in a sorry state of affairs. Illiteracy, lack of basic education, inadequate medical facilities and poor health awareness, inaccessibility of safe drinking water and proper sanitation facilities, malnutrition and high infant mortality, etc. constitute its salient features. As such, socio-economic development in the rural areas is a crying need. In order to achieve its goals, whether in the field of education, health and sanitation, etc., a medium is required to reach to the teeming millions of rural populace, and to act as an interface between the planners and the people. That medium can be provided by the Panchayati Raj.

Under the official Indian policy of "Education for all", several programmes have been launched: *District Primary Education*

Programme (DPEP), for promoting universal primary education; *Midday Meal Programme,* for- providing nutritional support to primary education; *Operation Blackboard (OBB), Adult Education Programme,* for spreading education among people who failed to get educated in their childhood, and *Open Learning System* (OLS), for providing education to those who are unable to learn through full time institutional system. The popular participation and the wide fora ensured by the Panchayats can help to effectively carry out these programmes. The government officials in various states can work in close tandem with the Panchayat for better performance.

Moreover, the Panchayats can arrest certain causes of failure of the programmes fostering the rural people, especially regarding universalisation of education. Lack of interest in education of the girl-child, has been acting as an impediment to larger enrolment of children in schools. Besides the disinterest and social taboos, certain practical causes also result in a large dropout rate: teacher absenteeism, poor teaching methods compounded by the fear psychosis regarding the teacher, and poor curriculum design. The problems can be discussed at the Panchayat meetings and adequate measures adopted. In fact, the Panchayats can do a lot in solving these problems. Rural guardians can be motivated to send their wards to schools by generating awareness regarding the importance of education among them. Schools can be made attractive to the rural children. The teaching in schools can be suitably monitored, and the teachers can be inspired, so that they do not fail in their duties. Funds can be mobilised to provide necessary infrastructural facilities to the schools. The Panchayat bodies ought to be vested with adequate power, in that regard. And certain states have in fact made requisite legislations in that line.

The Zilla Parishads and the Anchalic Panchayats, after their formation in the various states, have indeed made remarkable progress in providing educational facilities to the rural folk. They have been able to increase not only the total number of educational institutions under them, but also the enrolment of students there in states like Karnataka and Nagaland, after the self-government institutions started monitoring the village level schools directly teacher absenteeism and dropout rates have shown a significant decline while the overall quality of education showed a noteworthy improvement. These local bodies have also helped in spreading literacy through programmes like *Total Literacy Campaign (TLC)* under the *National Literacy Mission.* In fact, the literacy levels are higher in the states with well-established Panchayati Raj system, as can be deduced from the figures shown in Table II. Naturally, the primary educational scenario is also brighter in such states.

Thus states like Kerala and Maharashtra which have strong active Panchayat bodies, have high literacy rates both for the rural population as well as for the general population. On the other hand, in states like Bihar and Rajasthan, where Panchayats are not that developed, literacy rates are low both for the rural population as well as for the general population.

Table II : Literacy Levels by States

(Figures in Percentage as per 1991 Census)

Sl No. *State*	*Rural Literacy Rate*	*Overall Literacy Rate*
State with Empowered Panchayati Raj Institutions:		
1. Kerala	89.9	89.8
2. Maharashtra	55.5	64.9
3. Gujarat	53.0	61.3
4. Punjab	52.8	58.5
5. West Bengal	50.5	57.7
6. Karnataka	47.7	56.0
States with Disabled Panchayati Raj Institutions:		
1. Bihar	33.1	38.5
2. Rajasthan	30.3	38.6
3. Uttar Pradesh	36.7	41.6
4. Madhya Pradesh	35.9	44.2
5. Orissa	45.4	49.1
6. Assam	49.3	52.9
All India	44.7	52.1

Source : Centre for Monitoring Indian Economy India's Social Sectors, February' 96, Mumbai.

Further ensuring good health among the rural masses, proper organizational support is required in the rural areas. That support can be provided by the Panchayats. The Panchayats can create health awareness among the rural people, can organise rural health camps, and can help in the successful implementation of disease eradication programmes. Besides, the Panchayats can co-ordinate with other departments like Health, Public Works Department, Public Health

Table III : Rural Health Indicators in Selected States by Extent of PRI Empowerment

Sl No.	State	Crude Birth Rate, Rural 1996	Crude Death Rate, Rural 1996	Infant Mortality Rural 1996	Life Expectancy at Birth Rural 1994	Total Fertility Rate, Rural 1989-93	Population %age under 15 years, Rural	Female Lateracy Rate, Rural 1991
State with Empowered Panchayati Raj Institutions:								
1.	Maharashtra	24.9	8.7	58	62.0	3.2	35.6	52.3
2.	Tamil Nadu	19.9	8.7	60	60.5	2.2	32.2	51.3
3.	Gujarat	26.8	8.2	68	59.1	3.3	34.2	48.6
4.	Andhra Pradesh	23.5	9.1	73	59.7	2.7	33.7	32.7
5.	Karnataka	24.1	8.6	65	60.1	3.1	35.1	44.3
6.	West Bengal	25.3	8.0	57	60.0	3.4	37.8	46.7
State with Disabled Panchayati Raj Institutions:								
1.	Uttar Pradesh	35.2	10.6	88	55.0	5.6	39.9	25.3
2.	Madhya Pradesh	34.2	11.8	102	52.3	4.7	38.3	28.9
3.	Rajasthan	33.9	9.5	90	55.6	4.8	39.6	20.4
4.	Bihar	33.1	10.6	74	57.7	4.2	41.6	22.9
5.	Orissa	33.1	11.1	98	54.9	3.2	34.4	34.7
6.	Assam	28.9	10.1	79	54.1	3.6	40.6	43.0
	All India	29.3	9.7	78	58.0	3.8	37.6	39.3

Source : Foundation for Research in Health Systems (1997). Health Monitor, Ahmedabad.

Engineering, etc. for providing safe drinking water, proper sanitation, and adequate medical facilities in the villages. As a matter of fact, the local bodies have started working in that line. Therefore, the health indicators are better in states with empowered Panchayati raj institutions, as apparent from Table III.

Natural Resource Management

Natural Resources broadly include pastures, forests, minerals, wastelands, threshing grounds, waste dumping places, watershed, drainages, ponds, tanks, river/rivulets, and riverbeds. During the colonial and the plan era, these natural resources of the country were more or less centrally managed. The idea was that the land, the water, the forests, and so on, in order to be conserved, ought to be protected from the "onslaught" of the local users. Laws were framed to that effect and the various government departments viz. the Forest Department, the Irrigation Department etc. were established to control the use and conservation of the resources. The roles and duties of the departments were rigidly demarcated through stringent Acts and Rules; and a large part of their energies were utilized in keeping away the local people from the resources. As a result, the local communities which had been using these resources for centuries and were dependent on these, were alienated. Exclusion of these people also meant that a lot of traditional knowledge regarding conservation developed over centuries of experience, were lost. That coupled with ruthless commercial exploitation led to large-scale degradation of the very resources.

On realisation of the dangers involved in that faulty turn taken by the trajectory of natural resources management (NRM) in India, the State along with several NGOs started exploring the possibilities of the participation of the common people in that resource management. Certain model projects were designed in that line by the research institutions, by NGOs, and even by government departments on individual initiative of a few innovative officials. Thus, Joint Forest Management (JFM) and Watershed Development came into being. Today, Joint Forest Management (JFM) by the government agencies like the forest department and the civil administration, and the forest dwellers, has become the method for the effective protection of the country's diverse flora and fauna. Same is the case with other forms of natural resource management involvement. But that to be successful, the people of the forest areas must have an organised forum, a forum that is given by the Panchayat.

Therefore, consequent to the 73rd Amendment, the Indian Statute has given the Panchayats the functions of natural resource management (NRM) viz. agriculture, soil conservation, watershed development, social forestry and farm forestry, fuel and fodder, and maintenance of community assets, vide the XI Schedule of the Constitution. The process would engender the participation of the common people and make them responsible, and ameliorate the situation of the colonial and plan times, as has been mentioned above.

Besides, the mobilisation of the natural resources, including human resources (especially labour), locally via the Panchayats would ease the development work greatly, and reduce costs considerably. Work then would not be dependent much on the availability of funds from above.

Moreover, the use of the natural resources can be properly regulated only by strong local institutions like the PRIs. The illegal encroachment of these resources at, the hands of private interests can be effectively thwarted by the PRIs. Fresh encroachment can be prevented if the PRIs exercise the administrative control vested upon them, and strictly implement the already existing rules and regulations relating to encroachment. Carefully considering the legalities involved in removing existing encroachments, the PRIs can be entrusted with the power to evict encroachers of common land within their jurisdiction. The PRIs can also use the Gram Sabhas to educate the villagers about the benefits of conserving the common resources, and to formulate strict rules not only in discouraging the existing encroachments but also to halt any future encroachment. Thus, the PRIs can ensure collective responsibility in the regulation of the natural resources.

However, the people's participation in NRM via the medium of Panchayats is beset with certain basic problems. First, the user communities whose participation is actually necessary in NRM, generally do not happen to be the communities represented by the local political bodies such as the Panchayats. Panchayats function in a much wider area and are dominated by the local elite who may not actually identify with their constituent villagers. Although managing the projects through the user groups would be much more beneficial to them, the Panchayats are sustainable institutions with a mandate to work for local development, and have the capability to integrate NRM with wider development strategies. In such a situation is it desirable to continue with NRM via, the Panchayats, or to entrust responsibility directly to the user groups , or to have a structure wherein both can co-ordinate for efficient NRM? In that respect, we can take note of the Ostrom Principles. In her pioneering work, *"Governing the Commons"*, Elinor Ostrom mentioned a few principles for long enduring organisations managing natural resources:

1. They must have clearly defined boundaries so that everyone knows what is being managed and for whom;
2. There must be congruence between appropriation and provision rules and local conditions i.e. rules restricting time, place, technology and/or quantity of resource units are related to local conditions;
3. Most individuals affected by the operational rules can participate in modifying the operational rules.
4. Monitors, who actively audit the common pool conditions and appropriator behaviour, are accountable to the appropriators or are the appropriators.
5. Appropriators who violate operational rules are likely to be assessed graduated sanctions by other appropriators or by officials accountable to these appropriators or both;
6. Appropriators and their officials have rapid access to low cost local arenas to resolve conflicts among appropriators or between appropriators or between appropriators and officials, and
7. The rights of appropriators to devise their own institutions are not challenged by external Governmental authorities.

These principles are universal and relate to the Indian conditions as well. On close scrutiny, we find that the Panchayati Raj Institutions and the Community Based Organisations (CBOs) of the user communities together mentioned all the principles, but not alone.

PRIs satisfy four of the above fulfill principles: 1, 4, 5 and 6. PRIs have well defined boundaries, officers who acts as monitors of the PRIs and actively audit the common pool conditions and appropriator or behaviour, have to report to the PRIs, who are the appropriators, as the common pool resources belong to these institutions. The graduated sanctions, if imposed on violators of operational rules, can be enforced, as the PRIs have the powers to sue and be sued. Conflict resolution mechanism is in fact built into the PRI structure itself. But the PRIs fail to fulfil the other principles: 2, 3 and 7. PRIs cater to several user communities; and as their appropriation and provision rules have to be uniform, they cannot relate to all the local conditions, these conditions varying from community to community. Since PRIs (excluding the Gram Sabha) are only representative bodies, the participation of all individual users of natural resources is not possible. The rights of appropriators to devise their own institutions are extremely limited under the PRIs, as these institutions have to function within the constitutional framework.

On the other hand, CBOs satisfy the three Ostrom principles which are not satisfied by the PRIs: 2, 3 and 7. Under the aegis of the CBOs, appropriation and provision rules are discussed in the open meetings of the users and are related to the local conditions. Collective-choice arrangements do exists in the CBOs, as the individuals affected by the operational rules are also members of the CBOs and have a say in the modification of the rules. The rights of the users to devise their own institutions are not challenged by the government, as they themselves have actively participated in the formation of the CBOs. And the CBOs fail to satisfy the four principles which are satisfied by the PRIs: 1, 4, 5 and 6. The CBOs do not have clearly defined boundaries, and their areas of operation (unlike that of the PRIs) have not been fixed by the government. The monitors of the common pool resources are neither the appropriators under the CBOs (i.e. the users), nor are they accountable to them. While graduated sanctions can be applied to the violators by the CBOs, they cannot be enforced in most cases. There is no conflict-resolution mechanism readily available to the CBOs.

Therefore, the best way to ensure sustainability in NRM in the Indian context, as per the Ostrom principles, is to link the CBOs with the PRIs. The link can be established either by some sort of representation of the CBO in the PRIs, or by institutional collaboration between the CBOs and the PRIs; so that the two can function in a complementary fashion and protect the natural resources and the interests of the user groups.

Secondly, the creation of Common Pool Resources under NRM by popular participation is liable to be counter-productive. The Common Pool Resources are a subject of public goods with finite or subtractive benefits: if an individual uses more of the resources, less remains for others. As noted by Wade, each individual has an incentive to ignore the social costs of his resource use for fear that others will capture the benefits of the resource before he can. Garret Hardin visualised in his essay, *Tragedy of the Commons:*

> *In a pasture open to all, it is to be expected that each herdsman will try to keep as many cattle as possible on the commons ... Therein the tragedy. Each man is locked into a system compels him to increase his herd without limit in a world that is limited. Ruin is the destination towards which all men rush, each pursuing his own best interest in a society that believes in the freedom of the commons. Freedom in a common brings ruin to all.*

Common Pool Resources are, therefore, potentially subject to congestion, depletion, or degradation. However, the solution cannot be complete privatisation of the resources, as advocated by the capitalist school. That would lead to the exclusion of millions of users, create the problem already mentioned, and defeat the very purpose of rural development.

What then is the solution? The solution lies in supplementing an effective monitoring system under the Panchayats, with educating the ordinary users of the Common Pool Resources not to kill the proverbial goose that lays the golden eggs. The NGOs have an important role to play in that respect.

Promotion of Rural Entrepreneurship

Panchayats can play a big role in encouraging rural entrepreneurs and thereby promoting village (both cottage and small-scale) industries. Several self-employment measures like TRYSEM, JRY, etc. have been initiated by the government for that. For proper utilisation of such schemes, to encourage the rural youth in that regard, and to guide them properly, the Panchayats have to help out.

The success of Grameen Bank of Bangladesh in this field have led the Indian Government to adopt many of its features in its schemes. For example, the formation of self-help groups for utilisation of bank micro- credit in the newly announced schemes like Swarnajayanti Gram Swarozgar Yojana, Jawahar Gram Samriddhi Yojana. The individual rural entrepreneurs can come together to form self-help groups via the forum of Panchayats. The measures have been a great success in states like Andhra Pradesh, effectively replicating Grameen Bank.

Moreover, even monetary resource can be generated by the Panchayats for the implementation of the development schemes. The constitutional provisions provide for the local level tax collection by the Panchayats not only for their smooth functioning but also to finance rural entrepreneurship.

Better Micro-Planning

The Panchayats being a local level body and entrusted with the task of helping in the decentralised planning can guarantee the inclusion of the actual needs of the villages in the micro-planning process. Grass-root level decisions always address to local requirements and even adapt plans made by experts from above accordingly. In fact, the planning process of the Panchayats involves:

1. Initial contact and motivation in the Panchayat, followed by in-depth discussion and identification of active representative leadership.,
2. Collection of relevant information and basic data of the Panchayat, and preparing an inventory of prioritised needs of individual households and community villagewise, along with an inventory of resources (natural resources: water, vegetation, land and minerals, livestock; human resources, and financial resources);
3. Matching the aforesaid prioritised needs and resources into a Five Year Plan of the Panchayat and approval of the draft plan by general assemblies of small villages;
4. Systematic presentation of the Five Year Plan broken-up into Annual Plans, and its approval by the Panchayat;
5. Final approval of the above plan by the general assemblies of small villages, and finalisation of approved and modified plan.

The achievements of such type of planning are quite apparent in states like West Bengal, Kerala and Andhra Pradesh.

Check on Corruption and Diversion of Development Funds

The Panchayats have been vested with the powers to oversee the various development agencies. In fact, according to the procedures established, the implementing agencies like the District Rural Development Agency (DRDA) and the Development Blocks under them, are under the control of the Panchayat bodies, manned by the people or their local representatives. That can provide a check on corruption, and thwart the diversion and misappropriation of development funds.

To conclude, we can say that although Panchayati Raj has now been in existence in almost all the states of the Indian Union, certain lacunae have been experienced in the system, which have hindered its role as the harbinger of rural development. All of the 29 subjects earmarked for the Panchayats by the constitution have not been transferred by the respective state governments. There has been little infrastructure development of these local bodies as no funds have been provided for that. In many states, there is hardly any provision for training of the Panchayat people. Besides, the statute is silent or ambiguous on a number of matters related to the Panchayats. Once these issues are addressed, and the people learn to use the system effectively, the Panchayati Raj system is definitely going to play an important role in the rural development process. At the same time, we ought to understand that the system cannot be the proverbial Aladdin's lamp.

REFERENCES

Acharya, Poromesh; 2002, Education-Panchayat *and* Decentralisation; *Economic & Political Weekly*, Vol 37 No. 8

Alam, K: 1999, The Graméen Bank Micro-Credit and the Poor, *Assam Economic Review*, Vol 7.

Balakrishnan, Dr V. *and* Surjit, V., 2000, People's Plan in Kerala; *Kurukshetra*, Vol 48, No. 5.

Biswas, S. K: 2000, Microplanning Education- Chandrapur Experience; *Kurukshetra*, Vol 48, No. 4.

Buch, Nirmala: 1999, *From Oppression to Assertion - A Study of Panchayats & Women at Madhya Pradesh, Rajasthan & Uttar Pradesh*; Centre for Women's Development Studies, New Delhi.

Ibid: 2000, *Women's Experience in New Panchayats; The Emerging Leadership of Rural Women (Occasional Paper No.35);* Centre for Women's Development Studies, New Delhi.

Chand, Dinesh: 1999, Drinking Water Supply to Villages; *Kurukshetra*, Vol. 47 No. 10

Dadibhavi, R. V.: 2001, Management of Common Property Resources- Some Policy Issues; *Kurukshetra*, Vol 49 No. 11.

Deodhar, D. S.: 2000, Rural Health- Emerging Scenario; *Kurukshetra*, Vol 49, No. 1.

Dutta, Bishakha, (ed): 1998, And Who will make the Chappatis? A Study of All women's Panchayats in Maharashtra; *Stree*, Calcutta.

Dwarakanath, H. D.: 2000, Strategies to Improve Primary Education in Rural India, *Kurukshetra*, Vol 48, No. 4.

Ghatak, Maitreesh *and* Ghatak, M.: 2002, Panchayat System in West Bengal; *Economic & Political Weekly*, Vol. 37 No.1.

Jodha, N. S.: 1986, Population Growth and Rural Poor in Dry Region of India; *Economic & Political Weekly*, Vol 21 No. 27.

Joshi, R.P.(ed): 1998, *Constitutionalisation of Panchayati Raj – A Reassessment*; Rawat Publications, Jaipur.

Kulkarni, V. *and* Parikh A: 2000, Community Participation and Universalisation of Education – A Case Study, *Yojana*, Vol. 44 No. 10.

Meenakshisundaram, S.S. : 2001, Panchyati Raj Institutions in Natural Resources Management: Findings from Kerala; *Kurukshetra*, Vol. 49 no.12.

Mishra, R.K. *and* Davies, MR: 1999, VLW-as Catalyst for Rural Development: A Comparative Study of India and South Africa, *Indian Journal of Public Administration*, Vol 45 No 2.

Naganatha M, Jyoti-Sivagnanam *and* Gulnaz, Baby: 2000, Primary Education in Tamil Nadu–Challenges Ahead; *Kurukshetra*, Vol 48 No 4.

Ostrom, Elinor: 1994, *Governing the Commons: The Evolution of Institutions for Collective Action;* Cambridge University Press, Cambridge.

Padmaja, G *and* Lakshmipathi-Raju, M.:1999, Janmabhoomi–A New Dimension for Rural Development; *Kurukshetra*, Vol 47 No. 5.

Prabhakaran, S: 1990, Voluntary Agencies for Rural Development; *Kurukshetra*, Vol 38 No 9.

Ramachandran, Vimala: 2001, Community Participation in Primary Education-Innovations in Rajasthan; *Economic & Political Weekly*, Vol 36 No. 25.

Reddy, D.V. Narasimha: 1999, Kalva: Symbol of women's Power, *Kurukshetra* Vol 47 No 8.

Sastry, K.R. : 1999, Panchayati Raj in Andhra Pradesh-Recent Developments, *Kurukshetra*, Vol. 47 No.7.

Singh, J.L. *and* Pande, G.P.: 1998, Fifty Years of Panchayati Raj and Rural Development; Mark Publications.

Singh S. K: 2000, PRIs in Health Care–Future Strategies; *Kurukshetra*, Vol 49 No.1.

Sundar-Raj, D: 2000, People's Participation in Rural Development; *Kurukshetra*, Vol 48 No. 5.

Vyasulu, Poornima *and* Vyasulu, Vinod: 1999, Women in Panchayati Raj, *Economic & Political Weekly*, Vol.34, No 52.

5

PEOPLES' PARTICIPATION IN RURAL DEVELOPMENT IN NORTH EAST INDIA

Gorky Chakraborty

Introduction

The scientific study of rural society as a specialized area of sociology is a development of the twentieth century and prior to World War II had its growth principally in the United States[1]. This might be true from the sociological stand point but in terms of other branches of human knowledge, rural set-up, their relations of production, patterns of human habitation and occupation, culture and tradition influenced the study of human civilization from ages around the world. As overwhelming majority of the human race resided in rural areas, their study invariably was related (mainly) to these areas only. The percentage of the world's population living in localities of less than 20,000 was 97.6 in 1800, 95.7 in 1850, 90.8 in 1900 and 79.1 percent in 1950. For major world areas, estimates of the percentage of population living in places of less than 20,000 in 1950 were: Africa 91; Asia 87; Central America 79; South America 74; USSR, 69; Europe (excluding USSR) 65; North America 58 and Ocenia 53 percent[2] respectively.

The overwhelming number of rural population has made the agrarian question one of the central abiding concerns of classical political economy at least from the time of physiocrats. The Physiocrats contemplated a society where both the social product and surplus product originated in agriculture and therefore their treatise and discussions revolved around the rural set-up. Quite surprisingly, in the present world of globlisation, this agrarian question persist strongly in all global economic deliberations in general and issues concerning the developing world in particular. Agriculture and its practitioners hold the key to various current interrelated issues ranging from social, economic and political to that of patents, traditional rights and bio-diversity in today's world. Therefore the agrarian question persist as a global phenomenon and involves more particularly those areas which are yet to industrialize.

As Byers[3] points out, the agrarian question is a political question regarding the attitude of peasantry and their role in the transformation of social formations. What would be the posture of different strata of peasantry? What kind of alliances could they form with other classes or social strata who have shared interest? What kind of agrarian programme is necessary to mobilize the support of the peasantry or at least a section of it? The second aspect is social which relates with the class formation in agriculture or the differentiation of the peasantry. The third aspect is economic which concerns with the linkages between agriculture and the overall development of the entire social formation in particular to the process of industrialization in general. The role of agriculture as a major source of surplus for primitive accumulation, prior to self-sustaining accumulation of industrial capital therefore come into sharp focus. Thus agriculture and rural development occupies an important role to understand issues related to the growth of domestic markets for industrial products to the process of understanding the causes for shrinking of traditional and common property resources in a socio-economic set-up like ours.

Rural Development in India

India resides in villages, is an age-old adage and therefore issues related with rural development occupied an important position in the thoughts and philosophies of our thinkers and nation-builders. From Gandhi's *'Nai Talim'* and *'Swaraj'* to Tagore's concept of *Polli Somaj* rural development happened to be the key for an upright, humane and prosperous India. The ideal village community or village republics has been upheld by both of them as a model of village self-sufficiency and self reliance. They wanted to revive the village communities as a non-political base for social-regeneration in rural India. Rural reconstruction has therefore been the very basis of their nationalistic thoughts.[4] How much could we understand their ideals and implement them in our effort of national reconstruction is debatable and it seems that overwhelmingly we have failed to translate their ideals into reality. Nevertheless the values of Gandhi's 'austerity' and Tagore's 'aestheticism' remains true and unless today's mechanical man' is replaced by the 'creative integral man' within the framework of a decentralized economy[5] their ideals will remain ineffective in all models of rural development anywhere around the world.

Considering the ideals of rural development of our national leaders during freedom struggle, the support of peasantry to the freedom movement as well as their despicable plight for centuries, it was logical that ameliorating the condition of the rural masses should be the first priority of Independent India. The Five Year Plans through their Community Development Programmes ushered in a new era of rural development for the nation. Rural poverty and joblessness were sought to remove through various self employment and wage employment programmes. Since then it has been more than five decades of planning and rural development programming in India and whatever positive in terms of foodgrain production, land reforms, reduction of unemployment and poverty, it has been due to the implementation of these programmes. Starting from SFDA, MFAL, ICDS, DPAP, DWCRA, IRDP, TRYSEM, JRY to the present Swarna Jyanti Rozgar Yojna it has been a long list of programmes which have been initiated and implemented both at the national as well as the state level in India. There has been no dearth of programmes, finances and implementation agencies for rural development in our nation and therefore the important question arises that how far have we fulfilled the promises of our freedom struggle or are those ideals nothing but distant dreams? What do the current indicators indicate? Where have we failed and what is the way out?

Current Indicators

Agriculture has grown steadily during the last fifty years of planning in India yet if we consider it in terms of non-agricultural sector, the growth seems to be far from desired. There has been a widening gap between agriculture and non-agriculture sector in the Indian economy. Table 1 illustrates this fact.

Bhalla states that low farm incomes on sub-marginal holdings combined with employment growth rates in the economy which have fallen increasingly below population growth rates place a large sub-set of the rural population in a situation where they have limited options.[6]

This has led to the ever-widening gap between the agricultural and non-agricultural sector. In other words, one sector has grown at the cost of the other. However considering the state of Indian industries, it can be easily concluded that even their growth is far from satisfactory.

Table 1 : Per capita Incomes in Agriculture and Non-Agriculture from 1950-51 (Rs. in constant 1970-71 prices)

Per capita / year Per capita net domestic product at factor cost	*1950-51*	*1960-61*	*1970-71*	*1980-81*	*1990-91*
1 In Agriculture	402	427	427	417	483
2. In Non-Agriculture	588	831	1,080	1,252	1,742
3. Ratio of 2 to 1	1.46	1.94	2.53	2.93	3.61

Source : Bhalla, 1993

The dampening growth rates in the primary sector continued during the decade of 90's and in fact became more acute during the end of the decade. Table 2 highlights this fact.

Table 2: Annual Average Growth Rates in Primary Sector

Period	*Growth Rates*
1986-90	5.72
1991-95	3.77
1996-00	1.95

Source : Patnaik, Prabhat, 2001.

Low growth in agriculture has hampered the process of rural development in India. The agricultural sector has remained trapped within a vicious circle of excessive labour force, lower yields, traditional practices and deep rooted poverty. If we follow the NSS data it is evident that rural poverty ratios declined sharply during the 80s but during 90s it has exhibited a disturbing trend. (See Table 3).

Patnaik states that although there is a small decline in rural poverty between 1993-94 and 1990-2000 yet there has been no decline in 1998-2000 relative to 1990-91.[7] In other words, the basic proposition that the 1990's have been bad for poverty stands true.

Table 3: Head Count Poverty, Rural Areas (in percentage)

NSS	Period	Rural Ratio
32	July'77-June'78	50.6
38	Jan.'83-Dec.'83	45.3
43	July'87-June'88	39.6
46	July'90-June'91	36.4
50	July'93-June'94	38.7
51	July'94-June'95	38.0
52	July'95-June'96	38.3
53	July'97-Dec.'97	38.5
54	Jan.'98-Jul.'98	45.3

Source : Patnaik, Prabhat, 2001.

An increase in the poverty ratio has been the fall out of pathetic annual rate of growth of total employment in India in general and rural areas in particular during the last decade. (See Table 4).

Table 4: Annual Rate of Growth of Total Employment (%)

Period	*Rural*	*Urban*
1983 to 1987-88	1.36	2.77
1987-88 to 1993-94	2.03	3.39
1993-94 to 1999-00	0.58	2.55

Source: Patnaik, Prabhat, 2001.

Low rates of employment growth had two consequences, firstly, a rise in unemployment rate and secondly, reduction in participation rates. The current daily status unemployment rate rose between 1993-94 and 1999-2000 for rural males, rural females and urban males (except for urban females), the rise for rural males have been steepest at 29 percent. Similarly between January 1994 and January 2000, there has been a decline in worker population ratio for all categories. This decline has been steeper in rural areas than urban centres. Taking both males and females the decline has been from 444 per thousand to 419 in rural India and from 347 to 337 per thousand in urban India. (For India as a whole it has dropped form 418 to 395).[8] These statistics speak for themselves about the despicable plight of the millions in rural areas despite frequent launch of schemes concerning rural development in India.

The effect of dismal sectorial growth rates, falling income and employment have resulted in a fall in annual per capita availability of foodgrains for human consumption. Since more than 70 percent of our population are in rural areas and had falling income and opportunities, it can be logically concluded that fall in per capita availability of foodgrains has been much steeper in rural areas than urban centres. From Table 5 it is evident that average annual availability of foodgrain has declined to 159.9 kg from 173.5 kg, i.e., by 8.5 percent' during the last decade of economic liberalization in India.

Table 5: Per capita Availability of Foodgrain, 1989-90 to 2000-01

Period	Cereals	Pulses	*Annual Per Capita Availability* foodgrains (in kg)
1989-90 to 1991-02	159.3	14.2	173.5
1992-93 to 1994-95	156.5	13.6	170.1
1995-96 to 1997-98	156.6	12.7	169.3
1998-99 to 2000-01	148.1	11.8	159.9

Source : Patnaik, Utsa, 2001

These indicator themselves highlight the dismal scenario of rural India and thereby call upon for an alternative model of rural development where there is growth with equity and social justice.

Scenario in India's North East

The aspect of rural development as a foundation of economic development of the region is unquestionable. However, considering the milieu of the North East, the task of rural development seems not only diverse but intriguing too. The hill-plain continuum along with the tribal-feudal one makes the development issue difficult. This diversified existential reality has often been missed by the planning authorities and implementation agencies concerned with rural development in north east India. The customary and traditional values, occupation and practices has been just brushed aside in many cases as methods and models of development alien to the indigenous people have been thrust upon them in the name of development. What Narmada Bachao Andolan[10] had to say about these patterns of imposition over the tribals of the Narmada region in the name of development holds true for the people in the north eastern region too. The imposition of capitalist conception of private ownership of land is the only recognisable right and *sine qua non* of social development has not only encroached upon customary corporate rights and often extinguished rights to common property resources of the tribals, but has also weakened their relative egalitarian, communitarian and co-operative ethos. Prabhu[11] a well-known tribal activist adds that the individual oriented developmental process available to a small fraction, is geared not only to co-opt and assimilate the few but also to facilitate the entry of capitalist interests into in essentially pre-capitalist matrix. These schemes and the imposition of alien cultures have further damaged their ethics of sharing, values of cooperation, consensus politics, heritage of self-control, and management of forest resources, marine and animal life. So in the name of connecting to the mainstream and ushering in an era of development in this alien terrain according to Roy Burman certain elite groups were created in these societies which were internally alienated and externally frustrated.[12] These structures which the development model has created within the society of north east are in conformity with the structures that colonialism created in Indian society as a whole.[13] Issues concerning rural development and agrarian reforms are not much different from the projections as stated in this section.

For the north-eastern region as a whole the rural scene particularly the agricultural scene is beset with lower yields, large scale poverty and lack of employment opportunities. Traditional methods are often sought to be substituted by so-called modern methods of cultivation and livelihood. *Jhumming* or slash and burn cultivation bears one such testimony. There are more than 100 tribes in the hill regions of north east who practice shifting cultivation and the state machinery is trying to replace it with sedentary terrace cultivation for the last 50 years. This effort has met with little success as terrace cultivation doesn't fit into the local milieu and secondly, due to lack of high energy inputs such as fertilizers, weedicides and pesticides it become unproductive. As the soil cover is thin in majority of areas in north east, the nutrient losses are heavy and therefore large quantity of fertilizer is required to sustain the practice of terrace cultivation. Although it is true that the jhumming cycle which earlier had been 20-30 years have drastically come down to 5 years or even less yet is highly debatable whether this is the result of rise in population of hill dwellers vis-a-vis settlers on one hand or due to large scale timber extraction over the years.[14] However the greatest cause for failure of the schemes to replace *jhum* cultivation has been due to lack of people's participation in those areas where it has been proposed to be implemented.

While the replacement of shifting cultivation with terrace cultivation in the hills has been far from desired in the plains, the picture in terms of enhancing productivity of foodgrains have been similar. There are no lack of schemes on issues concerning rural development and raising of agricultural productivity yet mainly due to lack of peoples participation, the results never match the proposed targets. The yield rates of foodgrain in the north eastern states has been lower than the all India average and this has widened more after 1990-91. Table 6 shows the difference in yield rates.

Table 6: Yield Rates of Foodgrain in India and North Eastern Region

(kg/hectare)

Period	*India*	*NER*	*Difference*
1987-88	1,328	1,162	-166
1990-91	1,392	1,315	-77
1995-96	1,491	1,370	-121
1997-98	1,551	1,400	-151

Source: Scanned from Basic Statistics, 2000.

This pattern is similar for all principal crops grown in this region compared to that of the all India average.

Table 7: Proportion of North Eastern Region to All India Foodgrain Production, 1985-86 to 1997-98

Period	*Total Foodgrain Production (in lakh tonnes)*		
	NER	*India*	*% of NER in Total Foodgrain Production*
1985-86	42.18	1504.99	2.80
1990-91	48.83	1762.30	2.77
1995-96	50.87	1804.15	2.82
1997-98	52.60	1924.34	2.73

Similarly the proportion of Northeast to all India foodgrain production has remained unchanged over the years. The average foodgrain production of the region to all India foodgrain production has stagnated around 2.8 percent although it inhabited 3.7 per cent of India's total population. Table 7 illustrates this fact.

Thus it is evident that neither in the hills nor in the plains of northeast, desired results have been achieved in case of agricultural practices or its productivity. Despite planning and implementation of various schemes related to rural development it is felt that the process has been slow and less than desirable. Other than lack of infrastructure, irrigational facilities, better inputs etc. the single most important factor resulting in hampering of the rural development process has been lack of people's participation. Until and unless, the people of rural areas for whom the policies are framed and implemented are involved in the process, sustainable development of rural areas will remain a far cry.

People's Participation

From the belief that industrial revolution fostered an era of agricultural revolution, technology and capital continued to hold the sway for rural development over a long time. The aspect of community and people's involvement and participation in the process of rural development therefore were not the priorities among the policy framers. It took them sometime to realise the importance of 'participation' by the people for desired change. People being the subjects and not the objects, the premise should be that the projects are for the people and not people for projects. It is only through participation that the urge for development emerges from within the people and the process of imposition of alien development models become redundant.

Various scholars have defined participation in their own ways depending on the circumstances and the projects in which they were involved. Paul[15] states that in the context of development, community participation refers to an active process whereby beneficiaries influence the direction and execution of development projects rather than merely receive a share of project benefit. Santhanam[16] forwards several possible ways of involving people in development projects based on various case studies. It includes i) convincing the people about the importance of programme; ii) need for better planning with people; iii) need to consult local organizations before launching a programme; iv) inviting the villagers for discussion before introducing a programme; and v) taking into consideration the felt needs of the people. So instead of centralisation, peoples participatory concept advocates decentralization and that too not from one level of government to another but from the bureaucratic level to that of people through a democratic process. Here the Panchayati Raj Institutions can play a major role in motivating people to participate, formulate and implement programmes for rural development.

Mishra[17] has dealt extensively with the process and levels of people's participation. He is of the view that first of all the policy framers should have proper understanding about the community since these are rarely homogenous groups. Then the positive and negative attitudes of the community towards a particular set of activities are to be ascertained. During this process there should always be an eye on some prospective group leaders. These informal leaders help in creating a consensus among heterogeneous communities thereby avoiding friction. Then identification of the priority needs of the community are to be ascertained by group meetings which with due approval can be framed into a programme/project. With proper networking of funding the project can be initiated keeping in view about the local or community's contribution towards total cost of the project. Then the project managers can train for proper implementation with due involvement of the beneficiaries. The implementation can then start fruitfully at the hand of beneficiaries who themselves decide the ways and means of proper implementation. At this stage the project managers play a passive role of facilitator thereby making the people confident about themselves. This process leads to self-generating development programmes.

Case Studies

The note on people's participation as discussed in the preceding section if followed meaningfully can be implemented in a sustainable way thereby bringing about a sea-change in the approach towards rural development. This is particularly true in case of India's northeast where traditional values and community principles are often mistakenly equated with factors inhibiting change and development. After all, all human behaviour aims at satisfying a need or an aspiration, and people will only agree to change their habits when they are convinced that it will be to their advantage. So it is through informing, motivating and encouraging the people that we can best hope to improve their living condition. Their lies the importance of people's participation.

Three case studies are presented which emerged from various field trips in different villages. While the first maintains its activities within its community practices, in the second case by forming an organisation a traditional livelihood pattern is practised while in the third the organisation takes up a new venture quite in tune with the development model of globalized world. However, in all the three instances, the organisations have achieved success, solely due to the participatory approach followed among the members both planning and its implementation. This has provided the sustainable edge to these projects.

Case study : I

In Chetia Kaivarta Gaon[18] of Sibsagar district few villagers encroached upon adjacent government land to increase the size of their agricultural holdings used for cultivation. This process of encroachment has never bothered the Land Revenue authorities but the community has taken up an unique measure to deal with it. Those who illegally occupied government land, had to pay a nominal sum to the village community fund which is utilised for various community based programmes in the village. Moreover, harvest in the encroached land is divided between the individual encroachers and the community as a whole. This has helped to create a buffer stock in the village which is utilized during exigencies or festivals. This feature is unique in the sense that the land which otherwise has been left barren is cultivated and a part of the produce is kept aside as community fund and food stock. The process of penalising the encroachers by forcing them to part with a portion of their produce has been beneficial for both the parties. Since it is a truism that wherever a piece of land lies empty or abandoned there will be encroachers and considering the present state of affairs, the government machinery is bound to fail. So the best viable alternative is to solve the problem at the village level through local institutions as initiated in Chetia Kaivarta village. This example portrays how a flexible management principle within the community set up can play an important role both in penalising and also enhancing the community principles pragmatically

Case study : 2

This is an example of how an organisation maintaining their community relations and practising traditional livelihood patterns have undertaken sustainable projects through People's participation. An women organisation with the name of "Deori Jagaran Mahila Samity"[19]

comprising of plain tribals mainly belonging to the Deori tribe of two adjacent flood prone villages namely Adarsha Deori Gaon and Kololowa Deori Gaon of Khowang Block in Dibrugarh district have been undertaking various programmes of production and marketing such as weaving of shawl and *gamocha*, preparation of pickles, squash, jam and also imparting training concerning weaving and food processing to fellow women in these two villages. The organisation maintained their records and accounts professionally. Cash is deposited in their bank account No. 6378 of United Commercial Bank in Khowang Ghat. The organisation is registered under the Societies Act bearing a Regd. No. 3319. Moreover they also conducted meeting both of the Executive Members and General Members at regular intervals.

The President of this organisation came into contact with CAPART which encouraged the organisation to carry out suitable rural development programmes locally. After due discussion with the members of the organisation a project was finalised related to piggery and poultry development. Evaluator and Monitors were sent by CAPART to ascertain the skill, capacity and sustainability of the project and its beneficiaries. Piggery and poultry being traditional occupation of the Deori's, the women beneficiaries of this project had little difficulties. The project was granted by CAPART whereby grants were made and guidelines for scientific management were forwarded. About 20 percent of the project cost have been by means of local contribution both in cash and kind from the beneficiaries (10 percent from the organisation and 10 percent by beneficiaries). The project has been completed successfully and the beneficiaries have benefited not only monetarily but also in terms of skill and confidence too. Due to which the beneficiaries have themselves continued the project and added manure and compost programme along with their piggery and poultry programmes.

Table 8 : Status of Self-Help Groups

Group No.	*Date of Establishment*	*Total Savings* (Rs.)	*Total Lending*	*Bank Account No.*	*No. of Members*
1	29-4-2000	6,500	6,050	SBI, AS/3/217	15
2	7-7-2000	3,735	3,050	SBI,AG4/2/25	16
3	19-9-2000	4,505	4,300	SBI,AG4/3/223	18
4	27-9-2000	5,910	5,000	SBI,AG4/3/228	15
5	28-9-2000	2,184	2,000	SBI,AG4/3/226	16

Here within the traditional set up and traditional livelihood pattern this organisation has benefited due to people's participation and therefore enhanced the process of rural development meaningfully in the concerned village.

Case Study : 3

This case study is concerned with another organisation named the Tinisukia Gaon Tribal Mahila Samity[20] in a distant place (in terms of its distance from National Highway 37) in Tinisukia Gaon of Barbaruah Block of Dibrugarh district comprising of poor tribal women. This organisation have been involved in income generation projects such as pig and goat rearing and small business activities other than imparting training related to weaving. The organisation organises camps on issues concerned with environment protection and family welfare. The organisation has an Executive body and a General body, the members of which meet at regular intervals. They maintain a regular account of their meetings as well as 'that of finances. It has a Savings Account No. CSI/20 at State Bank of India, Lejai SAB. The organisation is registered under the Societies Act and bear a Regd. No. 451. This organisation is popular in its locality for active intervention and participation on issues concerning women.

The President and an Executive member of the organisation attended a Training Programme conducted by Rashtriya Gramin Vikas Nidhi (RGVN) in Guwahati on formation of Self-Help Groups (SHG's) and Micro-Finance Programmes. After their training at RGVN, they convened a general meeting of the members of their organisation and motivated them to form SHG's. Due to their participatory nature, 80 members came forward to form SHG's. Within 3 months 5 SHG's were formed who took up micro-finance programmes. The current status of these groups are as follows:

Each member contributes equal amount to the group savings and in turn, collection amount is deposited in the bank. If they required credit, the member can apply for the credit mentioning amount required and also the purpose of loan. Then all the members of the group decide the loan application.

Considering the success of the existing SHG's the organisation has chalked out a project proposal for forming 40 SHG's in 4 villages namely Binoy Khuti No. 1 and 2, Dewan Bari and Lalmati involving women of these respective villages. As it is an enormous task concerning large number of people in 4 villages, they have forwarded the proposal to CAPART for evaluation and approval.

This is thus a successful case of women empowerment by an organisation in a distant village by means of modem concept. They have retained their traditional structures yet imparted modern approach of micro-finance programme among their members. The key to their success is again nothing but participation and sharing.

In Lieu of Conclusion

In order to foster a meaningful and sustainable pattern of rural development in India's north-east certain existential realities are to be noted in its historical context. Without understanding the ethos of community practices, traditional skill and patterns of livelihood and occupation any development programme imposed upon the societies of northeast are bound to have halfhearted if not distorted results. Historical patterns of occupational specialisation result in development of distinct skills and competencies in different communities. When development strategies require these communities to diversify into new occupations, the time and effort this transition requires is often underestimated. Again an important element of transition from tradition to modernity is the replacement of authority based transactions to contract-based exchange relations[21] and in communities steeped into tradition and customs, peoples participatory approach seems to be the viable alternative for bringing about rural development in these areas. The case studies highlighted in the paper revalidated this aspect strongly.

NOTES AND REFERENCES

1. Sills, David. L (ed.), *International Encyclopedia of Social Sciences*, Vol. 13, The Macmillan Company and Free Press, 1968.
2. *Op. cit.*
3. Breman, Jan and Mundle, Sudipto (eds.), *Rural Transformation in Asia*, Delhi : O.U.P., 1991.
4. Mandal, Gobinda, C., *Rural Development : Retrospect and Prospect*, New Delhi : Concept Publishing Company, 1992.
5. See no. 4
6. Bhalla, Sheila, 'The Dynamics of Wage Determination and Employment Generation in Indian Agriculture', *Indian Journal of Agricultural Economics*, Vol. 48, No. 3, 1993.

7. Patnaik, Prabhat, 'Ten Years of Economic- Liberalization', *The Marxist*, Vol. 17, No. 2, 2001.

8. See no. 4

9. Patnaik, Utsa, 'Falling Per capita Availability of Foodgrains', *People's Democracy*, September 30, 2001.

10. Towards Sustainable and Just Development, Baroda, *Narmada Bachao Andolan*, 1992).

11. Prabhu, Pradip, 'Sustainable Tribal Development'. *The Indian Journal of Public Administration*, Vol. 39, No. 3, 1993.

12. Roy, Burman, B. K., 'Challenges and Responses in Tribal India', as quoted in no. 11 above.

13. Roy, Burman, B.K., 'National Movements Among Tribals, as quoted in no. 11 above.

14. Ramkrishnan, P.S. 'Sustainable Development in Weaker Sections of the Society - Where do we stand?, *The Indian Journal of Public Administration*, Vol. 39, No. 3, 1993.

15. Paul, S., Community Participation in Development Projects : The World Bank Experience', *Readings in Community Participation*, Washington, The World Bank, 1989.

16. Santhanam, M.L., 'People's Participation - Some Psychological Dimensions', *Journal of Rural Development*, Vol. 3, No. 4, 1984.

17. Mishra, S. N., 'People's Participation for Sustainable Development', *The Indian Journal of Public Administration*, Vol. 39, No. 3, 1993.

18. Chakraborty, Gorky, 'Whithering of Community Resources : A Few Case Studies in Assam', *Man & Development*, Vol. 19, No. 1, 1997.

19. This organisation has been under my supervision in the capacity of Project Evaluator cum Facilitator for Council for Advancement of People's Action and Rural Technology (CAPART), Regional Centre, Guwahati.

20. I am currently monitoring this organisation as a Project Evaluator cum Facilitator for Council for Advancement of People's Action and Rural Technology (CAPART), Regional Centre, Guwahati.

21. Shall, Tushaar, 'Institutional Dimensions of Agricultural and Rural Development in India', *The Administrator*, Vol. 40, No. 1, 1995.

6

PANCHAYATI RAJ IN ASSAM
Understanding the Politics of Democratic Decentralisation and Rural Development

Girin Phukon

In a vast country like ours, Panchayati raj institution assumes great significance from the point of view of democratisation of the political system. As is well-known, effective functioning of a democratic system depends upon the degree of political participation of the people. In order to ensure political participation, the devolution of power and authority to the rural people is necessary so as to enable them to take part in development administration. The participation of people at the grass-root level in managing their local affairs is possible only through the institution like the Panchayats. Democratic decentralisation is a popular concept in the arena of political discourse. It makes possible the extension of democracy at the grass root level. This paper is intended to examine how far rural people have been able to effectively exercise the powers given to them through the institution of Panchayat. Why decentralisation of power to the people has degenerated into decentralisation of corruption and power over the people ? However the paper is limited to understand the case of Assam in this context.

I

Panchayat as a system of local self-government had its genesis during the British rule. Lord Ripon may be regarded as the father of local government in India. He attempted to establish self-government at the grass root level in the country by introducing provision for non-official element in the local government. Since then various efforts have been made towards the reform of Panchayati raj system. After independence, local self government institutions received a new impetus, particularly in rural sector. A number of provincial governments organised village panchayats as the unit of rural local self government and endowed them with powers and authority to carry out various important functions to satisfy the needs of the people at the lowest level of public administration. This idea was incorporated in the part IV of the Indian Constitution which provides for Directive Principles of State Policy. Accordingly Article 40 of the Constitution maintains that the state shall take steps to organise village Panchayats and endow them with powers and authority as may be necessary to enable them to function as units of self-government. Thus it appears that the ideal of participatory democracy through grass root level institution like Panchayats was envisaged in India's constitutional framework. After adoption of the Constitution, Panchayats have been constituted in rural areas all over the country in variation in forms from state to state,. But the working of Panchayati raj institutions shows that in many states they have become ineffective due to the reasons such as not holding of periodic election regularly, prolonged supersessions, inadequate representations to weaker sections like ST/SC and women, lack of adequate financial resources and inadequate devolution of powers to them. In fact, the goal of power to the people through Panchayati raj institution turned into power over the people. In view of this, 73rd amendment of the Constitution was made in 1992 which came into force in 1993. Under this Act State Legislature is supposed to devolve powers and responsibilities to the local bodies to enable them to function as institution of self-government. Further, the State Legislature is obliged to transfer necessary financial powers and resources. Although many states have already implemented this Act, Assam is yet to materialise the Assam Panchayati Raj Act, 1994 adopted in accordance with the 73rd amendment of the Constitution.

II

After independence, the first Panchayati Raj Act was the Assam Rural Panchayat Act, 1948. The Act provided for two-tier Panchayati raj system-Primary Panchayats at the village level and Rural Panchayats at the apex level. For the first time the Act provided for an election of Panchayati raj institution on the basis of universal franchise. In 1957 a committee was constituted under the chairmanship of Balwant Rai Mehta to recommend for an effective institutional mechanism to involve local people in the process of development. The committee recommended the three-tier Panchayati raj institution with a real devolution of powers and resources. In the line of this recommendation the Assam Panchayat Act, 1959, was enacted with three-tier Panchayati raj institution i.e., Gaon Panchayat at the village level, Anchalik Panchayat at block level and Mahkuma Parishad at the sub-divisional level. However, in order to revitalise the local self-government, 1959 Act was replaced by Assam Panchayati Raj Act, 1972, and a two-tier structure was introduced. Mahkuma Parishad at the subdivisional level and Gaon Panchayat at village level, covering a population of 15000 and not more than 20,000. The state again came back to three-tier system of Panchayat institution with the enactment of Assam Panchayati Raj Act, 1986.

All these Acts provided scope for people's participation in rural decision making process along with reservation of weaker section of the society. Besides the Acts contained provision of holding election for Panchayat institutions at regular interval. But the supersession, dissolution, delays in holding election and suspension of election for an indefinite period had crippled the institutions resulting reduction of importance of Panchayati raj institution in the process of decentralisation of power to the grass root level. This situation was further aggravated by installations of ad-hoc bodies replacing the elected one. Further acute financial constrain cropped up in Panchayati raj institution. The financial resources collected by way of imposing taxes, fees etc. have become absolutely inadequate to support the developmental work without grant-in-aid from the state government.

In 1986, Government of India has set up a Committee to prepare a scheme on the revitalisation of the Panchayats. The Committee recommended that Panchayats should be constitutionally recognised and protected by inserting a new provision in the constitution The committee further suggested that the provision should ensure regular, free and fair election of the Panchayats. In conformity with these recommendation the 73rd Constitutional Amendment Act, 1992 came into effect from April 24th 1993. As per this Act, the government of Assam enacted the Assam Panchayati Raj Act, 1994, repealing the Assam Panchayati Raj Act, 1986. The new Act again introduced the three-tier Panchayat system, i.e. Gaon Panchayat at the village level, Anchalik Panchayat at block level and Zila Parishad at the districts.

IV

Despite frequent changes of structures of Panchayati Raj institution, it has not been able to fulfil the expectation of the people due to lack of political will, paucity-of funds, over dominance of administration, factionalism and corruption, over dependence on government grants are some of the major causes behind failure of local bodies to act as the arm of democratic decentralisation. It needs to mention that in a situation where a large majority of the people live below poverty level and are illiterate, there may hardly be any scope for peoples' active participation. Besides, the peoples' participation at grass-root level has been limited by the political leadership which comes from a particular class of people. Therefore, although a number of Panchayati raj institutions have been created at the grass-root level in order to operationalise the concept of "democratic decentralisation" and devolution of power to the marginalised people, wide-spread poverty and illiteracy of the people have facilitated the dominance of corrupt politicians and bureaucrats and the privileged class of the society monopolise the political power. This class normally refuge to share power with the disadvantaged groups of the rural masses. As such decentralisation of power to the people bound to degenerate into power to the powerful. In effect, decentralisation of power to the rural people degenerate into decentralisation of corruption. The bureaucracy is more interested in government subsidy schemes, a large part of which is shiffoned way by the politicians, middlemen and contractor nexus involving in rampant corruption.

The democratic institutions like Panchayats are expected to reflect the will of the people and respond to the popular needs to a considerable extent. But in a developing countries like India where political awareness is limited and public opinion is incapable of asserting itself effectively, the democratic process suffers from many inherent maladies. Therefore, the working of participatory democracy with democratic decentralisation in India during last few decades has demonstrated an unhealthy political culture emanating from the rise of popular authoritarianism, political corruption, criminal-political nexus highlighting the role of money and muscle power which has led to the decline of social and political values challenging the credibility of the democratic institution and the State apparatus. As a result, bureaucracy has more or less ceased to be an effective instrument of development and social engineering rather it has been highly politicalised. Similarly, the Parliament and Legislative Assemblies of different states ceased to be a forum for serious and purposeful discussion on the issues of public importance. In such a state of affairs how one can expect that the local bodies will be exception to their creators. Therefore, the working of Panchayati Raj Institutions in Assam will have to understood in the context of totality of this objective situation.

V

In view of the facts noted above, it is necessary to understand the basic character of Indian state for the purpose of assessing the working of Panchayati raj institutions as they are inseparable parts of the larger whole i.e. totality of the system. India has adopted a system of bureaucratic capitalism. In fact, it has accepted the capitalist path of economic development which obviously resulted in uneven economic development in the country. The centralisation of state power is a reflection of law of centralisation inherent in the capitalist development. In other words, the law of centralisation is inherent in the capitalist path of economic development . It may not be out of place here, even if, by way of digression, to note that such a tendency towards centralisation and concentration of political power has been a universal phenomenon in the constitutional evolution of all liberal democracies. Obviously, therefore, centralisation and concentration of power is inherent in the Indian Constitution itself. By and large, India's democracy is essentially a bourgeoisie democracy as it seeks to protect and reproduce socio-economic system based on private property. There is a logical connection between capitalism and liberal democracy. Therefore, the liberal democratic institution such as the Panchayati raj is bound to serve the interest of privileged bourgeois class rather than the general masses. But interestingly, with the creation of Panchayati raj institution through necessary enactment, an impression has been created that powers are decentralised to the marginalised people to enjoy the fruits of democracy. The argument that democratic decentralisation makes possible the extension of democracy at the grass root level, decentralisation lies at the core of democracy because it aims at making democracy real by bringing the millions into the functioning of representative government at the lowest level are nothing but lip services made for perpetuating and concentration of power in the hands of authoritanian regime at the centre controlled by bureaucratic capitalism. Empowerment of the rural people and the toiling masses may be meaningful only if a drastic change of the existing socio-economic structure of our country could be made for which the masses need to be educated to the extent of generating political consciousness. The working of Panchayati raj institution in Assam and elsewhere in the country may be better understood under this framework and also in the context of totality of character and role of Indian state.

7

PEOPLES' PARTICIPATION IN RURAL HEALTH CARE PROGRAMME
Insights from three Blocks of Kamrup District

Suranjan Sarma

Introduction

The rural development programmes are designed to improve the economic and social life of the people at the lower end of income distribution - the poor and those that are marginalized because of their gender, caste, lack of education and residence. However for better social return from investments in such a development programme like primary health care programme, basic education etc., perhaps greater involvement of the community is required. The process of people's participation helps to counteract the denial of access to development resources by the poor.

The meaning of people's participation varies in different settings depending upon the conditions prevalent in a community as well as the approach of a rural development programme. The easiest and perhaps the most widely practiced form of people's participation in development programme is consultation with members of the community about their development needs (Tandon, 1994). Thus in implementation of development programme apart from imparting actual service, the extension work for information, discrimination and motivating the common people to avail the services take an important place. Spreading of awareness helps in greater community involvement that would make community oriented health care programmes like prevention and eradication of communicable diseases much easier to implement. Therefore, in case of a primary health care programme whether initiated by the non-government organization or by government, generally, health workers are expected to interact on a regular basis with the community to define its health needs. Consultation may be held with the individuals, with families or with formal groups such as village health committee to acquaint them with information of health programme.

In Assam, the Government of Assam has been running a lot of primary health care programmes like 'maternal and child health' (MCH)[1] and various 'disease control programme'[2] to fight against common infectious, endemic and communicable diseases through a network of primary health centre[3] in the rural areas. A large number of extension workers like multipurpose workers (MPW), *anganwadi* workers (AWW), health guides, auxiliary nurse midwifes (ANM), dais etc., are being associated with different health care programmes. This induced the author to take up a study about the role and effectiveness of the extension work in implementation of various health care programmes. The present paper, which is a product of that study, is organized with the following objectives:

(1) to study the effectiveness of extension work for information dissemination and motivating the common people to avail the health care services; and,

(2) to discuss the emerging policy implications for increasing involvement of the people with the development programmes.

Data Source and Methodology

The field study on which the present work is based was carried out during the first quarter of 1998. The study was confined to three primary health centre areas/ blocks of the Kamrup district of Assam. These three locations namely, Sonapur, Kamalpur and Chaygaon primary health centre areas were selected keeping in view two factors (a) the selected areas should be geographically scattered in different parts of the district; and (b) the population in the areas should be representative of the different social and ethnic groups inhabiting the district.

A sample of households was drawn from each of the selected primary health centre areas through a process of two stage random sampling. In the first stage six villages from each primary health centre area were selected. In the second stage ten percent of the households from each selected village were drawn as ultimate sample unit. A total of 250 households thus selected from 18 villages of the primary health centre areas of Sonapur, Kamalpur and Chaygaon were covered in the field survey. However, out of 250 households under survey 113 households had their children in the age group less than 5 years. All total 157 numbers of children comprised the sample. The children were classified into two categories (1) children born recently (infants up to 2 years old); (2) children born earlier (2< age >5). The classification was done with the view to examine the progress of immunization over time, whether the infants born recently are better immunized or not.

Discussion of the Results

Role of Extension Work in Implementation of Various Health Care Schemes

Progress of Immunization: The progress of immunization against infectious and communicable diseases like measles, polio, tetanus etc., among infants and child bearing/ pregnant mothers of the sample households is presented in Table 1.

Table 1: Progress of Immunization Among Infants and Child Bearing Mothers of the Sample Households

	Immunization of Infants			Immunization of Child Bearing Mothers		
	Age <2	2<age>5	Total	Recently Child Bearing Mother	Earlier Child Bearing Mother	Total
Fully Immunized	67 (84.62)	61 (78.20)	128 (81.50)	54 (68.36)	47 (60.25)	101 (64.30)
Partially Immunized	7 (8.86)	9 (11.53)	16 (10.20)	16 (20.25)	16 (20.51)	32 (20.38)
Non Immunized	5 (6.32)	8 (10.25)	13 (8.30)	9 (11.39)	15 (19.23)	24 (15.28)
Total	79 (100)	78 (100)	157 (100)	79 (100)	78 (100)	157 (100)

Figures in brackets indicate the percentages of column total.

The table shows that about 81% of the infants under survey were fully immunized, 10% were partially immunized and the remaining percentage were out of getting the facility. The rate of progress of immunization in case of recently born infants (which is 85%) compared to earlier born ones (which is 78%) is not very significant, nevertheless it is a considerable increase. Thus, the progress of the programme is to some extent satisfactory, although the fulfilment of target lags still behind to achieve the national norm of 95% immunization of the infants. On the other hand, out of total 157 childbearing mothers, only 64% were fully immunized, which is much less than the national target of 100% immunization of pregnant and lactating mothers. Of course, the data depicts a positive increase in case of recent childbearing mothers.

The further examination of the progress of the programme across the block primary health centre areas reveals that the rate of immunization of infants was maximum in Sonapur (about 91%) and minimum in Chaygaon (57.5%). In both Kamalpur and Sonapur the rate of immunization in case of recently born infants increased considerably than the infants born earlier. The sample data of Chaygaon shows a rather exceptional picture. In this area non-immunization rate in recent times increased highlighting a serious cause of concern for the policy makers. Another significant cause of concern is that in Chaygaon only 27 % of the mothers were fully immunized, and other 45% were covered partially.

The individual block wise enquiry gives the idea that the rate of immunization among infants and their mothers in Sonapur can be related to the good extension work (imparting the people to avail the free immunization facility supplied by public sector) of health workers like multipurpose workers, auxiliary nurse midwifes, anganwadi workers and doctors etc. In Sonapur health workers motivated about 80% of the households. It is the Chaygaon primary health centre area where both rate of immunization and the extension work by the health workers are poor. From investigation in the sample area it is found that health workers rarely visit the field area. They rather record their presence in the primary health centre. The extension work by the health workers is also poor in Kamalpur, but it is almost redundant among population in this socio-economically developed area where about 56% of sample households were equipped with self information about the need of immunization (Table- 2).

From field study it is found that about 36 percent children were born in their own home without any outside help. The utilization of doctor's service slightly increased in case of infants born recently than the infants born earlier. Taking together all the infants it is found that the percentage of uses of trained dais/ auxiliary nurse midwife and

Table 2: Sources of Information about Immunization used by Households Having Infants

Sources	Households											
	Kamalpur			Sonapur			Chaygaon			Total		
	A	B	T	A	B	T	A	B	T	A	B	T
Self-informed	15 (55.5)	9 (56.2)	24 (55.8)	1 (3.7)	5 (14.2)	6 (9.6)	3 (27.2)	0 (0.0)	3 (13.6)	19 (29.2)	14 (22.5)	33 (25.9)
Told by neogh-bours, relatives	11 (40.7)	7 (43.7)	18 (41.8)	3 (11. 1)	3 (8.5)	6 (9.6)	4 (36.4)	5 (45.4)	9 (40.9)	18 (27.6)	15 (24.1)	33 (25.9)
Health workers	1 (3.7)	0 (0.0)	1 (2.3)	22 (81.4)	27 (77.1)	49 (79.0)	4 (36.4)	5 (45.4)	9 (40.9)	27 (41.5)	32 (51.6)	59 (46.4)
Others	0 (0.0)	0 (0.0)	0 (0.0)	1 (3.7)	0 (0.0)	1 (1.6)	0 (0.0)	1 (9.1)	1 (4.5)	1 (1.53)	1 (1.6)	2 (1.5)
Total	27 (100)	16 (100)	43 (100)	27 (100)	35 (100)	62 (100	11 (100)	11 (100)	22 (100)	65 (100)	62 (100.	127 (100)

Note:
A - Recently Born Infants.
B - Earlier Born Infants.
T - Total.

1. Self Informed
2. Total By Neighbours, Relatives etc.
3. Health Workers (ANM, MPW, Doctors etc.)

Figures in brackets indicate the percentages of column total.

doctor's services are 11.46 and 23.56 percents respectively. The rate of non-utilization of any outside help is the highest in Chaygaon and rate of utilization of doctor's service is maximum in Kamalpur. Exceptionally both trained and untrained dais, play a significant role in Sonapur (14.4 and 53.6 percents respectively) helping the mothers to care their new-born babies.

Extension Work and Various Disease Control Programmes in the Field Study Areas: Apart from immunization programme the health workers are supposed to play an active role in other ongoing health programmes like Control of Diarrhoea, National Malaria Eradication Programme, Control of Tuberculosis, Control of Goitre etc. With respect to these programmes the coverage of extension work shows similar pattern across blocks as in case of immunization. In other words, extension workers are much more active in Sonapur area whereas their presence is less felt by the sample households in Kamalpur and Chaygaon areas. In Sonapur area nearly four fifths of the sample households reported that during last one year (from the date of survey) health workers visited their house/ area and discussed about health needs and problems. In contrast only 10 percent of sample households in Kamalpur and none of the sample households in Chaygaon could remember a visit by health workers during last year to enquire and talk about health problems or health needs.

Table 3: Literacy of Mothers Having Different Degrees of Immunizatior by Their Infants

Immunization of Infants	Literacy of Mothers		TOTAL
	Literate	Illiterate	
1	2	3	4
Fully Immunized	72 (56.2)	56 (43.8)	128 (100)
Partially Immunized	5 (31.3)	11 (68.7)	16 (100)
Not Immunized	1 (7.7)	12 (92.3)	13 (100)
TOTAL	78 (49.7)	79 (50.3)	157 (100)

Figures in Brackets indicate the percentages.

From the field study it was also clear that the percentage of literacy of mothers is the highest in the fully immunized group and much less in partially immunized group and very low in non-immunized group. Individual block wise the literacy among mothers has been found highest in Kamalpur and lowest in Chaygaon. The high literacy rate among mothers apparently had a strong positive affect on the progress of immunization at Kamalpur in spite of deficiency of extension work in that block.

Conclusion

From the above analysis it is observed that the progress of immunization rate among infants in the sample areas is more or less satisfactory, but the immunization rate in case of pregnant mothers is much less than the national target of the programme. The positive relationship between spread of women's literacy and progress of family welfare is confirmed by our findings on progress of immunization programme in the field study areas. Similarly it is also established that the extension work of health workers like multipurpose workers, anganwadi workers, health guides and doctors etc., obviously have a positive impact on the spread and implementation of immunization and other health care programme particularly in backward areas. Among the three sample block areas under survey, in Sonapur about eighty percent of the households were motivated by the extension workers to avail the health care facilities supported by the government. On the other hand, in Chaygaon both extension work and the rate of implementation of health care programmes are poor, although both Sonapur and Chaygaon resembles in socio economic background. At the same time the extension service is found almost redundant in the economically developed areas like Kamalpur where majority of households, who are economically well off and literate, are self informed about the health needs. From the analysis it is found that although for promoting people's participation in health care programme the extension workers play significant role, the uniform expansion of the extension work in all the areas cannot be expected. Thus in the socio economically backward areas, which are also suffering from poor female literacy rate, it is an urgent need to consider empowerment as a basic strategy for promoting community participation in health programmes. For this, significant efforts, time and energy should be devoted for empowering the community in those areas. Thus for empowering the community a special thrust for spreading information network among the people should be given by the government in selected areas. Our findings, however confirms that the extension service is redundant in developed areas. Therefore the findings suggest a policy for an uneven network of health information service throughout the state. It should be focused in only those areas, which are backward not only in terms of income but also in terms of literacy, particularly female literacy.

Notes and References

1. Maternal and Child Health programme: under maternal and child health programme a target of immunization of 95 percent in case of infants and 100 percent in case of pregnant mothers against infectious and communicable diseases like measles, polio, tetanus and tuberculosis etc., are taken.
2. Disease Control Programme: Under disease control programme measures to prevent common; endemic and infectious diseases like malaria, diarrhea, goitre etc., are being implemented by the Government of Assam with financial support from the Central Government of India.
3. Network of Primary Health Centre: The network of primary health centre is organized in a three tiers system. At the bottom there are the sub centres catering to a population about 5000 in general/ 3000 in areas with concentration of scheduled caste and schedule tribe populations. At the middle level there are the mini primary health centres/ dispensaries or even a primary health centre (PHC), which are better equipped in man and material than the sub centres. All these institutions operate under a community health centre or block primary health centre, which forms the apex of the network in a community development block area.

Rajesh (1994), 'Where are the People? Community Participation In Health', in *Reaching India's Poor*', ed., Saroj Pachauri, Sage Publications, New Delhi, 1994.

8

NGO AND RURAL DEVELOPMENT
A Note on YVU of Manipur

Rajmani Singh

In Manipur more than 200 NGOs have been working in different areas for rural development. Among them some 20 NGOs have their foreign funding agencies besides assistance from the central and the state government from time to time. NGOs of Manipur work sincerely and more efficiently in rural areas. They operate over a wide range of activities such as the governments anti-poverty programmes, training of rural youth, promotion of safe and good drinking water, rural housing, promotion of science and technology, waste land development, health care and family welfare, education and women credit and thrift fund project etc.

Among the few selected prominent NGOs in Manipur, Youth Volunteers Union (YVU) is one of the leading agency for the welfare of community and rural development in different parts of Manipur particularly in Thoubal district. Since inception, YVU has been ceaselessly endeavouring for bringing about socio-economic and rural development in the state of Manipur by giving a supportive hands so on to shape their destiny. Various Programmes have been taken up to achieve its mission in different areas of Manipur covering remote villages. Following are some of the important activities undertaken by Youth Volunteers Union:

1. As an agricultural development activities YVU has constructed 11 km long irrigation canal From Wanghem, Phaodel to Thoubal

Nongankhong and inter village connecting road of 5 villages inhabited by the schedule tribes.

2. In collaboration with AFPRO, New Delhi, YVU has organised north eastern level training courses in project formulation and management, accountancy, agriculture, livestock, people participatory process and participatory rural appraisal etc.

3. Youth Volunteers Union established a Women Credit and Thrift Project Bank at Thoubal district headquarter during 1995-96. The main objective of the Bank is to develop the habit of saving among the women and establish their own small business. The Women Credit and Thrift Project Bank was introduced for the first time in Manipur with assistance from SIDBI a sum of Rs 4,50,000 as soft loan and Rs 50,000 as grant towards the implementation of the project.

4. Under the sponsorship of SIDBI, YVU established a project called 'Mahila Vikas Nidhi'. Under this project 100 cottage juice extraction units were established by distribution of hand juice extractor to 100 scheduled tribe women trained in extraction and preservation of juice. EZE Germany also provided financial support in the establishment of central food processing centre located at the campus of YVU, 24 boys and girls were given full time employment in this centre.

5. For the first time among the voluntary organisation, YVU established a fruit processing plant 'WAIFRUIT' at the union's campus. WAIFRUIT is the biggest processing unit run by a voluntary organisation in the north eastern region of India. It is equipped with automatic, semiautomatic machinery with a capacity of 250 MT per annum. 100 fruit extraction unit has also been established benefiting 100 schedule cast, scheduled tribe and other backward classes of women in Senapati and Thoubal districts of Manipur.

6. Youth Volunteers Union helps in development of 147 acres of wasteland into a pineapple orchard benefiting 1 acre each of 147 scheduled tribe families in Lishamlok, Poirou Kabrang and Lembakhul in Saikul block, Senapati district, Manipur

7. Since 1982 Youth Volunteers Union is running a printing press at Thoubal Bazar. It provides full and part time employment to unemployed youth, training facilities to educated unemployed

in the field of printing, binding and cutting of books. It also provides a main source of income to the union.

8. Youth Volunteers Union established a Dairy foundation farm 'WAIVIEW DAIRY FARM" at Thoubal. The farm has 22 milking cows, 14 heifers and calves. Besides giving full time employment facilities to educated unemployed youth, the farm gives income to union. It has giver 6 cows to 6 selected farmers under its 'Passing on the Gift Scheme'

9. Community fishery programme was introduced by YVU in Sikhong village of Thoubal district. The union formed the selected beneficiaries into a cooperative society. This society is the first of its kind in the state. 50 individual fish farm has also been established.

Besides above, Youth Volunteers Union is also undertaken various rural development programmes like rural drinking water project, low cost sanitary latrine, health education training programme, sloping agricultural land technology programme, public library cum information center, and rural women institute.

To conclude, most of the state and local NGOs have, been actively involved in the movement for fighting exploitation of weaker section, menacing poverty and insurmountable unemployment. From the above highlighted achievement made by the union it is clear that YVU have been playing a major role to link up between state agencies and intended beneficiaries for the development and upliftment of rural poor in different areas of Thoubal district, in particular and Manipur in general. While executing its developmental activities YVU faces some problems in the area of construction, transportation, marketing and procurement of raw materials. Here the central and state government should come forward to help and support in providing financial and technical requirement in time to those NGOs which are actively involve for the development of rural areas.

INDUSTRY, ENTREPRENEURSHIP AND MARKET

9

THE STATE OF MANUFACTURING IN MEGHALAYA

Resource-Industry Linkages

Gurudas Das

Official data collected and collated by different government departments and agencies, relating to manufacturing activities/units, etc., follow a certain pattern and hardly reveal the 'factual state of affairs" which, more often than not, varies from the "official state of affairs". By way of illustrations it may be pointed out that the statistical handbooks published by the governments, reports on the number of industrial units registered with the Directorate of Industries which also provide information on the volume of investments and size of employment proposed in them. But after registration how many units keep on functioning and how many of them have gone for liquidation – no such information is usually available. Moreover, the official reports contain no grain of information about the unregistered industrial units, which usually exceed far more in numbers as well as value additions compared to their registered counterparts [for problems with official data relating to manufacturing, scc, Das (1995)]. However, in spite of these limitations, official data are of immense value which may be used as benchmarks for conducting sample surveys in order to estimate the ground realities.

This paper is based on the official data and hence makes no claims of representing the exact ground realities. It suffers from ambiguities that are inherent in official data. However, the purpose here is to focus on the broad trends of manufacturing activities and to assess whether these trends commensurate with the comparative advantages arising out of the resource base and overall economic development of Meghalaya or not.

II

State of Manufacturing

Official data relating to manufacturing units in Meghalaya are available in three categories - (i) registered factories, (ii) registered small-scale industries, and (iii) Khadi and Village industrial units. Starting with the first category, the rate of growth of registered factories during the last 25 years in Meghalaya has been around 53.33 percent. From 45 units in 1974-75, their number has gone up to 69 in 1998-99 (Table 1). However, the figures for registered factories released by the State Government do not tally with the same published by Central Statistical organization (CSO). The latter counts their number at 43 during 1997-98 (Where do we stand in 2000, p. 39).

Table 1: Growth of Registered Factories in Meghalaya

Year	*Number of Units*	*Number of Employees*
1974-75	45	2945
1980-81	55	3075
1985-86	56	3574
1990-91	58	3345
1995-96	58	2800
1998-99	69	3079

Source: Statistical Handbooks, Meghalaya, various issues.

A category-wise/type-wise distribution of the registered factories is not officially available for all the years. A type-wise distribution given for the period 1978-83 (Table 2) reveals:

(i) 26 percent of them are based on forest resources,

(ii) 9 percent are based on agro-horticultural resources,

(iii) 32 percent are demand based service units,

(iv) 10 percent are based on water,

(v) as the cement producing units are clubbed with others, the relative numerical position of the mineral based units cannot be deduced.

Table 2: Registered Factories by Type (1978-83)

Sl. No.	*Category*	*Number*
1	Printing Press	7
2	Plywood Manufacture	2
3	Repairs of motor vehicle	11
4	Canning and preservation of Fruits	2
5	Saw milling	10
6	Rice and flour milling	3
7	Furniture and fixture	3
8	Generation and transmission of electricity	6
9	Others*	13
	Total	57

*Includes cement, beverage, motor assembling, pumping, cotton gunning and mineral processing, etc.

Source: Statistical Handbook, Meghalaya, 1983, Directorate of Economics, Statistics and Evaluation, Meghalaya, Shillong.

Taking up the second category, i.e., small-scale industries, it may be noted (Table 3) that they have registered a growth of about 1198 percent during the last 25 years. The growth in this sector is, indeed, spectacular during the 1990s.

Table 3: Growth of Small-Scale Industries (Registered) in Meghalaya, 1974-75 to 1998-99

Year	*No. of SSIs*	*No. of Employees*
1974-75	252	1645
1980-81	180	1440
1985-86	671	4240
1990-91	1558	9248
1995-96	2533	14791
1998-99	3270	18585

Source: Statistical Handbooks. Meghalaya, various issues

A typological analysis of small-scale industries for the year 1998-99 (Table 4) reveals:

(i) more than 50 percent of the SSIs are engaged in need based/demand based production activities (both services and goods),

(ii) in the need based/demand based sector, the number of service exceeds to that of goods producers,

(iii) about 18 percent of SSIs are forest based,

(iv) about 8 percent of the SSIs are mineral based,

(v) about 1 percent of the SSIs are leather based

(vi) since industries clubbed as others, which form 22 percent of the total SSIs (3270), are not specified, the resource classification linkages is not exhaustive.

Table 4: Small-Scale Industries in Meghalaya by Type 1986-87 and 1998-99

Sl. No.	*Industry Type*	*No. of Units*		*No. of Employees*	
		1986-87	*1998-99*	*1986-87*	*1998-99*
01	Motor repairing, servicing	66	179	501	1270
02	Wooden furniture	75	330	383	1714
03	Leather based industries	10	36	46	162
04	Bakery	90	249	509	1317
05	Flour and rice mills	48	242	180	1077
06	Tailoring	49	399	281	1853
07	Printing	27	49	242	439
08	Cement based industries	90	159	497	856
09	Knitting and embroidery	55	150	144	447
10	Steel based industries	25	164	206	997
11	Tyre retreading works	17	70	98	362
12	Saw mills	30	79	389	1175
13	Stone crushers and sandstone chips	11	37	103	623
14	Cane and bamboo works	35	172	111	708
15	Weaving	12	164	61	950
16	Lime making	6	73	76	1207
17	Others	156	718	1122	3428
	Total	802	3270	4949	18585

Source: (1) Statistical Handbook, Meghalaya, 1987.
(2) Pocket Statistical Handbook Meghalaya, 2000.

Coming to the third category, i.e., Khadi and Village industries (KVI), it is difficult to comprehend as to whether there is any overlapping between this category and registered small-scale units or not. Moreover, figures relating to KVI industries are simply provided in official reports without bothering to append any note regarding the change in criteria, if any, so that one can understand how much of temporal fluctuations in figures is caused due to change in definitive criterion. Khadi and Village industries have registered 88 percent negative growth between 1986-87 and 1998-99 (Table 5). The sudden and spectacular decline from 5400 units in 1995-96 to 42 units in 1998-99 needs to be explained.

Table 5: Growth of Khadi and Village Industries in Meghalaya (1986-87 to 1998-99)

Year	*No. of Units*	*No. of Employees*
1986-87	344	4517
1995-96	5400	12520
1998-99	42	246

Source: (1) Statistical Handbook, Meghalaya, 1987.
(2) Pocket Statistical Handbook, Meghalaya, 2000.

A typological analysis (Table 6) of KV industries reveals that:

(i) about 10 percent of them are forest based,

(ii) about 52 percent are agro-horticulture based,

(iii) about 12 percent are based on minerals, i.e., lime based, and

(iv) about 19 percent are demand based foot loose industries.

III

Contribution of the Manufacturing Sector to Income and Employment

Table 7 and Table 8 exhibit a secular decline of the share of the manufacturing sector to Net State Domestic Product (NSDP) of Meghalaya. Table 7 exhibits a secular; decline in the share of the primary sector to NSDP during last 25 years. For the secondary sector, its percentage share has increased from 7.05 percent in 1973-74 to 19.95 percent in 1980-81. But thereafter, it has declined continually. The decline in the percentage share of both the primary and secondary sectors has been compensated by a secular rise in the share of the tertiary sector. These trends in Meghalaya, however, correspond to the structural change in the national economy.

Table 6: Activity-wise Distribution of Khadi and Village Industries in 1998-99

Sl. No.	*Type of Industries*	*No. of Units*	*No. of Employees*
01	Cane and bamboo	2	12
02	Carpentry and blacksmithy	2	14
03	Pottery	2	8
04	Processing of cereals and pulses	7	19
05	Lime industry	5	40
06	Fruits and vegetable industry	15	95
07	Electronic	1	2
08	Bone crushing	1	4
09	Plastic polymer	1	10
10	Textile	3	6
11	Tyre retreading (service)	3	36
	Total	42	246

Source: Pocket Statistical Handbook, Meghalaya 2000.

As the secondary sector, besides manufacturing, also includes the income originating from construction as well as electricity and water supply activities, the overall performance of this sector while compared with the other two sectors does not reveal the true strength of the manufacturing in an economy. Hence a further breakup of the contribution of the secondary sector is called for. Table 8 exhibits that the share of manufacturing to the secondary sector income is subject to a secular decline, whereas the same for construction has registered a secular rise.

Table 7: Percentage Distribution of Sectoral Contribution to NSDP of Meghalaya

Sector	*1973-74*	*1980-81*	*1990-91*	*1999-2000 (Q)*
Primary Sector	65.11	44.62	33.58	30.19
Secondary Sector	7.05	19.95	17.00	11.02
Tertiary Sector	27.84	35.43	49.42	58.79
NSDP (at current prices) (in crores)	65.41	149.35	794.61	2806.20

Source: State Domestic Product and Per Capita Income of Meghalaya 1973-74 at current prices. Government of Meghalaya. Statistical Handbooks, 1987, 1994, 2000.

Q = Quick estimates

Table 8: Percentage Share of Manufacturing, Construction and Electricity and Water Supply to the Total Secondary Sector Income of Meghalaya

Sub-Sector	*1973-74*	*1980-81*	*1990-91*	*1999-2000 (Q)*
Manufacturing	36.88	22.15	17.66	15.76
Construction	34.71	64.03	69.96	76.76
Electricity and Water Supply	28.41	13.82	12.38	7.48
Total Secondary Sector Income (in crores)	4.61	29.80	135.11	309.21

Source: As in Table 7.

The performance of the manufacturing in Meghalaya in terms of employment is no better. Table 9 exhibits the following revelations:

Table 9: Percentage Distribution of the Main Workers according to Industrial Category in Meghalaya

Sectors	1981	1991	2000(E)
Primary Sector	74.74	74.80	77.52
Manufacturing	0.41	2.15	2.23
Others	24.85	23.05	20.25
Main Workers	308946	715587	798568
%	(100)	(100)	(100)

Source: Compiled from (i) Basic Statistics of North Eastern Region, Statistical Handoooks, Meghalaya, 1996, 2000.

Note: E - Estimate

(i) While the percentage of total main workers engaged in agriculture and allied activities remained the same throughout the 1980s, the same has increased during the 1990s.

(ii) Manufacturing sector employs only insignificant percentage of the total main workforce. While the percentage of main workers engaged in the manufacturing sector has increased by less than 2 percent during the 1980s, no significant growth has been registered during the 1990s.

(iii) The category "others" in Table 9 includes the tertiary sector plus construction plus electricity and water supply. There has been a secular decline of percentage workforce engaged in this category since 1981.

The following trends and implications may be observed from Tables 7-9.

(i) While the share of primary sector in NSDP of Meghalaya is declining, the additional labour force is taking refuse in this sector. As agriculture is subject to diminishing returns, this trend will eventually likely to affect the productivity in this sector, and, if not reversed, this may, in the long run, lead to the elimination of whatever surplus this sector is producing; and also lead to the shortening of *jhum* cycle, wherever practiced, thereby causing environmental degradation. With rising workforce and declining share in NSDP, the pauperisation of the people engaged in this sector may only be apprehended, once the culturable land reaches to the threshold limit.

(ii) With percentage of labour force engaged in the tertiary sector declining and, the same in the manufacturing sector remained stagnant throughout the 1990s, unemployment problem in the state will have no easy way out. Since the educated unemployed labour force usually seeks to enter into manufacturing or the service sector rather than into the primary sector, unless the absorbing capacity of these former two sectors is enhanced, higher level of socio-political unrest may only be apprehended.

One of the possible options to counter the negative implications mentioned above is to take refuse into the process of industrialization. A brief account of the resource-base, which, to a large extent, determines the perimeter of industrial growth is in order.

IV

Meghalaya is rich in natural endowments – a storehouse of a number of mineral resources having significant bearing for industrial growth. A list of the economically efficient and commercially viable minerals and their estimated reserves is given in Table 10.

The industrial structure of Meghalaya outlined in section II only reveals a very weak linkage with the resource base. Minerals like coal, sillimanite, Kaolin, are being extracted and sold directly without any value addition. The forward linkages in the form of industrial units/ products are yet to be established in these cases. Only limestone is used as industrial inputs in the production of cement. There are five cement producing plants operating in the state including the Mawluh Cherra Cement Limited under the public sector.

Table 10: Estimated Reserves of Minerals in Meghalaya

Sl. No.	*Mineral*	*Reserves (in million tones)*
1	Limestone	4147.000
2	Coal	563.500
3	Kaolin	4.440
4	Clay	80.970
5	Sillimanite	0.046
6	Glass Sand	2.540
7	Quartz	0.077
8	Feldspar	0.128

Source: Directorate of Mineral Resources. Meghalaya.

Besides this rich mineral resource base, the state is also having marketable surplus in a number of agro-horticultural products (Table 11).

Table 11: Area, production and estimated Surplus of Selected Agro-Horticultural Products in Meghalaya, 1994-95

Crop	*Area (hectares)*	*Production (tonnes)*	*Estimated surplus (tonnes)*
Potato	18093	121240	84900
Ginger	6683	39968	39000
Turmeric	1354	1756	1400
Pineapple	8568	76888	53800
Banana	4774	60549	30390
Citrus Fruits	7749	32838	26300
Cotton	7509	5317 (bales)	5 100 (bales)*
Jute and Mesta	8945	56694 (bales)	53900 (bales)**
Misc. Fruits	N.A.	37124	27800
Vegetables	N.A.	68000	27200

Source: For figures in col. (2), Pocket Statistical Handbook, Meghalaya, 1996
For figures in col. (3) and (4), Ninth Five Year Plan 1997-2002, and Annual Plan 1997-98, Draft Proposals, Vol. II, Part I, Agriculture and Allied Services, Government of Meghalaya.

Note : Production estimates of crops presented above do not tally with that of Handbook, Meghalaya, 1996

* bales of 180 kg ** bales of 170 kg.

However, only a portion of the limestone mined annually enters into the production of cement in the state. A significant portion of limestone is being exported to Bangladesh as inputs for the production of cement at Chatak Cement Company. Apart from cement, limestone is also used for the production of limes which are then used as inputs in the tea gardens and paper mills in Assam and bleaching powder industries elsewhere.

Table 12: Potential for Resource Based Industries in Meghalaya

Resource Base	*Potential Industry*
Lime Stone-Based Industries	* Cement * Lime and hydrated lime * Precipitated and Activated calcium carbonate * Calcium carbide * Acetylene Black
Coal-Based Industries	* Formed coke * Low temperature carbonisation plant * Coal parqueting and high temperature carbonization plant * Low ash coke
Kaolin/China Clay/Fire-Clay based Industries	* Low tension/high tension insulators, switches, cut-outs, etc. * Wall/flour tiles * Earthen wares (crookeries, novelties, etc.) * Stone wares (Sanitary wares, etc.) * Fire bricks * Aluminium sulphate * Clay washery
Other Mineral-based Industries	* Granite mining and polishing * Sillimanite refractory and allied industries * Cement based mosaic tiles
Agro-Horticulture based Processing Industries	* Fruit processing industries * Turmeric processing industries * Ginger processing industries * Potato chips * Starch processing industries * Mushroom processing industries

The resource-industry linkage in case of agro-horticultural products is no better. Although there are 4 fruit processing units operating in the state, no potato processing unit has come up to utilise huge surplus production of potatoes in the state. Starch processing units which provide the forward linkages for the agricultural surplus are yet to come up. Similar is the case of Meghalaya turmeric. In spite of being one of the finest variety having curcumine content as high as 7.5 percent, except a few cottage industries, there is no worthwhile turmeric processing industry in the state. Besides agro-horticulture sector, the topography and climate of Meghalaya also carry immense promises for the growth of tea-plantation and floriculture. Tea plantation has recently been started in the state. The experiments with the small tea growers in the state have produced encouraging results.

Meghalaya has distinctive comparative advantage in three lines of production, i.e., mineral-based industries, agro-horticulture based industries and plantation. The 1997, Industrial policy of Meghalaya has identified all these three areas of state's comparative advantage. Accordingly the Meghalaya Industrial Development Corporation (MIDC) has identified a number of potential resource-based industries (Table 12) for future development.

V

Having studied the industrial structure, mapped the resource-base and located resource-industry linkages, only, one side of the prospect of industrialization is taken care of, i.e., the supply side. But the resources will be lying idle until and unless there is sufficient demand for them. In fact, the market signals emanating from the operation of the national economy are not strong enough to bring the resources of Meghalaya into immediate use. The resource exploitation here warrants first the scarcity of a particular natural resource product to go up to such a level that can justify the higher price at which it can be supplied in the national market by using the resources from peripheral states like Meghalaya (Das, 2002). Whatever resource extraction is taking place here is largely in response to the demands across the border in Bangladesh (Das, 2001). The peripheral location of the state within the political geography of our country is standing on the way of immediate utilisation of her natural endowments (Das, 1998). The time-horizon required for the development of any meaningful resource-industry linkages that provide sufficient resilience to the local economy largely depends on how long time will be required for the market demands to go up to such a level that can justify the use and exploitation of resources of Meghalaya. In view of indefinite time-frame for the national economy, the alternative is to integrate the resource-base of Meghalaya with the demand in the markets across the borders in neighbouring countries through cross-country subregional development cooperation.

REFERENCES

Das, Gurudas, 1995, *Tribes of Arunachal Pradesh in Transition*, Vikas Publishing House, New Delhi.

Das, Gurudas, 1998, "Limits to Economic Development of North-Eastern Region: An Analysis of Contradictions between Economic Goals and Social Choices", in: Datta Ray, B. and Prabin Baishya (eds.), *Sociological Constraints to Industrial Development in North-East India*, Concept Publishing Co., New Delhi.

Das, Gurudas, 2002 "Geo-Economy of Arunachal Pradesh: The Cross-Border Dimension", in: S. Dutta (ed.), *Cross-Border Trade of Norrh-East India*, Hope India Publications, Haryana.

Das, Gurudas, 2001, "Trade Between North Eastern Region and Bangladesh: Nature, Trends and Implications for Development Cooperation', *Dialogue*, Vol. 2, No. 4, April-June.

Government of Meghalaya, Were Do We Stand in 2000: Meghalaya in North East and India and the World, Directorate of Economics and Statistics, Shillong.

Government of Meghalaya, *Statistical Handbooks*, Various Issues, Shillong.

Government of Meghalaya, *Industrial Policy*, 1997.

Government of Meghalaya, Ninth Five Year Plan 1997-2002 and Annual Plan 1997-1998, Draft Proposals, Vol. II, Part I, Agriculture and Allied Services, Planning Department, Shillong.

North Eastern Council, *Basic Statistics of North Eastern Region*, 1992.

10

RURAL INDUSTRIAL EMPLOYMENT IN ARUNACHAL PRADESH

B. Panda

In developing economies, for a long time, modern formal manufacturing sector and the ever expanding public sector were considered to be bastions of employment creation. However, of late, with the rising capital intensity in the former and initiation of structural adjustment programmes to downsize employment in the latter; these economies are not in a position to absorb the growing labour force. Elasticity of employment with respect to output has been diminishing in a number of sectors in these economies. This falling elasticity of employment in the formal sector as well as in agriculture, makes Rural Non-Farm sector to be seen as a viable sector for solutions of the problem of rural unemployment and rural poverty. Rural Non-Farm Sector has a number of components. Rural Manufacturing or Industrial Employment (here after referred as RIE), is an important component of it. A large number of studies in Indian context have been undertaken on various aspects of Rural Non-Farm Employment (RNFE). Most of the studies were, either macro level ones or based on other regions of the country. Even the micro studies don't take into consideration the case of a hilly tribal state like Arunachal Pradesh. This author had undertaken a study of various aspects of RNFE in the state of Arunachal Pradesh in 1997 which also prominently included the sectoral composition of RNFE. The present paper is based upon this study. All data incorporated in this paper are from the various census reports of Government of India.

Table 1 : Composition of RNFE in India and Arunachal Pradesh; 1971-91

Industry category	*Percentage share in RNFE*				*Annual Growth rate(1971-91)*	
	India		*Arunachal Pradesh*		*India*	*Arunachal Pradesh*
	1971	*1991*	*1971*	*1991*		
Mining & Quarrying	2.67	2.64	0.01	0.77	2.77	28.06
Manufacturing(a+b)	36.26	43.29	1.65	8.97	2.24	12.81
Household mfg	21.16	20.20	1.53	0.68	0.05	(-)0.48
Non-household mfg	15.11	20.04	0.12	8.29	4.30	28.17
Construction	4.88	5.88	0.48	19.79	3.80	24.90
Trade & Commerce	16.10	18.51	1.93	8.87	3.56	11.87
Transport, storage and communications	5.38	6.97	0.02	3.10	4.18	32.63
Other services	34.69	33.78	95.91	58.50	2.71	1.14
Total	100.00	100.00	100.00	100.00	2.84	3.67

Source: Author's calculation based on various census reports.

Rural Industrial Employment and RNFE

Trends in the composition of Rural Non-Farm Employment (RNFE) and the share of Rural Industrial Employment (RIE) in the context of A.P. and India are given in Table 1.

From Table 1, it is evident that at the national level in both points of time i.e. 1971 and 1991, manufacturing or industrial sector employment formed the highest share among all the sectors of RNFE, whereas at Arunachal level, it was the other services sector employment which formed the highest share in RNFE. In 1971, rural industrial (mfg) employment in Arunachal formed only 1.65 of total RNFE and here the household mfg. sector employment formed 1.53 percent and non-household manufacturing sector employment only 0.12 percent. The implication is that in 1971, rural industrial employment was negligible in total employment and whatever little employment rural industries provided, most of it was in the household industries segment. In 1991, i.e. 20 years latter, rural industrial employment in A.P has increased to 8.97 percent of the RNFE, suggesting creation of more jobs is in the rural industrial sector. But when one looks into the composition of the rural industrial sector employment in 1991, the non household sector provided almost all the jobs, making the household sector virtually a non-entity (only 0.68 percent of RNFE). In terms of growth rate over this period 1971-91, rural household industrial employment in fact has experienced a negative growth rate of 0.48 percent. This has happened mostly because the rural household industries could not withstand the competition from the modern formal industrial sector and change in the tastes and preferences of rural consumers due to integration of the region with the national market network.

Comparing the national figure with that of Arunachal from growth rate angle, it is seen that over this period i.e. 1971-91, at the all India level, it is the non-household industrial employment in RNFE which has experienced the highest growth rate followed by employment in transport, storage and communications sector; whereas at the state level, it is employment in transport, storage and communications sector which has experienced the highest rate (32.63%) followed by employment in the non-household industry group (28.17%). However, one thing is very clear, i.e., in terms of rural industrial employment, Arunachal lags much behind the national figure, the latter being 5 times more of the former. This clearly suggests that rural Industrialisation is still in its infancy in Arunachal Pradesh.

Determinants of Rural Industrial Employment

Since RIE is a constituent of RNFE, it is assumed here that the variables/factors that determine the level of RNFE do also determine the level of RIE. Generally, agricultural growth, urbanisation, literacy percentage, infrastructural development, rural poverty, rural unemployment and public policy have been the most talked of factors determining the magnitude of RIE in an economy. However, the job of an analysis involving these variables in the context of Arunachal Pradesh has been a difficult one in the sense that proper data with regard to many such influencing variables are not available in the state. Given this limitation, an attempt is made here to study the effects of a handful of variables/factors on the level of RIE through a multiple correlation model. These variables are, (i) fruit crop yield per hectare (X_1), (ii) food crops yield per hectare (X_2), (iii) urban population percentage in 1991 (X_3), (iv) Literary percentage in 1991(X_4), (v) Road length per 100 sq km (X_5), (vi) number of bank branches (X_6). Variables (i) and (ii) have been incorporated to know the effects of agricultural growth on RIE. Variables (iii) and (iv) are self explanatory and have been included to ascertain the effects of urbanisation and literary growth on RIE. Variables (y) and (vi) are infrastructural variables and have been included in the model to know if infrastructure development has anything to do with growth of RIE. A multiple correlation analysis has been undertaken to find out the nature of such relationships and their significance. The data used are cross sectional ones and pertain to 11 districts in existence in 1991. Year 1991 has been chosen as this is the latest census year for which data are available at present. The cross sectional data of probable determinants of RIE in Arunachal Pradesh have been given in Table 2.

From the correlation matrix, it is evident that RIE is positively correlated with fruits yield per hectare, food crops yield per hectare, urbanisation and literacy percentages. This positive correlation is the highest with literacy percentage. However, none of these positive correlation is statistically significant. Hence, we can not with certainty attribute this little growth in RIE to any of these given variables. Further, the correlation of RIE is negative with both the infrastrucutural variables. The implication from this is that, (i) banks have played little role in promoting rural industrialisation in A.P., (ii) much of the rural industrial activity is area/village specific with very less in the form of interregional trade. Finally, although the positive relationships of RIE with literacy and fruit yield are not statistically significant, yet it can be inferred that,

Table 2 : Select Economic Indicators and Determinants of RIE in various Districts of Arunachal Pradesh

District	*Fruit yield per ha (1991-92) kg*	*Food crops yield per ha (1991-92) kg*	*Urban population (%) in 1991*	*Literacy rate (%) 1991*	*Road length per 100 km²*	*Number of Bank branches (1992)*	*% share of RIE to total rural main employment (1991)*
	X_1	X_2	X_3	X_4	X_5	X_6	X_7
West Kameng	1590	1586	10.02	46.31	14	7	2.68
Tawang	2410	1706	0.00	29.78	43	3	0.77
East Kameng	1800	1330	0.00	26.20	19	2	0.64
Lower Subansiri	830	896	25.50	41.57	13	16	0.86
Upper subansiri	goo	1134	0.00	38.31	10	3	0.86
East Siang	2350	1277	13.23	44.30	22	12	1.2
West Siang	3520	1467	14.72	45.64	10	8	1.31
Lohit	4890	1506	21.19	49.21	12	4	3.95
D. Valley	1920	1207	16.20	46.88	5	2	4.67
Tirap	1680	1160	8.30	32.06	50	4	3.79
Changlang	2000	1459	0.00	43.19	20	4	4.39

Source : (1) Census of India reports for 1991 (11) Statistical Abstract of A.P, 1992 (iii) Arunachal Agriculture in Brief(Series-3), 1994. The resultant coefficient matrix of these cross-sectional data is given in table.3

in days to come, education and agricultural growth (horticulture included) may hold keys to further expansion of rural industrial base and rural industrial employment in Arunachal Pradesh. My earlier analysis which explains agricultural growth as a statistically significant determinant of rural non farm employment in AP, further strengthens this inference. At this juncture, whatever growth in RIE has happened might have happened because of some other exogenous factors such as Government's policy towards industrialization and rural industrialization, which have not been accounted for in this model.

Table 3 : Correlation Coefficient Matrix of Percentage Shares of RIE and Other Variables

	X_1	X_2	X_3	X_4	X_5	X_6	X_7
X_1	1	–	–	–	–	–	–
X_2	0.669	1	–	–	–	–	–
X_3	0.297	-0.366	1	–	–	–	–
X_4	0.380	0.026	0.636	1	–	–	–
X_5	-0.087	0.181	-0.387	-0.664'	1	–	–
X_6	-0.167	-0.421	0.629	0.327	-0.162	1	–
X_7	0.267	0.096	0.171	0.456	-0.033	-0.368	1

Significant at 6% level.

Conclusion and Limitations

Arunachal is an industrially backward state. The volume of rural industrial employment as a percentage of total rural main employment was negligible in 1971. However, its rural economy has experienced a continuous sectoral shift in favour of Non-Farm Employment during the period 1971-1991. Although, 'other services sector' still constitutes the sector having the highest percentage of rural non-farm employment in 1991; the share of rural industrial sector employment has experienced a modest increase. Much of this increase has happened in the non-household industrial sector The household industrial sector employment has rather experienced a negative growth over this period of 1971-81. This trend needs to be arrested. The modest increase in the share of RIE during 1971-91 can not be very definitely attributed to any given factor, as shown in our correlation model. However, given the nature of positive correlation, we can, of course, with caution assume that, spread of education and agricultural (including horticulture) growth have played some role in enhancing the share of RIE in Rural Non-Farm Employment. They need to be consolidated in coming years. Secondly rural industrial investment and marketing network need to be improved. Finally, it is felt that, state policy on industrialisation in general and rural industrialisation in particular matters a lot here. In our present analysis we have not been able to capture this because of data constraints. This certainly remains a limitation of our analysis. In addition to all these, the sociological factor is also an important factor influencing industrialisation in any given society and more so in the rural segment of it. In this model, it has not been possible to capture its effect on rural industrialisation and RIE in Arunachal Pradesh because of obvious complexities involved. This is another limitation of our analysis.

11

BELL METAL INDUSTRY IN ASSAM
Problems and Prospects

Chayanika Goswami

The Assam: rural economy of Assam is basically predominated by agriculture. This agrarian economy is supported by the traditional subsistence village industries, the role of which can nevertheless, be neglected.

Since agriculture is already overcrowded, additional workforce in the rural areas must be put to rural development programmes and governmental employment generation schemes. But the village industries will continue to provide both primary and secondary support to the rural families.

The village industries of Assam are basically the cottage industries, which are carried on in the home of the artisan. It may be a subsidiary occupation together with agriculture or, in some cases it may also be a full time work. No power is used in it and the tools and implements used are also simple. One such industry is the Bell Metal Industry, which is considered to be a hereditary craft of Assam.

The Bell Metal Industry

Bell metal is an alloy of copper and tin. A large number of utility items are made out of this metal which has certain distinctive characteristic features of its own as compared to other metals. For example, food kept in the utensils made out of bell metal is not spoilt. For Bengali and Assamese families, it is a traditional utility cum gift item. They are in common use in every household because of some religious sentiments attached to it.

The main production centers in the North-East are located at Sarthebari, Titabar and Raha in Assam. In the states like Manipur and Tripura, there are a few more units, which produce occasionally some bell metal items. Sarthebari is the main commercial centre in the entire North East

In India, the bell metal industry is concentrated in states like Karnataka, Tamil Nadu and Kerala. The industry is well organized in Moradabad also, but the industry of Assam has some distinctive characteristics, which differentiates it from the rest of the industries throughout India. These characteristics are:

1. It is a typical example of perfect competition where all the items produced are similar in every way.
2. The items are completely hand made using simple tools and antiquated techniques.
3. It is the primary occupation of the people in Sarthebari area.

Brief History and Demography of Sarthebari

Sarthebari is an area in the Barpeta district of Assam comprised of 129 villages. It has a population of 7,707 according to 1991 census and more than a thousand families are engaged in the bell metal industry.

The industry is one of the oldest traditional cottage industries, which gained momentum especially during the Ahom rule before the advent of the British. There are sufficient historical data from which we can trace the time of emergence of this industry. The historical gifts presented to Harshavardhana by Kumar Bhaskar Barma of ancient Assam (Kamrup) consisted a lot of traditional crafts along with a *'Kanjapatra'* made of bell metal. From this information, the historians claim that this industry has been surviving in Assam since 7th century A.D. One Jeudhan Kahar of Sarthebari received the *'Tamrapatra'* from Lord Siva Sinha for his sophisticated bell metal works. The famous legendry of Sarthebari, late Pushpa Kahar was honoured by Queen Victoria for his crafts of bell metal exhibited in an agro-crafts exhibition held at London.

The Products of Bell Metal

The range of products produced includes a wide variety of utility and decorative items of bell metal. These are locally known as: *Kahi* (plate), *Bati* (bowl), *Bota, Sarai, Ban, Lota, Barkahi, Hati Khujia bati, Safura, taal* (cymbal), *Bhortal,* etc.

Raw Materials

The basic raw material used in this industry is bell metal, which is an alloy of 78% copper and 22% tin. Other raw materials required are charcoal, clay, lac and mustard oil. Lac is used for polishing the finished product and the oil is used to smoother the interiors of the moulds.

Sources of Raw Materials

The main raw materials viz, copper and tin are collected from Kolkata and Delhi while the other materials like charcoal, clay, lac etc. are gathered locally. The products are also manufactured by recycling of scrap collected from different areas throughout Assam.

The Process of Manufacturing

Manufacturing of bell metal crafts is not an easy task. The crafts are a product of phase wise creation. So it can be said to be an outcome of joint or group effort. The group comprises of five to six members under a head known as *Ojah Kahar.* The instruments used by them are locally termed as *Haturi, Niyari, Reti, Cheni, Khanta, Chatli Kund, Oa, Bhati etc.*

The whole process of manufacturing can be described in seven stages as follows:

Weighing: The weight of the scrap metal is determined by the weight of the article to be made plus the quantity required to compensate the melting losses.

Melting and Pouring: An open-hearth furnace is prepared in the ground for melting the metal. A hand driven blower is used to blow a slow blast of air through the coal or coke and as the flow increases combustion sets in. A crucible basically made of burnt clay is kept on the fire and the bell metal scrap is melted in it. The molten bell metal is pored into the mould and allowed to air cool.

Smoothing: By shaking the mould, the cooked metal, which has assumed the shaped of the mould's concavity, is taken out and beaten with a light hammer while hot in order to get a curved sheet metal of uniform thickness. Any gas locked up also gets released by beating and blowholes are eliminated. The curved metal sheet is now ready for shaping.

Shaping and Cooling: The curved metal sheet is heated in the furnace and when it is red hot, beated to shape with a heavy hammer. The shaped metal is immersed in water kept in a vessel. The shaped metal after complete cooling is beaten with gentle strikes by a light hammer in order to loosen the black layer that formed during cooling on the surface.

Cleaning: The black layer is removed on the surface by scrapping and after scrapping the edges are filed out to remove extra metal sticking out.

Finishing: The finishing operation is done on a revolving workbench. The article to be finished is fixed to the free end with lac. As the job revolves against the workbench, it is being scraped, filed and polished.

Riveting: For making articles having more than one distinct part, riveting is done.

It takes approximately one day to complete one pair of Kahi-bati (plate and a bowl) and three to four days in making a bota (traditional item of Aassamese society used to offer betel leaves and nut). The time consumed by each item depends upon the design and amount of art on the item; the more complicated design the more time it consumes and accordingly there is variation in price also.

The Cooperative Society at Sarthebari

There are many cooperative societies of producers in Sarthebari region but they are mostly unorganised. There is an apex society known as the Assam Cooperative Bell Metal Utensils Manufacturing Society Ltd, which is to some extent organized. This is the only cooperative society that is operating at present. One Kuhiram Das, who was the first honours graduate from Barpeta district, established it in 1933. This society helps its members by supplying raw materials i.e., copper and tin or bell metal scrap and also in getting some financial help,

At present, there are 248 manufacturing units under the cooperative sector and including the private units the total number of units are estimated to be 350. It is found that the whole village is divided into different areas and the artisans of each area manufactures basically a single item.

The cooperative society has its head office at Sarthebari itself and nine branches spread throughout Assam. Out of these four are located at Guwahati and one each in North Lakhimpur, Tezpur, Jorhat and Sibsagar.

The annual production figures under the cooperative sector are shown in the Table 1 below:

Table 1: Bell Metal Production in Assam

Year	*Annual production (in kilos)*
1990	27,998.420
1991	16,487.140
1992	22,289.960
1993	20,160.000
1994	23,955.890
1995	24,528.590
1996	21,301.590
1997	23,257.580
1998	18,118.130
1999	22,000.000
2000	28,289.000

Source: Assam Cooperative Bell Metal Utensils Manufacturing Society Ltd., Sarthebari.

The above figures show the picture of the production in the cooperative sector only. The majority of the people producing in the private sector do not keep a proper record of their production. Hence it is not possible to get a true picture of the total annual production figures of the whole area. However it is found that the total annual production of bell metal products in that area is roughly three times of what is produced in the cooperative sector. As such, we can arrive at the total annual production figures of the combined private and the cooperative sector by multiplying the production figures of the cooperative sector by three, as shown in Table 2.

The demand of the bell metal products within the state will more or less remain the same. But the demand outside the state can be increased to a large extent. At present bell metal products are exported to Burma, Bhutan, Thailand and a few other South East Asian Countries in addition to the metropolitan states of India. But the export is in very small quantities. Moreover, there is always exploitation of the manufacturers by the middlemen involved in its export.

Table 2: Bell Metal Production in Assam

Year	*Annual production (in kilos)*
1990-91	83995.26
1991-92	49461.42
1992-93	66869.88
1993-94	60480.00
1994-95	71867.67
1995-96	73585.77
1996-97	63904.77
1997-98	69772.74
1998-99	54354.39
1999-2000	66000.00
2000-2001	84867.00

The products of bell metal have its own charm and beauty. Besides it is strongly built and the quality is also consistent. But there are certain disadvantages on part of the producers, for which they are not able to augment the production and popularise the products among masses. The industry has many prospects for development if it is properly maintained. Below we suggest some measures, which would help in its development.

1. Mechanisation to a certain extent

The bell metal products being completely hand made, consumes a lot of time and energy. If the process of production is mechanized to a certain extent, for example, by introducing rolling machines, there would be economies of scale as a result of which not only production will increase but also the cost of production would reduce and the quality of the products would be better.

2. Availability of raw materials

At present the basic raw materials, copper and tin, are acquired from places like Kolkata and Delhi through agents but if the government allots the quota of importing these materials to the producers, they can increase their scale of production.

3. Variation in designs

The items of bell metal produced at present are of the same traditional patterns and designs. So the use of these items has remained confined to a particular region. Thus, variation in the products by incorporating innovative designs would increase its demand to a large extent.

4. Marketing of the products

One of the most important reasons for this "industry being backward is that the products have very less popularity. In fact, many people from the North East India itself are not aware of the existence of such industry. If proper marketing of the products is done it would certainly yield beneficial results.

For proper marketing of the products, the producers would have to know about the tastes and preferences of the customers of different regions and accordingly design the products. But while doing so care should be taken so that the originality of the designs is not totally lost. Moreover, there should be proper channels of marketing. Display of the products in showrooms and exhibitions will also accelerate its promotion.

5. Export promotion

It is found that the present consumption of the products is more in the domestic market than the foreign markets. Only about 2 to 5 % of the total production is exported at present. This is mainly because the people from other regions are unaware of the use and utility of these products. Promotion of export by increasing popularity of the product among the masses would help in the development of the industry.

6. Government assistance

The major impediment in the growth of the industry is inadequate government assistance. The North East region being geographically isolated from the rest of India and due to the problem of terrorism, private entrepreneurs shy away from investing in the region. So development of the industry is only possible through government assistance.

In the ultimate analysis, it is seen that the bell metal industry, with its unique features, has much scope for development but due to production and marketing constraints it is not being able to grow in a proper way. For proper growth and development of the 'industry certain strategies should be chalked out. Popularising it in the market through proper marketing and distribution would increase its consumption and increase in consumption of the products would lead to increase in the demand for these goods. For satiating the growing demand production has to be increased. Increase in the number of units of production would also generate employment for the rural unemployed masses thus satisfying their need for employment.

Thus, development of the industry through government assistance and cooperation of the people would make it a successful institution and will also improve the economic scenario of the rural life in the region.

12

SMALL SCALE INDUSTRIES IN MANIPUR: Problems and Prospects

G.P. Prasain

Small Industry: Concept and Definitions

Small scale industries exist in every country. But in a developing country like India the small scale sector occupies a special place in the industrial structure. In our country manpower is abundant but capital is relatively scarce. Small scale industries tend to be labour intensive. Therefore, these industries are better suited to the country's resource potential. In view of the vast potential of small scale industries, the Government of India and various state governments are encouraging the growth of this sector. An industrial undertaking is regarded as small scale industry if its investment in plant and machinery whether hold on ownership terms or on lease/hire purchase basis, does not exceed Rs. one crore since December, 1999. The investment level was Rs. three crores from December 1997 to December 1999. Prior to that, from April 1991 to December 1997, it was Rs. 60 lakh only.

An ancillary industrial undertaking is one which is engaged or is proposed to be engaged in the manufacture or production of parts, components, sub-assemblies, fooling or intermediates, or the rendering of services, and the undertaking supplies or renders or prepares to supply and render not less than 50 per cent of its production or services, as the case may be, to one or more industrial undertaking. Its investment in fixed assets in plant and machinery whether held on ownership terms or on lease/hire purchase basis does not exceed Rs. one crore at present. This investment limit was Rs. three crore from December 1997 to December, 1999. Prior to that, from April 1991 to December 1997, it was Rs. 75 lakh. No such undertaking shall be subsidiary of or owned or controlled by one other industrial undertaking. Parent enterprise can be a small, medium or large unit.

An export oriented small scale industrial unit is one which is started with an obligation to export at least 30 per cent of its annual production by the end of the third year of commencement of production and having investment in fixed assets in plant and machinery up to Rs. three crore at present. Earlier, from April 1991 to December 1997, the investment level was Rs. 75 lakh. A unit is regarded a tiny enterprise, if its investment in fixed assets in plant and machinery does not exceed Rs. 25 lakh. Earlier from April 1991 to December 1997, the investment level was Rs. 5 lakh only. Small scale service and business enterprise is an enterprise rendering industry related service/business with investment level in fixed assets, excluding land and building, up to Rs. 10 lakhs (from September, 2000). The investment level earlier, from April 1991 to September 2000, was Rs. 5 lakh. The concept was introduced in 1982. Such enterprises are admissible for benefits applicable to micro sector enterprise, and will be eligible for coverage under priority sectors lending. For computing the value of fixed assets, original price paid by the original owner will be considered, irrespective of the price paid by the subsequent owners.

Rational of Small Business

The rational behind small business has been summarized in the Industrial Policy Resolution of 1956 as under: "They provide immediate large scale employment, they offer a method of ensuring a more equitable distribution of the national income and they facilitate an effective mobilisation of resources of capital and skill which might otherwise remain unutilised. Some of the problems that unplanned urbanisation tends to create will be avoided by the establishment of small centres of industrial production all over the country". Small scale industry can out-compete with large scale industry in certain circumstances and in selected products. Example of such industries are bricks and tiles, fresh baked goods and perishable edibles, preserved fruits, goods requiring small engineering skill, items demanding craftsmanship and artistry. Small industry can fill in the gaps between large scale production and standard output caused by large scale units. Small industry has been a complementary to its large counterparts. In the real world many small units produce intermediate products for large units. Under such complementary relationship, small units function under the tutelage of the large units and enjoy the advantage of protected markets for their products. Then, the flourishment of such small units remains under doubt. Attracted by the high profits of large units, small units can also take initiative to produce the particular product. If succeeds, the small grows to large over a period of time. Some small scale units distribute and sell their products through large scale units. For example, Hindustan Lever Limited distributes soaps and cosmetics produced by some small firms. Footwear, refrigerators, voltage stabilizers manufactured by many small firms are marketed by large firms.

Small Scale Industries in Manipur

Manipur is a small state located in north-eastern part of India bordering with Nagaland, Assam, Mizoram and Myanmar in the north, west, south and east with an area of 22,327 sq. km. About 90% of the total geographical area of the state is covered by hills and only 10% is valley. There are nine districts in Manipur, out of which five are in hills and four are in valley. The total population of the state is about 23 lakhs. Manipur continues to remain as an industrially backward state with all the nine districts under the category of "No Industries District" by all India standard. Although Manipur's economy is basically traditionally agriculture based, the role of secondary and tertiary sector can not be under estimated in the transition of economy. Though the economy of Manipur does not posses any basic and key industries to make a break through in initiating economic development, it has a limited number of industries mostly medium and small scale to initiate the process of industrialization.

Industrialisation is one of the important areas for growth and development of economic activities, alleviation of poverty, generation of employment opportunities, removal of regional economic imbalances etc. In view of its importance the Government of Manipur has been making efforts to bring about rapid industrialisation in the state by adopting industrial policies and plan economic programmes. It has been decided to focus attention on the small scale industries and agro based industries. This will hopefully serve the objective of employment. For achieving balanced growth, greater emphasis is now being placed on the development of medium and small scale industries by providing a package of incentives to the intended entrepreneurs in the state. It is also felt that the development of small scale industries is essential keeping in view its distinct advantages over large scale industries.

Number of SSI, Production, and Investment in Manipur

By the end of March, 1999, the number of permanent small scale industries both SIDO and non-SIDO stood at 9247 with an investment in plant and machinery of Rs. 33.84 crores, employing 47,157 persons with an annual production of Rs. 140.86 crores. The growth of small industries over the year in Manipur is shown in Table 1.

Though the growth in employment and investment is inevitable along with increase in the number of SSI units, yet looking at these two aspects per unit reveals striking features. A continuous decrease in some year (1992 to 1994) per unit indicates that the erstwhile labour intensive SSIs have tended to become more capital intensive over the years. But average employment in Manipur in most of the year is almost same and there is not much change. This is explained by the corresponding increase in investment per unit from Rs. 0.31 crores to Rs. 0.37 crores. This is mainly due to the definitional changes that has taken place in SSIs from time to time. The periodic revision of SSI investment limits is primarily aimed at compensating for inflations, encouragement for technical development and greater export thrust.

Another important feature which is found in Manipur is that the already limited number of industries in the state is highly unevenly distributed among the districts within the state which is clearly revealed from the cursory look of figures in table 2. 52.50 percent of units in 1999, are concentrated in Imphal (west and east) district alone, 12.92% in Ukhrul district and 6.94% in Bishnupur district, thus, pronounced in these three districts amounting for a total of 72.36 percent units. Only 27.64 percent units were located in the remaining five districts. This is, by any standard, a lackadaisical and lopsided industrial development highly skewed in favour of developed district. The two distinct features emerged out of the Table 2 are worth mentioning. First the industrial activity in the state like else where in India concentrates on the areas with proximity to road, to urban centres and market, (Papola 1979: 208 and Khanka 1994: 26-34). A recent study on the impact of new economic policies on small size firms also shows that the entrepreneurs operating within a cluster have much better resilience to policy changes than operating in isolation (Krishna and Awarthi: 1994).

Table 1: Districtwise Distribution of Regd. SSI Units in Manipur as on 31.03.1999 (Since inception)

Sl. No.	*Name of District*	*No. of Units*			*Production value (Rs. inCrores)*	*Investment (Rs. inCrores)*	*Nos. of Employment*
		SIDO	*Non-SIDO*	*Total units (3 + 4)*			
1	*2*	*3*	*4*	*5*	*6*	*7*	*8*
1.	Imphal West	3157	2264	5421	79.12	18.81	27,885
2.	Ukhrul	787	103	890	14.54	2.95	4,521
3.	Senapati	279	51	330	4.97	1.48	1,728
4.	Churachandpur	450	107	557	9.61	1.91	2,876
5.	Tamenglong	284	208	492	7.72	1.91	2,551
6.	Chandel	230	130	360	5.67	1.26	1,902
7.	Thoubal	384	115	499	8.44	2.72	2,574
8.	Bishnupur	479	172	650	9.66	2.60	2,846
9.	Imphal East	40	7	47	1.13	0.15	244
	Total	6090	3157	9247	140.86	33.84	47,157

Source : Directorate of Commerce & Industries, Government of Manipur, Imphal, 1999.

Secondly, the higher growth in number of industries in relatively less developed semi-urban areas followed by their increasing share in the total units in the state in the yesteryears (1988-99) implies that possibly due to the Governments promotional policies the industrial activity has started dispersing from urban to semi-urban and backward areas. This indeed, augurs well for the future industrial development of the state.

Table 2 : Percentage of Growth rate of SSI Sector in Manipur

Sl.No.	*District*	*Number of SSIs (SIDO)*		*Percentage growth*
		1988	*1999*	
1.	Imphal	870 (41.87)	3197 (52.50)	267
2.	Ukhrul	375 (18.05)	787 (12.92)	110
3.	Senapati	110 (5.29)	279 (4.58)	154
4.	Churachandpur	194 (9.34)	450 (7.39)	132
5.	Tamenglong	135 (6.50)	284 (4.66)	190
6.	Chandel	54 (2.60)	230 (3.78)	326
7.	Thoubal	148 (7.12)	384 (6.31)	159
8.	Bishnupur	192 (9.24)	479 (6.94)	149
Total		2078 (100.00)	6090 (100.00)	193

Source: Directorate of Commerce & Industries, Government of Manipur.
Note: Figures in brackets refer to percentage to total.
SSI (SIDO) units as on 31st March of the respective years.

Growth of Small Scale Industries in Manipur

The growth of small scale industries in this state has been very tardy, in spite of various facilities and incentives offered. Main reasons for slow growth of SSIs are lack of adequate infrastructure, entrepreneurial shyness etc. The trend of growth of small scale industries in the state may be seen from Table 3 and 4.

In 1990-91, the state had 6788 SSI units as against 13,78,485 units in country and amounted for a share of mere 0.49 percent. The share of the state in the development of SSI sector is not improved to a certain extent during the year 1990-91 to 1991-92. In 1991-92, the state had 7392 SSI units as against 14,98,193 unit in the country and amounted for 0.49 percent of the total SSI sector of the country. In 1996-97, the total number of registered SSI units in the state were 8916 as against

22,06,742 in the country and amounted for 1.40 percent of the number of small industries in the country. Table 4 reveals that the growth does not appear to be significant. But the other state have developed much more rapidly than the growth rate found in Manipur.

Table 3 : Growth of employment and investment in SSI in Manipur at the end of the year

(Rs. in crores)

Year	*Number of Units*	*Employment*	*Average Employment*	*Investment in plant & machinery*	*Average investment*	*Production*
1987-88	3996	19900	4.98	12.30	0.31	67.26
1990-91	6788	33390(67.79)	4.92	21.66(76.10)	0.32	91.81
1991-92	7392	36910(10.54)	5.00	23.59(8.91)	0.32	101.45
1992-93	7696	38400(4.04)	4.99	24.57(4.15)	0.32	106.90
1993-94	8096	39680(3.33)	4.90	25.70(4.60)	0.32	116.70
1994-95	8341	42720(7.66)	5.12	27.37(6.50)	0.33	123.16
1995-96	8612	43949(2.88)	5.10	30.19(10.30)	0.35	127.65
1996-97	8916	45469(3.46)	5.10	31.39(3.97)	0.35	132.05
1997-98	8916	46390(2.03)	5.20	32.05(2.10)	0.36	134.89
1998-99	9247	47157(1.65)	5.10	33.84(5.59)	0.37	140.86

Source : Directorate of Commerce & Industries, Government of Manipur, Imphal, 1999.

Note : Figures in brackets refer to percentage growth over previous year.

Table 4 : Growth of SSI units in Manipur vis-a-vis India 1990-91 – 1996-97

Year	*Manipur*	*India*	*2 as Percentage of 3*
1990-94	6788	13,78,485	0.49
1991-92	7392	14,98,193	0.49
1992-93	7696	16,37,812	0.47
1993-94	8096	17,72,455	0.46
1994-95	8341	19,43,519	0.43
1995-96	8612	20,84,639	0.41
1996-97	8916	22,06,742	0.40

Source: Government of India, Small Industries Development, Annual Report for data 1990 to 1999.
Government of Manipur, Directorate of Commerce & Industries, Government of Manipur, Imphal, 1999.

Note : No. of industries unit regd. both SIDO and Non-SIDO in Manipur are taken. for India only SIDO are taken.

Problems of SSIs in Manipur

The economy of Manipur is largely influenced by the imperatives of the fundamental backwardness, i.e., the handicap imposed by the geophysical location. The extensive share of the hill and hill areas to the extend of 90 percent of the total geographical areas suggests the necessity for a possible departure from the national strategy for development. However, till now, Manipur has been largely following the national policy although from time to time special programme of action are undertaken for the backward sector of the economy. In spite of the investment in the successive plans, the growth of small scale industrial sector remains very low and it appears that there is acute problems of structural stagnation.

There is lack of infrastructural facilities and service support for the growth and development of SSIs in Manipur. Transport and communications facilities is very poor. There is shortage of power supply. Flow of institutional finance is negligible in Manipur. Recovery rate of loan sanctioned by the banks and financial institutions is very poor. There is no proper industrial policy of the Government which is suitable for the growth of SSIs. Government also does not have sound policy

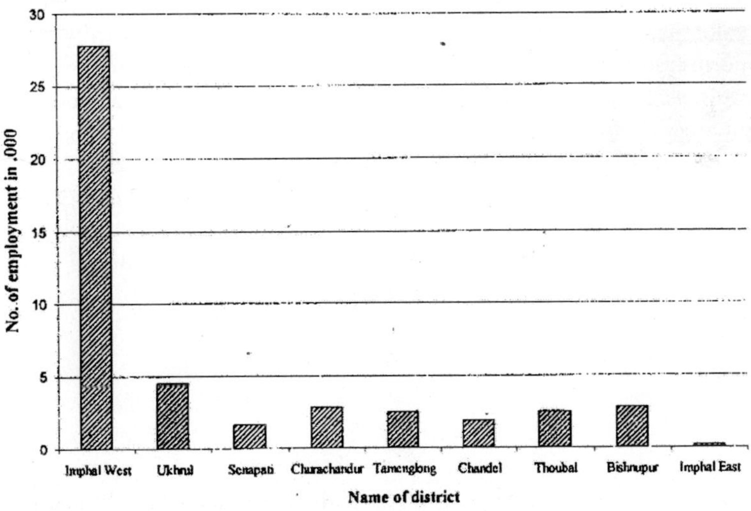

Diagram No. 1
Districtwise Distribution of Employment in SSI as on 31-03-1999

planning and follow up programme. The market of the products of small scale and tiny products depends only on the local buyers whose choice and preference is also changing as foreign made goods are available in plenty in Imphal as a result of opening of Indo-Myanmar border Trade. All the important foreign made consumer durable goods are available in Imphal which are imported from various countries through Myanmar. The rate of return of state owned public sector undertaking is negative. There is no Foreign Direct Investment in Manipur. There is also lack of resource inventory and competitive production technology. The law and order situation in Manipur is also deteriorated business and income. Due to law and order problems, investment environment gets endangered and looks unattractive in Manipur and as a result no entrepreneurs from other parts of country are interested to do any business in Manipur.

Prospects of SSIs in Manipur

Small scale industries play a vital role in the economic development of a state. More particularly its role in rural development is significant because of the importance of agriculture in the rural economy. Small scale industries help to improve the state income and lead to an equitable distribution of the same among different sectors and regions in the economy. Furthermore, they help to promote decentralisation of development in the economy. These industries generate employment opportunities on a large scale and contribute significantly to the process of self sustained growth. The economic prosperity of a developing economy depends on the forward and backward linkages of development process. Small scale industries lead to the creation of these linkages on a large scale by maximising complementarity of agriculture and industry. Improvement in agriculture productivity depends on a variety of inputs of industrial origin including fertilizers, pesticides, agricultural tools and implements etc. while agriculture in turn supplies to the industries not only wage goods but also raw materials.

Agriculture is the mainstay of the economy of Manipur and strong agro industry linkage will create demand on the one hand and adequate supply of locally available raw materials on the other. Without the development of agriculture and agro based resources, foundation for local resource based industrialisation will be weak. About 90% of the state is hilly region and development of primary sector will benefit the rural poor of the hills.

In the small scale sector in Manipur, there is prospect for industries like mechanical, electronic, glass and ceramic, auto-parts components and ancillaries, transport equipment, paper products, plastic products, lime products, rubber products, citronella oil, stationary items Oka Ink, electrical units, dairy products, bakery units, leather and tanneries etc. The indigenous secondary sector chiefly consisting of handicraft, reedmal, cane and bamboo wearing, pottery, embroidery, agricultural implements and aluminium utensils. There is a need to strengthen and modernise cluster of traditional industries to make them vibrant market and quality savvy, finished goods with high consumer demand made from locally available raw materials should be encouraged as thrust area.

Conclusion

Small scale industries can play a very important role in industrial development and solving unemployment problems in Manipur. SSI units should become competitive to face the challenges of liberalisation and globalisation, and also there should be no restrictions on SSI units to grow. Incentives should be made available for small units to grow into medium size. Periodic meeting of buyers and sellers should be hold. Small industries fair should be organised annually. Hence, the Indo-Myanmar Border Trade should be reviewed from time to time keeping in view the industrial potentials of Manipur. There is a need for technological upgradation and modernisation, adoption of cluster approach for quick and delivery of inputs to SSI sector, need to effective study tariff/non-tariff barrier under WTO, review of labour laws and steps for enhancing capacity utilisation of SSI units. There is need to increase employment and productivity per employee in the SSI Sector, to make it more competitive. Through simplifications of rules and regulations, and creation of friendly environment, SSI will help in reducing regional imbalances in industrial development, and utilisation of local resources and skills In a industrially backward state like Manipur.

REFERENCES

Khanka S.S. and Gupta C.B. (1996), *Entrepreneurship and Small Business Management*, Sultan Chand and Sons, New Delhi.

Mali, D.D. (2000), *Entrepreneurship Development in North-East India.*, IIE, Guwahati.

Mali, D.D. (2000), *Micro Enterprise Development, Policies and Programmes*, IIE, Guwahati.

Nagayya, D., (1998), Impact of Economic Liberalisation on Small Industry, Hyderabad, National Institute of Small Industry Extension Training (a study sponsored by the National Small Industries Corporation, New Delhi).

Singh N. Mohendro, Problems of Industrial Development in Manipur (A paper presented in Seminar on Development in Manipur).

Statistical Hand Book of Manipur, Directorate of Economics and Statistics, Government of Manipur.

13

ENTREPRENEURIAL BEHAVIOUR
A Study of Socio-Psychological Variables in Entrepreneurs of Tripura

Anjali Ghosh

As Bird and Jelinek (1988) note: "Entrepreneurship refers to the intentional creation or transformation of an organization for the purpose of creating or adding value through organization of resources.... Values added by entrepreneurial behavior result in increases in personal wealth (adding to personal and family well-being), increase in cash flow for a region (expanded business opportunities for others), new or better jobs (employment and worker satisfaction) and new or better products or services (alternatives for consumers)".

The potential of entrepreneurship for developing the talents and capabilities of young people and for creating a vibrant economy is increasingly being recognise in developing countries. Entrepreneurship does not emerge and develop automatically and spontaneously. Its emergence and development depend upon certain factors which we may call as supportive conditions. These factors can be broadly classified into economic and non-economic factors. While the economic factors consist of capital, labour raw materials and market, the non-economic factors include social and psychological variables.

Under the social and psychological variables, there are two most common approaches which are used for studying the characteristics of entrepreneurs. These are the trait approach and the demographic approach (Robinson *et al.*, 1991). In the trait approach, the entrepreneur is assumed to be a particular personality whose characteristics are key to explaining entrepreneurship as a phenomenon. And in the demographic approach, demographic information such as family background, age, education etc. are used to arrive at a profile of a typical entrepreneur assuming that people with similar backgrounds possess similar underlying characteristics (Bird, 1989).

Nowadays, entrepreneurial intentions and attitudes and the role of culture are taken into account for explaining entrepreneurial behaviour. The importance and role of entrepreneurs' intentions has been championed by Bird and her associates (Bird, 1988; 1989; Bird & Jelinek, 1988). Bird defines intentions as a state of mind that direct a person's attention toward he attainment of a particular goal or object, or towards the actions and behaviours towards the attainment of a particular goal or object, or towards the actions and behaviours that may be used to attain a more general goal. Entrepreneurial intention is observed to be a key determinant of entrepreneurial success and there are some exogenous factors which mediate the intention. These are demographic variables, personality characteristics, social and cultural factors.

Most of the studies have dealt either with psychological variables or demographic variables. Here in this study an attempt has been made to consider both socio-psychological and demographic variables for explaining entrepreneurial behaviour. The purpose of the study is to find out the role of certain socio-psychological and demographic variables which are important for determining entrepreneurial success in one North-Eastern state of India, namely Tripura. Under the socio-psychological variables we have considered task motivation, locus of control and individualism collectivism orientation of an entrepreneur. And in demographic variables we have taken into consideration age, educational qualification and status of the entrepreneur.

Method

Sample: Sample of this study constitutes 45 entrepreneurs who were running their small business enterprises in the West and South districts of Tripura.. They were selected randomly from the lists available from the District Industries Centre. The age range of the entrepreneurs were from 28 to 55 years with a mean age of 38.35 years. There were only 8 female entrepreneurs in this study. The group of entrepreneurs were mostly first generation entrepreneurs i.e. they have started their units on their own. On the other hand, the other group of entrepreneurs were traditional entrepreneurs which means they have inherited the enterprise from some source mostly from their family members. The type of enterprises studied here varies in nature ranging from handicrafts, handlooms to spices, food products and furniture.

Measures: The following measures were used in this study:

(a) *Task Motivation scale:* Entrepreneurial task motivation was measured by the scale developed by Ghosh (2001). This is a forced-choice scale developed on the basis of Task Motivation theory of Miner (1985). The scale consists of 26 triads in four areas of task motivation namely, Planning for the future, Personal Innovation, Self achievement and Risk avoidance. The items of the scale are scored as either positive, negative or indifferent. Split half reliability and Cronbach's alpha coefficient for the scale was found to be .80 and .75 respectively. The validity of the scale with different measures was found to be quite satisfactory.

(b) *Locus of control:* Rotter's locus of control scale (1966) was used in this study for measuring internal-external locus of control of an entrepreneur. Locus of control refers to one's generalized belief that the control of his or her own life in terms of positive and negative outcomes rests either on controllable internal factors or uncontrollable external factors. Internal locus of control of an individual refers to one's belief that his/her fate is largely in his/her own hands i.e., the action he/she performs that determines the outcomes. In contrast, the individual who has external locus of control believes that he/she has little control over his/her own outcomes, rather he/she perceives it as ruled by forces beyond his/her own control. It is to be mentioned here that high score in the scale indicates external locus of control and the low score indicates internal locus of control.

(c) *Individualism-Collectivism scale:* Individualism-collectivism scale developed by Triandis and Gelfand (1998), based on the original scale of Singelis et al. (1995), was used in this study. The scale has altogether 16 items, 8 items each for individualism and collectivism. Collectivism is described by interdependence with sociability and family integration whereas individualism refers to self-reliance and emotional detachment. The respondents were asked to indicate their responses on a seven-point scale ranging from strongly agree to strongly disagree.

(d) *Demographic Information Blank:* Some demographic information for example, age, gender, educational qualification, status i.e. whether the respondent is a first generation or traditional entrepreneur, were also collected.

(e) *Entrepreneurial success:* Entrepreneurial success was measured with respect to two indices i.e. turnover and profit of the organization. Success rate was calculated as the proportion of increment divided by the number of years the organization is in business.

All these information were collected from the entrepreneurs individually.

Results

The data collected from the entrepreneurs were first scored and then analysed for finding out the means, standard deviations and correlation of success rate with different variables. The values are presented in Table 1.

Table 1: Mean, Standard deviation (S.D.) and correlation values of success rate with different variables

Variables	*Mean*	*S.D.*	*r-value (St)*	*r-value (Sp)*
Task Motivation	9.93	5.03	.59**	.38**
Locus of Control	8.42	3.54	-.48**	-.51**
Individualism	46.96	4.70	.19	.24
Collectivism	43.04	7.69	-.50**	-.28

** Significant at .01 level

It is evident from Table 1 that success rate both in terms of profit and turnover are significantly related with task motivation, locus of control and collectivist orientation of entrepreneurs. The relationships with locus of control and collectivism were found to be negative which indicate that the entrepreneurs whose success rates are high are internal and also they are not so much interdependent and sociable or vice versa.

Next, multiple regression analyses were conducted to find out whether success as measured in terms of profit and turnover of the organisation can be predicted by these socio-psychological variables or not. The values are presented in Table 2.

Table 2: Multiple R^2 and F- values for success rate (Turnover & Profit)

Success rate	R^2	F- value
Profit	.45	8.13**
Turnover	.29	4.09**

** Significant at .01 level

The results reveal that profit of the entrepreneurs can be efficiently predicted in 45% of the cases whereas in case of turnover it is in 29% of the cases which indicate that these variables are more important for predicting profit of the entrepreneurs.

The group of entrepreneurs were subdivided into two groups i.e. high successful group and low successful group in terms of profit and turnover of the enterprise. This was done by splitting the group on the basis of mean success score. The entrepreneurs having above mean success score was termed as high successful group and those scoring at and below mean were termed as low successful group

T-tests were conducted to find out whether there is any significant difference between these two groups both in terms of profit (sp) and turnover (st) with respect to these variables. It was observed that there is significant difference between these two groups with respect to task motivation (t-values: sp= 5.81, $p<.01$, st=5.59, p<01), locus of control (t-values: sp=2.70, $p<.01$, st= 4.05, $p<.01$) and collectivist orientation (t-values: sp=3.36, $p<.01$, st= 2.95, $p<.01$). It indicates high successful entrepreneurs are more motivated toward the task, more internals i.e. believe on their own efforts for any outcome and less collectivist, i.e. do not give much emphasis on interdependence and sociability.

Demographic Variables

We have also considered certain demographic variables in our study. It was observed that the group of entrepreneurs studied here were mostly first generation entrepreneurs (77.8%), i.e. they have started their enterprise on their own. And there were some entrepreneurs who have inherited the business from some source mostly from family members. We have termed them as traditional entrepreneurs (22.8%). We wanted to find out whether there is any difference in the success rate due to the entrepreneurial status, age and educational level. This analysis with respect to gender was not done as there were very few cases of female entrepreneurs. We calculated the mean score of success rate (profit and turnover) on the basis of age and education and at the same time taking into consideration their entrepreneurial status. Therefore, we divided the group into four subgroups on the basis of entrepreneurial status and age: (a) traditional old entrepreneurs, (b) traditional young entrepreneurs, (c) first generation old entrepreneurs, and (d) first generation young entrepreneurs. This division was made by splitting the group on the basis of their mean age. Similarly, on the basis of educational level i.e. below secondary (low), secondary but below graduation (middle) and above graduation (high), three groups were formed and they were again subdivided according to their entrepreneurial status. Thus, there were six groups: (a) traditional high educated, (b) traditional middle educated, (c) traditional low educated, (d) first generation high educated, (e) first generation middle educated and (f) first generation low educated. But no cases were found in the traditional low educated group. The means for all the groups for success rate (profit & turnover) were calculated and are presented in Figures 1 and 2.

It is observed from the above figures that success index both in terms of profit and turnover are higher for traditional entrepreneurs than first generation entrepreneurs and this is also true for higher educated and old entrepreneurs. This indicates that maturity and education have important role to play in the success of an enterprise.

Conclusion

The findings of the study indicate that the group of entrepreneurs studied in Tripura mostly first generation entrepreneurs. The study reveals that there are some socio-psychological and demographic variables which are important for determining the success of the enterprise. It was noted that:

(a) There is significant positive relationship between task motivation and success rate both in terms of profit and turnover . Successful entrepreneurs were found to be more motivated towards the tasks.

(b) Success rate was found to be significantly and negatively related with locus of control of entrepreneurs. The high score in the locus of control scale indicates external locus of control (i.e. those who believe in fate or luck for any outcome) and the low score indicates internal locus of control (i.e. those who believe that their outcomes are the results of their own performance). Thus, the results indicate that the entrepreneurs who are more successful are internal or *vice versa*.

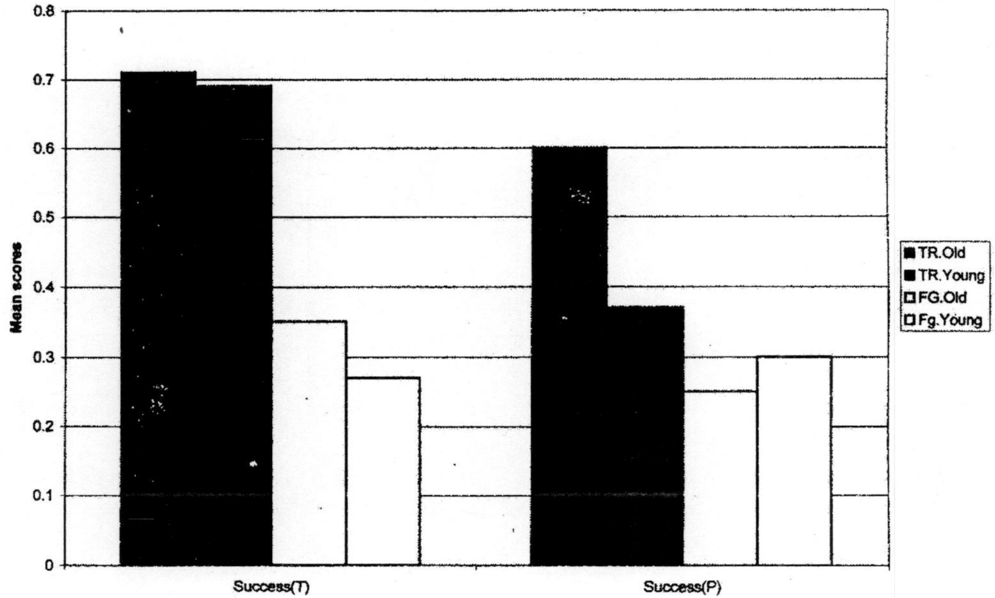

Fig. 1: Mean Success rate (Turnover & Profit) of entrepreneurs according to status and age

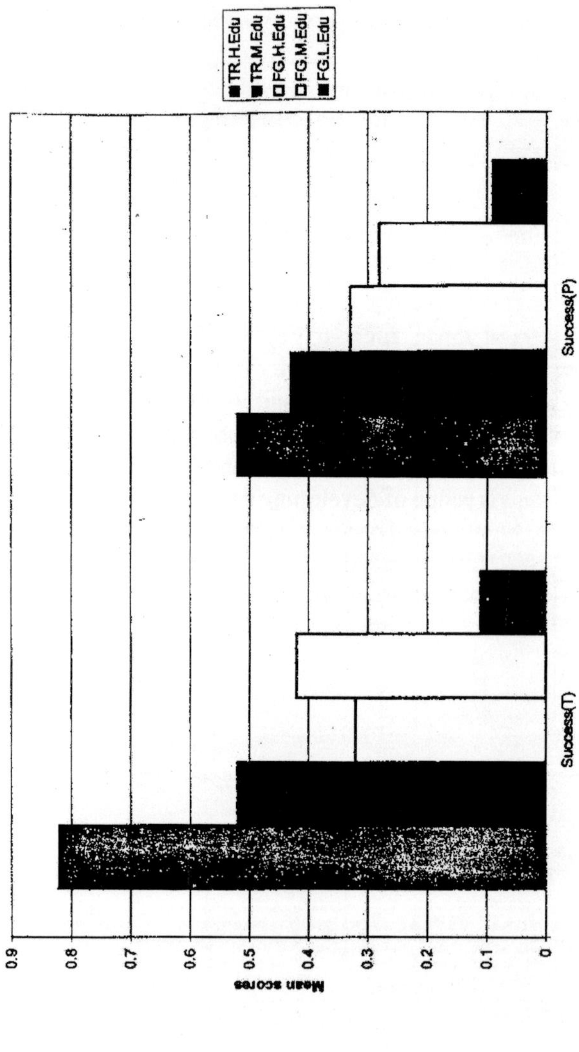

Fig. 2: Mean Success rate (Turnover & Profit) of entrepreneurs according to status and educational qualification

(c) Significant negative relationship was observed between success rate and collectivist orientation of entrepreneurs. This indicates that successful entrepreneurs do not believe in interdependence and sociability or vice versa.

(d) Individualistic orientation was found to be positively related with success rate but the relationship was not found to be significant. It indicates that the successful entrepreneurs are more self-determined and independent than the less successful entrepreneurs.

(e) Demographic variables were also found to contribute to entrepreneurial success. Traditional entrepreneurs with high qualification and matured age were found to be more successful than first generation less educated young entrepreneurs.

But apart from these socio-psychological and demographic variables, economic factors have important role to play for the survival of the enterprise. In Indian cultural set up, family support is very important. In our study, it was observed that the entrepreneurs who inherited their business from family members are more successful than the first generation entrepreneurs. There is scope of developing rural enterprises in the areas of fruit processing, bamboo and cane products etc. It was revealed during discussion with the entrepreneurs that there are problems of marketing, competition and other infrastructural facilities in this region. But still their attitude toward task, self-determination, initiative etc. are positive signs for future development.

REFERENCES

Bird, B.J., (1988), Implementing entrepreneurial ideas: The case for intention, Academy of Management review, 13 (3), 442-53.

Bird, B. J. (1989), *Entrepreneurial Behaviour*, Glenview, I-L: Scott, Foresman & Co.

Bird, B.J. & Jelinek, M., (1988), The operation of entrepreneurial intentions, *Entrepreneurship Theory and Practice*, 13 (2), 21-29.

Ghosh, A. (2001), Entrepreneurial Task Motivation: A forced-choice measurement scale, Technical Report, Indian Statistical Institute.

Miner, J.B. (1985), Sentence Completion measures in personnel research: The Development and Validation of the Miner Sentence Completion Scales, in H.J. Bernardin & D.A. Bownas (eds), *Personality assessment in organizations* (145-176), New York: Prager.

Robinson, P.B., Stimpson, D.V., Huefuer, J.C. & Hunt, H.K. (1991), An Attitude approach to prediction of Entrepreneurship, *Entrepreneurship Theory and Practice*, 13-3 1.

Rotter, J.B. (1966), Generalized expectations for internal vs. external locus of reinforcement, *Psychological Monographs*, 80, (1. Whole No. 609).

Singelis, T. M.; Triandis, H.C. Bhawuk, D.P.S. & Gelfand, M.J. (1995), Horizontal and Vertical aspects of Individualism and Collectivism: A theoretical and measurement refinement, *Cross-Cultural Research*, 29,3, 240-275.

Triandis, H. C., & Gelfand, M.J. (1998), Converging measurement of Horizontal and Vertical Individualism and Collectivism, *Journal of Personality and Social Psychology*, 59, 1006-1020.

14

ROLE OF PERIODIC MARKETS IN RURAL DEVELOPMENT
Study of a few Markets in Meghalaya

Sutapa Sengupta
Susmita Das

Markets, whether permanent or periodic, besides being the prime center of transaction of goods and services, also act as centers of diffusion of various programmes or even ideas. The size, frequency and distribution of such markets appear to be an indicator of economic development of the areas where they are held. This is even more specific in areas where urban types of permanent markets have not yet developed or are very few in number. In the rural and hill areas of this country, the periodic markets, however, are different from the typical '*mandis*', as they cater to a wide spectrum of demand. Thus, they have considerable significance in the economic development of the region, since they offer a high degree of interaction between groups of people who otherwise live in isolation and have limited scope of economic development.

In Meghalaya, the weekly periodic market is a phenomenon that has close connection with the social and economic aspect of human life particularly in the rural areas of the state. It is only in Shillong that a permanent market has developed which has both rural and urban characteristics in terms of its functions. Besides the Iewduh market of Shillong, most of the markets in the rural areas are either intra-village or inter- village periodic markets which act as the major place of sell of agricultural or any other rural surplus produces as well as any other kind of goods and articles which are imported by a group of sellers from outside the state or even outside the country. Thus, the rural periodic markets, most of which have existed from quite early times, remain as places of prime economic and commercial activities either for one village at a time or for a group of villages. It is in this backdrop, the present study undertakes to analyse the role of periodic markets in the economic development of the rural areas in Meghalaya. The periodic markets acting as the most important economic institutions in the rural areas of the state, lend a specific significance to this kind of study.

The present study focuses mainly to understand the nature of functioning of a few selected periodic markets of Meghalaya and also to analyse the role of these weekly markets in the rural development. The markets selected for the present study are Sohra (Cherrapunjee), Pynursla, Umsning, Umroi and Smit markets, falling respectively in Ri-War (Sohra, Pynursla), RI-Bhoi (Umsning, Umroi), and in Khynrium (Smit) areas.

The present work has been organized in three broad sections. The introductory section deals with the problem of study, objectives and the historical background of rural periodic markets in Meghalaya. This is followed by a section that discusses about the present pattern of functioning in the selected periodic markets. The final section analyses the impact of these markets and the nature of their functioning on the economic and social development of the rural areas of the state.

The rural markets in Meghalaya are more or less contemporary with the establishment of the British settlement in the north eastern region of the country in general and that in Meghalaya in particular. It is during that time the rural settlements in the state experienced some changes particularly in their size and structure. This changes led to the coming up of a few markets in Meghalaya like Sohra market, Smit market etc. The number of such markets multiplied rapidly in the post Independent period. However, a look at the location of these periodic markets of the state reveals that, most of them emerged at different transport lines signifying the importance of transport linkages in their evolution. The trading patterns in these rural markets have undergone a gradual process of change. To begin with most of these markets operated in an exchange system of commodities as was carried in barter trade of earlier times. Slowly with the influence of outside people like the Britishers, a proper system of transaction was introduced in these markets. The Khasi region of Meghalaya in particular had a very old commercial relation with their neighbouring regions. The principal commodities being sold out from the markets of Khasi hill areas to other places were lime, potato, oranges, betel-nut betel-leaves, bayleaves, pineapples, banana, irons and, coal limestone etc. A close look at the commodity structure of the present day markets reveals that, even today, the markets have considerable importance of trading in some of these articles. Thus, it is evident that, the periodic markets in Meghalaya, which were in existence in some form or other from a very early time in the state, are supposed to have considerable importance in the development of economic and social life of the people in rural Meghalaya.

FUNCTIONING OF PERIODIC MARKETS AT PRESENT

The commodity structure of a periodic market gives a reflection of the geographical environment of the region around the market. The amount of rainfall, temperature, soil type all influences the growth of different types of product. Again, the proximity to urban center, good road connectivity, facilitates the availability of different items in such types of a market.

The commodities available in these markets reveal two broad types i.e. goods of local origin and goods from outside areas. Keeping these two broad types in mind, the goods sold in these markets has been classified into ten broad categories (Table 1). A cursory look at the table reveals the predominance of perishable and semi-perishable products in the markets. This is obvious as in the rural areas meeting the basic requirements is the first criteria and as these two categories include items like vegetables, meat, fish, spices, betel leaf and nut, fruits and all types of groceries etc. their share in the markets remain significantly high. Next to it comes the share of non-perishable items which beside including stationary goods also includes commodities like clothes, utensils, cosmetics etc. apart from these a host of other items under different heads are also found in these periodic markets in different proportion.

Thus, as expected items of basic requirements mostly dominate these markets. However, the influence of Shillong (the urban center) could be felt in all the markets of the region in respect of the availability of wide range of items of urban usage.

Table 1: Commodity Structure

Type of Commodities	*Smit*	*Umroi*	*Umsning*	*Pynursla*	*Cherra*
Perishable food product	25.0	29.3	27.0	30.0	25.0
Semi-perishable product	15.4	10.7	30.0	35.0	20.0
Commodities beside food	15.4	14.7	5.0	12.0	4.0
Agricultural implements	11.5	5.3	3.0	3.0	9.0
Non-perishable items	15.4	26.7	20.0	10.0	20.0
Fuel	1.9	4.0	-	-	3.0
Medicine	3.8	2.7	-	2.0	4.0
Services	1.9	1.3	-	2.0	3.0
Electrical goods	1.9	2.7	-	-	4.0
Miscellenous	7.6	2.7	15.0	6.0	8.0

It is interesting to note that there is not much of an areal differentiation as far as the availability of commodities is concern.

The commodities traded in these markets are mostly generated from the Iewduh market of Shillong while some of the items do come from the surrounding areas of the market, like the vegetables, fruits, pork and chicken etc. This not only keeps the item fresh, but at the same time gives a platform to the cultivators generating some surplus production to sell. However, it may be said that the surplus amount is in no way comparable to the amount sold in most of the weekly markets in other parts of the country.

Items like fish, spices (beside the local ones), grocery, clothes, electronic and electrical items generally come from Shillong market only. Most of these items are sold in a few shops only and caters to a small number of customers. Grocery items has a lot of demand in all the periodic markets and the consumers are found to store items of their demand for the whole week. Kwai, which is consumed in large amount generally come from two areas. For markets that are located in the Bhoi areas, they come from Nongpoh and its surrounding areas, while markets of the War areas get them from Dawkai and nearby areas. Kwai coming from the southern part are considered to be of a better quality and as such fetch a higher market price. This particular commodity is sold in large quantity and in a number of shops in all the markets irrespective of their location. It may be mentioned here that at Pynursla market Kwai sellers overwhelmingly dominate the market transaction.

Dryfish, is yet another item with huge demand, finds its presence in all the markets of the region. Significantly in all these markets it comes from Dawkai and at times even from Bangladesh. Myllium happens to be the place from where all types of agricultural implements come to the periodic markets wherever they are located.

Besides the above mentioned items a host of other items are sold in the markets whose catchment areas varies depending on the location of the market as well as the season of their transaction.

Market participants i.e. both buyers and sellers play an important role as it is they who allow the market to function and carry out with transaction. The strength of the participants indirectly indicates the importance of the market. To site an example, the Cherrapunjee market which is considered to be one of the oldest market of the region attracts not only people of the surrounding areas but also of far off places.

Though there is no doubt that the importance of these markets have diminished recently, but the fact that they continue to function even today is enough an indication of the rural peoples dependence on them. It needs to be mentioned here that most of these markets are now looked after by the elderly generation and in spite of growing unemployment the younger group do not feel attracted to take it up as a viable alternative.

The buyers for most of these markets come from far off places but the sellers happen to be from among the local resident only. The only exception is the Cherapunjee market where people from as far as Pynursla, Shella-Bholagang, Shillong come to sell the product. It may be mentioned here that on an average people living close to the market generally visit. However, the mode and means of transportation does play an important role in explaining the area of origin and the distance that the buyers cover to reach a particular market.

PERIODIC MARKETS AND RURAL DEVELOPMENT

From the discussion held in the previous sections, it is evident that, these periodic markets in Meghalaya have emerged, if not as anything else, at least as a center of commercial interaction, which have considerable significance on the economic and social lives of the rural folk. The commodity structure and catchment areas of the commodities as well as the participation patterns in the markets clearly focuses the fact that these markets serve most of the basic needs of the rural population in the areas where the markets are held. The composition of commodities traded in these markets is quite varied and this composition is more or less same in all the markets. It implies that trade in most of the markets is done on the retail bases and specialised items is largely missing, which is otherwise the characteristic feature of the periodic markets in the rest of the country. Again, it is interesting to note that the commodities sold in the markets are often not the surplus produce of the village farmers, rather they are bought from some other sources (in most cases from Iewduh market in Shillong) and resold in these markets. The nature of commodities traded as such do not permit a large catchment area, which might have some impact on the more or less uniform commodity composition of all the markets. As far as the participation in the markets is concerned, it is obvious that the buyers come from different areas to all these markets. This indicates that, since the market do not usually specialise in the selling of any particular commodity, the buyers too do not have particular preference for any specific market.

The periodic rural markets in Meghalaya, when considered from a rural development point of view have but limited scope, since most of them have some limitation in regard to their commodity structure and composition, catchment areas, nature of participation and so on. However, in spite of all these drawbacks, the periodic markets in rural Meghalaya are operating and excepting a few villages which are very close to the Iewduh market in Shillong, most of these markets are in existence from a very early period of time. This very fact indicates that, whatever small may be their contribution, the weekly markets exert some control on the rural economic development of the areas where they operate.

It has been observed in many instances that, irrespective of the location of these markets, most of them can offer a set type of commodities catering to the immediate daily needs of the buyers in the market. As for instance, commodities like vegetable, fish, meat, milk, grocery items, utensils, animal feeds, etc. are present in all the markets right from Umsning which is on the Guwahati-Shillong highway to Pynursla with a quite interior location in the Ri-War areas. Thus, these markets are facilitating, to a considerable extent, the task of distributing the basic commodities to people of even very distant areas in the state. It has also been observed and confirmed through interview taken in the field, that, in the absence of any large permanent market in these specific villages or even in the nearby areas, the price of commodities is determined by the village headman and their councils. The price structure of these commodities is maintained in such a way that it is affordable by most of the people in the area. The periodic rural markets thus are offering services to the people in two important manners. They are not only saving people the expense of travelling from far off place to the major centers of markets, but also are offering commodities to them at reasonable and affordable prices. These markets have, therefore, emerged as indispensable socio-economic institutions of the villages in Meghalaya.

The periodic markets held on a weekly basis in Meghalaya do not as such require specialized infrastructural arrangements, such as warehouse, cold storages etc., since the markets at large do not trade in a few specific commodities on wholesale bases. However, in some markets one or two commodities are traded in wholesale basis at some time of the year. As for instance, ginger in Umsning market is sold in huge quantity and entirely on wholesale basis only. But the entire operation takes place in the open space of the market with certain make- shift arrangements. As such the cost of operation of these markets have still remained nominal. This could be one of the reasons that the markets are operating at various places, irrespective of their structure and arrangements.

The observation and queries made on the market participants reveal that there is a group of sellers in almost every market who do not sell the surplus produce of their respective farms, rather, they buy the articles from some other places and resell them in the weekly markets. The commodities sold by such traders can range from vegetables, fish, milk and other food items to all sorts of fancy items like costume, jewellery, bags, watches and alike. This indicates that, markets can offer small business opportunity to those who are otherwise not engaged in any land-based activities in the villages.

The operation of these periodic markets has enabled villages to get connected with transport and communication facilities. On all the market days a number of buses, taxis (mostly share) etc. are found plying between the market place with the nearby as well as far off places in order to bring both commodities and people. However, it was noticed while communicating with the residents of the villages that the smooth plying of vehicles happens only on the market days. As such the local population not only meet their basic requirement from these weekly markets, but also get a chance to go to other areas to fulfill different works.

Beside, the above mentioned functions which these weekly or periodic markets perform, a host of specific services (tailoring, repairing etc.) are also rendered on the market days, thus enabling the people of even remote areas to avail such facilities. Also a number of social gathering takes place on the market days as majority of the villagers remain present at some or the other point of time. Thus the market offers a place of social interaction between the different social groups. Through these gathering the market even help to spread the ideas and information.

The periodic markets in Meghalaya, as observed so far, no doubt have some impact on the rural development of the state. However, an insight into the different operational systems of the market reveal that there are certain limitation under which these markets are functioning.

The commodities traded in these markets, as mentioned earlier, lack in specialization. The traders thus have very little opportunity to build up a proper entrepreneurship in these markets, and as such they are not being able to earn high profit which is a must for development in any market based economy. It is due to this fact, that the markets are not gathering enough interest among the local youth to be involved in the market operations, which otherwise could have provided some alternative employment opportunities. The lack of specialization in the commodities, reflected the lack of infrastructural facilities in the markets. Due to a general absence of storage facilities, the commodities once brought to the market have to be sold on the same day. Thus, the traders have to sell their articles at a price that is quoted on the day. With the proper storage facilities, on the other hand, they could store the articles and sell them at the time when the higher price is available.

The market participation pattern reveals that the buyers in the markets do not come from any specific area, nor do they visit any specific market every week. This is mainly because the markets usually do not have monopoly on any particular item or a group of items. Thus, there cannot be any steady income as such from these markets.

It has been observed in several cases that proper weights and measures are not in use while selling the commodities. Special mention can be made of beef sold in Smit market. It is here that roughly about two hundred shops sell beef but none of them use any scientific measurement for selling, the use of which otherwise could have been profitable for both the sellers and buyers.

Thus to conclude it may be said that although these markets function with limitations, there is no denying of the fact that they play an important role in the social and economic life of the people. Efforts, therefore, needs to be made to improve the basic infrastructural facilities which might be able to solve many a problems that arises otherwise. These periodic markets) sheer presence is in itself an indication of their importance in the rural Meghalaya.

REFERENCES

Boshle, H.G. and Goettingen (1985), "South-Indian Weekly Markets: A Case Study in their Functions, Structure and Morphology" in Mukherjee and Ahmed, (eds.), *India: Culture, Society and Economy, Geographical Essays*, Inter-India, New Delhi.

Das Gupta, P.K. (1984), 'A Note on Shella Market", in J.B. Ganguly, (ed.), *Marketing in North East India*, Omsons, New Delhi.

Sharma, B.D. (1984), 'Marketing in Tribal Areas", in J.B. Ganguly, (ed.), Marketing in North East India, Omsons, New Delhi.

Singh, A.L. (1995), "The Periodic Markets as Rural Service Centres", in Hill Geographer Vol. XI, No. I & 2, Geographical Society of the North Eastern Hill Region (India) Shillong.

Syiemlieh, D.R. (1993), "Sohra or Cherrapunjee", in A.C. Sinha *et. al.* (ed), *Hill Cities of Eastern Himalayas - Ethnicity, Land Relations and Urbanisation*, Indus Publishing Co., New Delhi.

TECHNOLOGY, TOURISM AND COOPERATION

15

SUITABLE POST-HARVEST TECHNOLOGIES FOR THE RURAL AREAS

R.K.P. Singh
K.K. Satapathy

Introduction

In India, out of total production about 70 % is retained and stored by the farmers for various purposes like consumption, seed, animal feed, payment of wages etc. Only 30 % is marketable surplus that is handled by traders and different government agencies. Agricultural produce is perishable and semi-perishable in nature. At rural level grains are stored mostly from 3 months to 2 years, depending upon the need. Post-harvest losses occur both in quantity and quality. Due to lack of proper storage and processing technologies in rural areas, always there are glut during harvesting season and immediately followed by short supply. Thus growers are deprived of the remunerative price of their produce and possible income through value addition and processing technology. Moreover, nearly 10-15 % of food grains and 30-40 % of horticultural produce goes waste during post production system depending upon their perishability and lack of post harvest technologies applied. At least 50 % of this loss could be prevented using appropriate post harvest technologies and associated equipments and practices.

Use of improved post-harvest technology ensures loss reduction to farm produce, employment generation and augmenting income of rural people. It contributes to enhancement of skill of rural entrepreneurs and workers. At present post harvest techniques being followed by the farmers at rural level are rather more crude in north eastern hill region as compared to other parts of the country. The north eastern hills region also experiences hot and humid weather, which are highly hazardous from post harvest technology point of view. There is need to make farmers aware about various improved post harvest technologies so that post harvest losses could be reduced and value addition can be done at rural level.

Degree of Post Harvest Losses

There are significant losses of food grains between harvest and consumption. During storage, grain is attacked by insects, rodents, birds and micro-organisms. The stored grain pests not only eat away considerable quantity but also contaminate/spoil the grains in such a way that the grain, sometimes becomes totally unfit for human consumption. It is generally recognized that the losses in stored grains occur in decreasing order of magnitude by insects, rodents and fungi. While the insects migrate from the field at the time of harvest to storage, the fungus is brought in due to wet condition of the grain. Fungi and insects are often interrelated. Apart from this, the grain is contaminated by the excreta of the insects and hairs acid pellets of rats that lead to consumer hazards. The contaminated grain if consumed lead to several fatal diseases. The microorganisms can produce toxins, which are carcinogenous. If the storage losses are minimized we can enjoy greater benefits from the green revolution. It is estimated that about 15-25 percent of the total production of the country get lost in post harvest phase specifically during handling, storage, transport, processing and distribution. At least 50% of these losses can be reduced by adopting improved storage and processing technologies and saving to the tune of about Rs. 27,000 crore can be done (Table 1).

Where total post harvest losses in food grains ranges between 12-15 %, the total losses in fruits are estimated to be about 20-30 %. In a systematic study on post harvest losses of fruits, an estimate between 17.1 to 36.7 % in mango, 12 to 19 % in banana, 8.3 to 30.7 % in orange, 10 to 25 % in apple and 23 to 30 % in grapes has been made (Chadha, 1995). Post harvest losses of some vegetables are as high as 80-90 %. With a loss of about 10-15 % in fresh weight, vegetables appear shrivelled and stale thus lowering their market value and consumer acceptability considerably. The estimated loss for onion (16-35 %),

Table 1: Annual post-harvest losses and extent to which it could be saved using improved post harvest technology

Crop	*Prodn. in 1999-2000 (M tones)*	*Estimated loss as % of prodn**	*Avoidable loss as % of total loss***	*Volume of avoidable loss (M tonnes)*	*Value of *** avoidable loss (Rs. in Crores)*
Rice	88.0	15	60	7.9	4740
Wheat	74.0	15	60	6.7	3350
Coarse Cereals	32.0	15	60	2.9	2320
Pulses	15.0	15	50	1.1	1100
Oilseeds	25.0	12	50	1.5	1800
Vegetables	86.0	40	50	17.2	8600
Fruits	43.0	25	50	5.4	5400
TOTAL	362.0	20	55	42.7	27310

* Estimated loss includes losses during storage, handling, and milling/processing. It does not include losses at consumers end.

** Avoidable loss shows the component of the total post harvest loss that can be saved by using simple, economical improved post harvest technology like cleaners, graders, driers, metal bins for storage of food grains, improved milling equipment, and pre- coolers, waxing equipment, simple packaging and cold storage for fruits and vegetables.

***Assuming market price of rice, wheat, coarse cereals. pulses, oil seeds, vegetables and fruits as Rs.6000/-, Rs.5000/-, Rs.8000/-, Rs.10000/-, Rs.12000/-, Rs.5000/- and Rs.10000/per tonne respectively.

tomato (20-50 %), cabbage (37%), cauliflower (49 %) and lettuce (62 %) have been found relatively high (Singh and Seshadri, 1989). Considerable losses also occur during transport. This is merely a quantitative loss and that qualitative loss is beyond ones imagination. The control of post harvest losses has, therefore, been recognized as an effective means of increasing the availability of fruits and vegetables to the ever increasing population.

Recommended Storage Practice

Safe storage of farm produce has been a serious problem everywhere in north east India. A variety of structures are used and practices are being followed that vary from place-to-place. Still the extents of losses during storage are estimated to be very high. Losses at the level of farmers have been reported to be the highest in comparison to trade, and processor's level storage losses. The most important task for storage is the reduction of grain moisture to the safe limit and then maintaining it at that level during the entire storage period. Food grains being hygroscopic not only get remoistened through rain but can also absorb moisture from air depending upon ambient condition (temperature and humidity) and equilibrium moisture content (EMC) of the grain. Development of moulds begins when the air humidity is between 65 and 70%. For long-term storage, the moisture levels are to be kept even lower. Safe storage moisture contents of some food commodities are given in Table 2. To get best storage performance, the food grains must be:

(a) Thoroughly cleaned, graded and dried to the safe storage moisture level which is generally 10- 12% on wet basis (wb) for cereals and 7-9% wb for oilseeds for 6-12 months storage.

(b) Cleaned and dried grains should be kept in a storage structure which has been properly repaired, cleaned and disinfested.

(c) Structures should be strong enough to bear the load of grain stored and do not permit contact/exchange with outside humid air. The structure should be kept in the coolest part of the house/ farm.

To protect the grain in storage from damage following five golden rules should be applied :

1. Dry and clean the grain before storage.
2. Use dunnage to avoid damage due to moisture of the grains stored in bags.

3. Use metallic bins or other improved storage structure.
4. Fumigate with Ethylene Di-bromide (EDB) ampoules to avoid insect damage.
5. Use anticoagulants for the rat control.

Table 2: Recommended moisture content for some food commodities for their safe storage commodity

	Commodity	*Safe storage moisture* content (% wb)
1.	Maize, Wheat, Rice	13
2.	Paddy	14
3.	Cowpeas, Beans	15
4.	Millets	16
5.	Sorghum	12
6.	Soyabean	09
7.	Groundnut (pods), Rapeseed/ mustard, Sunflower	08
8.	Sesamum, Groundnut (kernel), linseed, Castor, Copra, Cocoa	07
9.	Safflower	06

Improved Storage Structures for Rural Area

The grains are stored mostly in rooms as bulk storage, which is prone to extensive damage by rats and insects. Storage structures are kept in corner of the house and they are rarely kept raised over a platform. Gunny bags are filled with grains and covered by wheat straw or *bhusa*. Though this type of practice keep bags free from moisture but they are not rat proof. Many places bamboo or wooden bins are used but bins are not properly covered with lids and grain is exposed to the vagaries of nature. These bins are also without rat proof cone. Most of the farmers are unaware of the use of chemicals in storage and improved storage practices. Indigenous storage structures are constructed from locally available material and most of them are not insect, rodent and moisture proof. Improved storage structures not only prevent the grain from rodents and insects but it also stops fungus and mould growth due to excessive moisture of the grain. Some of the low cost improved storage structures suitable for the rural areas are described below.

Metallic bin : The metallic bins are one of the best storage facilities with varying capacity. The bin having 240 cm length and 120 cm width made of G.I. sheets of 18 or 20 gauge having a capacity of 2 q costs about Rs. 500. Instead of GI sheet old bitumen drum can also be used for storage of food grains after certain modification like fitting of lids etc. The bitumen left in the drum is removed by burning. Lids made of metal sheet and latches and hooks are fitted. Later it is painted first with a printer (red oxide) and then with aluminium paint. These bins are of 520 mm diameter and 900 mm height. They can store 1.5 q of wheat and 1.2 q of Bengal gram. Hapur kothis are circular (G.I. sheet) bins of 2, 5, 7.5 and 10 q capacities and have potential of meeting requirements of even large farmers. Metal bins made out of aluminiurn sheets do not permit absorption of solar heat through bin wall by the grains and its life is also more.

Bamboo bin : These bins are made of two walls of bamboo with polyethylene lining in between and have varying capacities. It has been developed and tested at Akola, Coimbatore and Kharagpur centres of AICRP on Post Harvest Technology. These bins are suitable for short-duration storage and can be adopted by small and marginal farmers.

Baked clay bin : Baked clay bin of 7 q capacity (paddy) is made of 16 burnt rings (each 0.9 m in diameter and with a total height of 1.5 m) jointed by mud plaster, cement mortar and cow dung coatings one after another. The ends of the rings are made in such a manner that they fit into each other. These rings are kept on a polyethylene sheet covered and plastered platform (1.2 m x 1.2 m x 0.25 m) of brick masonry and cement sand mortar. An outlet is provided for the discharge of the grain. The top is covered with a mild steel lid. Paddy at initial moisture of 14.5-15.5% wb can be safely stored for 6 months. Because of the low cost and good performance this bin is particularly useful for small and marginal farmers who do not store their produce for longer duration.

Pusa bin : It is a modification of the ordinary mud storage commonly used in villages. To provide moisture-proof and air-tight conditions, polyethylene film of 700 gauge thickness has been embedded at the top, bottom and on all the sides of the mud bin. The embedding process provides mechanical support and safety to polyethylene film. The construction of outer walls with burnt bricks up to 45 cm height makes the structure rat proof as well. The Pusa bin is constructed with unburnt bricks on burnt bricks or concrete floor to avoid rat burrowing. The bin can be constructed for storing different quantities of grain ranging from 0.4 to 3.2 tonnes. Thoroughly dried (less than 10% moisture content) and cooled grain is loaded in well dried bin. The grain should be filled to full capacity. In the event of shortage of grain, farmers are advised to fill dried *bhusa* with the grain. The bin must be sealed at the filling hole. The grain and seed both remain safe in the bin for mere than 1 year when this precaution is followed. However, following precautions may be followed while using the above bins.

(i) Make sure that the grain is completely dried as the damp grain invites insect infestation and mould growth. Cereal grains stored below 11% and pulses 8-10% moisture will normally resist the insect attack.

(ii) Fill in the crevices and plaster the bin, if needed with white soil and cow-dung paste after each filling. Allow it to dry completely for a day or two.

(iii) Clean and fumigate the grain before filling.

(iv) Clean and disinfect (using 0.5% malathion spray/fumigant) the bin thoroughly.

(v) Fill the bin with grains to its full capacity and unload it only through the bottom outlet.

(vi) Maintain proper sanitation around the bin.

(vii) After filling, close the top cover and apply mud seal.

(viii) While disinfects or fumigating the bin and grain, expert advice from technical personnel like Village Extension Worker and Save Grain Campaign Agency may be obtained.

Other Technology Options for Rural Sector

Use of appropriate post harvest technology could go a long way in preserving the harvested produce and reduction in post harvest losses, generate gainful employment opportunities in rural, and semi urban areas near production sites and in value addition to the produce and hence additional income for the growers and traders. It also benefits to consumers in the form of better quality products at reasonable price and helps in development of an efficient market network. Large number of post harvest technologies has been developed by the ICAR institutes, State Agricultural Universities, All India Coordinated Research Project on Post Harvest Technology, CSIR Laboratories including CFTRI, Mysore and Regional Research Laboratories, which can be adopted in north eastern states specifically in small scale sector. Operation wise commercially viable options which can be used in north eastern states for various post harvest operations are described below:

Cleaning and Grading

For cleaning and grading of seeds, a large number of machines are commercially available. These come in different sizes ranging from 100 to 5000 kg/hr costing from about Rs. 25,000 to Rs. 20 lakh respectively. These machines are suitable for processing and upgrading various kinds of seeds by using the sieves of required size. Screens suitable for almost all crops like; paddy, maize, wheat, sorghum, barley, pearl millet, pigeon pea, chick-pea, rape seed/mustard, sunflower etc. are available. It can be operated with electric motor or diesel engine. Two screen and three-screen grain cleaner, perforated cylinder type cleaner, specific gravity cleaner/separators, magnetic separator, destoner, fruit and vegetable washer/grader, expanding pitch rubberized belt grading units etc. Hand operated swinging type double screen grain cleaner developed at CIAE, Bhopal, has a capacity of 200-300 kg/hr of produce cleaning and grading. It costs about Rs. 1000. A pedal-cum-power operated double screen grain cleaner and grader developed at CIAE can process about 300-500 kg/ha of wheat, pulses, and oilseeds. The machine costs about Rs. 12,000. It is easy to operate and maintain, and can be taken from one place to another easily. Paddy winnower developed at TNAU, Coimbatore, processes about 300 kg of material per hour. It winnows paddy threshed by the paddy thresher or by other means.

Grading of fruits is conventionally done manually by experienced persons through visual observations based on size, and soundness. The application of mechanical fruit graders have so far remained confined to processing industries only. An apple grader developed at GBPUA&T, Pantnagar, Uttaranchal, consists of six numbers of V-belts with 24 wooden pulleys mounted over four shafts. The distance between belts increases gradually from 20 mm from the feed end to 50 mm at the delivery end. It has a capacity of grading 500-700 kg/hr of fruits and costs about Rs.20,000/-. This machine can also be used for grading potato also. Similarly, a potato grader developed at PAU, Ludhiana, comprises of a frame, an elevator, feed conveyor, an intermediate receiving conveyor, a sizing conveyor with rubber spools, two identical driving rollers with helical grooves of gradually increasing pitch, collecting platform with partitions and gates, feeders, transport wheels and a power transmission system. The rods with the spools carry forward as the rollers rotate. The gap between individual spool goes on increasing gradually according to the pitch of the helix of the driving rollers. This leads to sizing of the tubers as these are carried forward over the sizing conveyor. Separation of the tubers of smaller size starts first and that of the bigger size towards the end of sizing bed. The accuracy of sizing depends on the uniformity of shape. Sizing accuracy is better in round shaped varieties than in oblong or irregular shaped.

Fruit grader developed at CIPHET with a rated capacity of 1000 kg/ ha round shaped fruits, runs on 2 kW electric motor, and costs Rs. 35,000. Gravity type, manually operated fruit grader of IIHR, Bangalore, has a capacity of 0.4-0.5 t/h for fruits like mango, oranges, etc. It costs about Rs. 5,000. Yet another unit of IIHR, Bangalore, can be used in fruit growing areas is a motor operated unit of 1.0 t/h capacity and costs about Rs. 25,000. A Multi-fruit grader that works on the principal of weight based grading has been developed at GBPAU&T, Pantnagar, having capacity of 300-400 kg/h for apples, pomegranate and oranges and costs Rs. 25,000. A vegetable washing machine developed at PAU, Ludhiana, uses tumbling of vegetables in a stream of flowing water that takes away the dirt and dust attached to the surface of vegetables. It enhances the shelf life, and market price. It is suitable for potato, tomato, and leafy vegetables etc. The machine is run on 1.5 kw electric motor and costs about Rs. 30,000.

Drying and Dehydration

Driers are essential gadgets for removal of excess moisture from agricultural material in order to protect them from fungi, molds, insects, and other biological agents. Though driers have been commonly used in chemical, pharmaceutical, and textile industry, these are yet to be used at farmers level and in small-scale agro-processing units. Driers basically utilize the principle of diffusion by creating suitable environment through regulating the temperature, RH, and rate of airflow across the bed of the material to be dried. A number of designs are commercially available. These could be batch type, or continuous flow type with recirculation facility. A typical batch type drier for batch capacity of 2 tonnes/batch of seeds may cost about Rs. 2.00 lakh.

A number of designs have also been developed in the country at several places. A solar cabinet drier developed at CIAE, Bhopal, is simple in design and does not require any prime mover. It can hold material in about 2 sq. m surface area of drying trays for thin bed drying. Electricity is not required. It is free from fire hazard. It is coupled with a chimney for accelerated airflow. It dries chilies, potato chips etc. in about one third time to that required for open sun drying condition. Similarly, CPCRI Solar Drier is made of a wooden frame and glass. A low cost poly solar drier using UV stabilized LPDE sheets and MS frame developed at CPCRI is also a gadget for farmers to dry products like copra, chilies and so on. Also, solar driers have been developed at CIFT, Cochin, for fish drying, and community grain drying at CRRI, Cuttack, and SPERI, Ballabh Vidyanagar.

Agricultural residues and by-products fired driers and rice husk fired crop driers have also been developed at several places in the country for drying of food grains, seeds, pulses, oilseeds, and fruits & vegetables. A continuous type grain drier developed at Pantnagar is a gravity fed continuous drier having two vertical descending grain columns each 17.5 cm thick with cross air flow and has a rang from 0.8 to 1.0 tonne per hour depending on the type of grain. Moisture reduction varies from 3.5 to 4.0 % (d.b.) in a single pass. The unit cost of drying per quintal per percent moisture reduction for wheat, paddy, maize and pigeon pea grains was found to be in the range of Rs. 50-70 per tonne. A solar heat treatment machine developed at RAU, Udaipur, could be used for stored grain insect's disinfestations by subjecting them to high temperature inside the machine. The unit consists of a cylindrical parabolic reflector made of aluminium sheet. A black body pipe is placed at the focal point of the parabola and has a screw conveyor inside it. One end of the pipe has a hopper for feeding the grain and the other end has a collector to collect the treated grain. The capacity of the screw conveyor is adjusted in a manner to treat the seeds efficiently so that the storability of the product increases.

Agricultural and Food Processing

Processing facilities for food grains and horticulture crops could not be developed adequately in north eastern states due to infrastructural deficiencies though potential is very high. Only some forest based plants such as timber, bamboo, has been utilized for development of agro based enterprises. Spices crop such as ginger, turmeric, large cardamom, black pepper, chilies etc. can open up new avenues for agro-based industries in north east. Soybean also grows extremely well in entire north eastern states with average productivity of more than 1000 kg/h and therefore, there is lot of opportunities to popularize various soya products and technology developed at Soybean Processing and Utilization Center, CIAE, Bhopal.

Processing techniques for various food crops, fruits and vegetables can also be used in this region since due to absence of storage facilities there is surplus in peak harvesting season followed by shortage immediately after. This will also help to increase income to the grower and employment to the rural mass. Establishment of model Agro Processing Center (APC) developed at different center of AICRP on PHT project as multi product processing enterprises using new appropriate technologies in rural area will help the small farmer to process their produce at door step. Various options apart from cleaning, grading and drying which could be included in the APC are rice sheller and polishing unit, mini *dal* mill, mechanical oil expeller, rice flaking unit, grinding of spices, full fat soybean flour, soy-milk and soy *paneer* unit, soy fortified cookies, maize/wheat/ sorghum/ragi flour unit, ginger powder, bleached dry ginger, tomato paste and ketchup, garlic powder unit, *papad* making unit etc.

Conclusion

The present status of agro-based industries in the region is not satisfactory. Post harvest technology being integral part of the agricultural system, needs to be developed at par with the developments in production agriculture. Considering the limited and dwindling land and water resources, slow growth in productivity and ever increasing population, minimizing post harvest losses is one of the most effectively and economical ways of increasing per capita food and fiber availability. Post harvest technology is commodity and location specific. However, the present requirement is to develop need based and market driven post harvest technology for loss prevention and addition to raw food materials of plant, animal and aquatic origin.

REFERENCES

Adam, A. 2000. Farm Mechanisation: Rising Energy Intensity. *The Hindu Survey of Indian Agriculture*, 2000.

Bisht, B. S. and Ilyas, S. M. 2001. Advances in Post Harvest Technology for Agriculture Specifically Suitable to North east Region. Paper presented during 5th Agricultural Science Congress held at AAU, Khanapara, Guwahati during April 4-7, 2001.

Chadha, K. L. 1995. Status of Post Harvest Technology of Fruits. Proc. of National Seminar on Post Harvest Technology of Fruits held at U. A. S., Bangalore, August 7-9.1995. pp. 1-6.

Singh, Kirti and Seshadri, VS. 1989. Vegetable production research and development in India. FAO publication on *Vegetable Production Research and Development in Asia and the Pacific Region*. FAO Regional office, Bangkok, Thailand. pp 169-188

Singh, R.K.P., Satapathy, K.K. and Sheo Govind. 1999. Present status of post harvest practices for fruits and vegetables in NEH Region. *Agricultural Engineering Today*, Vol(1-2), pp: 50-56.

Singh, R.K.P. 2000. Status report on ""Post Harvest Practices and Nutritional Availability Among Tribal of NEH Region" presented during workshop cum group meeting under NATP on "'House Hold Food and Nutritional Security Through Value Addition and Post Harvest Management" at CIAE, Bhopal, during May 1-2.

Singh, R.K.P., Satapathy, K.K, Gurmukh Das and Patil, R. T. 2001. ""Food and Nutritional Availability in North Eastern Hill Region of India"'. Paper presented during 88th Indian Science Congress held at IARI, New Delhi during January 3-7.

16

TOURISM AND ITS POTENTIAL FOR RURAL DEVELOPMENT IN ASSAM

Prasanta Bhattacharya

Introduction

There is no doubt that tourism is one of the flourishing industries in the present day world, which in most cases avoids the central and economically advanced places. In fact, in the developed world, it is being used to enhance the status of peripheral economy. Developed countries paid special attention to promote tourism on the principle of management. But in the developing world, which has tremendous potentiality in this regard, efforts for tourism development, by and large, tend to be of *ad hoc* nature. The scenario does not deviate much in case of India in general and Assam in particular, where development of tourism is not oriented towards specific directions and objectives.

Assam is one of the pioneering states of India to start tourism related activities way back in 1958. This is because of its rich natural and cultural resource potentialities. But it has not still attained the desired level. Uptil now, the development of tourism in the state has been confined to a few pockets only. However, it is felt that there is enough scope for tourism development by utilizing the physical and cultural tourist resources spread over Assam, especially in the rural areas. Considering the ability of tourism to strengthen local economy and generate job opportunity the paper attempts to highlight the possibilities of using tourism as a means of rural development in Assam, on the basis of intensive field experiences gained in different parts of the state.

Objectives

The objectives of the study are: (a) to evaluate the tourist resource base of the state on the basis of preference pattern of tourists, (b) to understand the existing spatial pattern of tourist demand, (c) to identify potential tourist destination of Assam on the basis of tourist demand and resource supply and (d) to highlight the present and possible role of the tourist resources and associated tourism activity, specially of rural areas, as a means of rural development.

Methodology

The present study is based on the primary data and information gathered by the author through a purposefully designed questionnaire survey conducted for tourist (covering 100 foreign mid 325 domestic tourists representing 5.3% and 3.5% of the total arrival respectively in 1995-96) visiting the state. It is also supplemented by intensive field survey carried out in the state for on spot evaluation of possible tourist resources (From 1995-98) of the state.

ANALYSIS

Recreational Demand of Tourists

For a better planning and development of tourism, an evaluation of the tourist resource base (both man-made and natural) is an urgent need. To identify the existing resource base and their significance, a recreational resource inventory of Assam was prepared and incorporated in the questionnaire. The inventory was prepared on the basis of the items of tourist attraction as campaigned in the various publications and tourist brochures of both government and private tourism promotional agencies. The inventory was then handed over to the tourists for their comment. The preference patterns of the tourists regarding 17 items of attractions of the inventory were then valued and ranked accordingly. The resulting preference pattern of domestic tourists (Table 1) indicates that there is a strong demand for three main tourist resources, viz. wildlife, National Park and scenery and natural landscape. The preferences given to these items are 76 percent, 63 percent and 57 percent respectively. These items obviously belong to environmental tourist resource-base of the state. A second thrust area includes items reflecting environmental as well as socio-religious resource base, which include places of pilgrimage (53 percent), hill resort (52 percent) and zoo visit (44 percent). The third and moderately significant cluster of attractions includes monument (37 percent) museum (34 percent),

Table 1: Demand of Tourists on the Basis of Preference Pattern

Sl. No	Attraction Category	Domestic Tourist		Sl. No.	Attraction Category	Foreign Tourist	
		No.of	% Tourist			No. of Tourist	%
1.*	Wildlife	248	76	1.*	Wildlife	74	74
2.*	Visit to National park	204	63	2.*	Visit to National park	71	71
3.*	Scenery & natural landscape	184	57	3.*	Scenery & natural landscape	66	66
4.	Pilgrimage	173	53	4.*	Native life and customs	66	66
5*	A stay at hill resort	169	52	5.*	Flora and fauna	57	57
6.	Zoo visit	144	44	6.*	Art and handicraft	48	48
7.	Monument	121	37	7.*	Trekking & mountaineering rock climbing, cycling, etc.	38	38
8.	Museum visit	112	34	8.	Monument	36	36
9.	Archaeological spots	109	33	9.*	Dance & festival	33	33
10.*	Native life and culture	107	33	10.	Archaeological spots	32	32
11.*	Art and handicraft	100	31	11.*	A stay at hill resort	31	31
12.*	Flora and fauna	99	30	12.	Museum visit	26	26
13.*	Dance and festivals	83	26	13.	Pilgrimage	18	18
14.	Recreation and entertainment	73	22	14.	Zoo visit	14	14
15.*	Water sports	69	21	15.*	Water sports	12	12
16*	Trekking & mountaineering rock climbing, cycling, etc.	52	16	16.	Recreation & entertainment	11	11
17.*	Angling	15	4	17.*	Angling	6	6

Source: Based on survey conducted by the author. * Indicates recreational resource base of peripheral areas.

archaeological spots (33 percent), native life and customs (33 percent), local art and handicraft (31 percent) and native flora and fauna (30 percent) of the state. A Comparatively less significant group of attractions include traditional dance, music, drama and festival (25 percent), recreation and entertainment (22 percent), water sports (21 percent) and trekking, mountaineering, rock climbing, etc. (16 percent). Angling is the last item of the inventory with only 4 percent of the tourists preferring it.

Unlike the domestic tourists, the priority areas of the foreign tourists include both environmental and cultural tourism resource-bases of the state. The items most sought after by the foreign tourists include wildlife (74 percent), visit to national park (71 percent), scenery and natural landscape (66 percent) and native life and customs (66 percent). The second group of items of attraction includes native flora and fauna (57 percent) and local art and handicraft (48 percent). The third and moderately significant attractions of the inventory includes trekking, mountaineering, rock climbing, cycling, etc. (38 percent), archaeological monuments (36 percent), dance and festival (33 percent), a stay at a hill resort (31 percent) and museum (26 percent). A comparatively less significant group of attractions of foreign tourists includes pilgrimage (18 percent), Zoo visit (14 percent), water sports (12 percent) and recreation and entertainment (11 percent). As in case of the domestic tourists, angling score least share (6 percent) of foreign tourists. A comparative account of the preference pattern of both domestic and foreign tourists reflects that major areas of demand continues to be wildlife, National Parks and natural scenery and landscape for the two groups. However, attractions like pilgrimage, zoo visit, native life and customs, art and handicraft flora and fauna and activities like trekking, mountaineering, rock climbing, cycling, etc. reflect a dissimilar nature of preference pattern between domestic and foreign tourists. For example, pilgrimage is one of the major motivating factors of travel for domestic tourists. Assam has the ancient seats of pilgrimage like Kamakhya, besides other least explored destinations, which attract a large number of tourists, domestic as well as local. However, there are very few foreign tourists who came to the state for the purpose of pilgrimage. It is observed that western tourists dislike to seeing animals in captivity, hence their preference for a visit to State Zoo is remarkably less. As the native life and customs, art and handicraft, dance and festivals are quite different and unique from the viewpoint of foreign tourists; their preference for such attractions is more. Similarly attractions for local flora and fauna are also more among them. Such dissimilar nature of recreational demands has also been witnessed in the areas like adventure activities, viz. water sports as well as in case of trekking and mountaineering, etc. As the present adventure activities practiced in the developing world, are poor imitation of those of the western world, hence they are less popular among the domestic tourists than foreign tourists. However, preference for water sports is relatively more among the domestic tourists because such facilities provide 'soft' activities like rowing and paddling in the closed lakes and ponds. As such activities are not 'hard enough' and lack adventure and thrill, they are found to be less popular among foreign tourists. It is observed that in general domestic tourists are soft enough in terms of physical stamina and hence prefer events like recreation and entertainment. Some of the attractions of the inventory viz. monument, archaeological spots and museum reflect similar nature of preference among both the group of tourists. Angling, the only item of the inventory has been found to be the least preferred attractions for both the groups of tourists, because this type of recreational activities are special enough and require proper campaigning to attract anglers by projecting the existing and potential angling spots of the state.

In general, the inventory of attractions helps to find out the similar and dissimilar nature of demands among the domestic and foreign tourists. Similarly it also helps in evaluation of priority areas for future tourism planning. Hence the tourism managers of both the government and private agencies should orient their developmental efforts according to the existing demand of the tourists. It is worth mentioning that out of the 17 items of the resource inventory 12 items (65%) are basically the ingredients of rural countryside. Hence proper orientation and projection of such resources will certainly attract tourist and gear up rural economy in near future. However, comparatively less significant areas require more publicity campaign to attract the attention of the target group of tourists.

Spatial Pattern of Tourist Demand

The locational preference pattern of tourists reveals an overall picture of tourists' demand regarding the existing tourist resources of the state under present mobility scenario. Table-2 indicates that the presence of both, domestic and foreign tourists is high in *Guwahati,* which serves as the gateway to the entire Northeastern region. The tourists usually prefer to have an overnight halt here, before going to

Table-2: Spatial Pattern of Tourist Demand in Assam

Domestic tourist				Foreign tourist			
Sl. No.	*Destination*	*No. of tourist*	*%*	*Sl. No.*	*Destination*	*No. of tourist*	*%*
1	Guwahati	325	100	1	Guwahati	84	84
2	Kaziranga	202	62.15	2 *	Kaziranga	81	81
3	Tezpur	26	8	3 *	Manas	11	11
4	Sibsagar	15	4.62	4	Sibsagar	9	9
5	Haflong	13	4	5	Tezpur	8	8
6*	Manas	11	3.38	6	Jorhat	5	5
7 *	Madankamdev	10	3.08	7*	Bhalukpung	5	5
8	Dibrugarh	7	2.15	8	Dibrugarh	5	5
9*	Bhalukpung	6	1.85	9	Mariani	4	4
10*	Sualkuchi	6	1.85	10	Lumding	4	4
11*	Hajo	5	1.54	11	Badarpur	4	4
12	Tinsukia	5	1.54	12*	Hajo	4	4
13	Silchar	5	1.54	13	Lakhimpur	4	4
14	Jorhat	3	0.92	14*	Sualkuchi	4	4
15*	Orang	2	0.62	15*	Majuli	3	3
16	Margherita	1	0.31	16*	Madankamdev	3	3
17	Naharkatia	1	0.31	17	Nagaon	2	2
18	Narnrup	1	0.31	18	Dhemaji	2	2
				19	Dhubri	2	2
				20	Duliajan	1	1
				21	Doomdooma	1	1
				22	Digboi	1	1

Source: Based on survey conducted by the author. * Peripheral destinations

Kaziranga, Shillong (Meghalaya) and other destinations of the northeastern states. Apart from it various government and private agencies of the city provide package tour and other related services of tourism. After Guwahati, *Kaziranga* attracts 62.15 percent of domestic and 81 percent of foreign tourists, as a result of gradually growing demand for nature based environment and associated tourist resources. This is also reflected by the preference pattern of the resource inventory. The author observed that domestic tourists prefer less physical effort during tour period, so their share in wilderness like Kaziranga continues to be comparatively less than that of the foreign tourists. Though National Parks are highly preferred by both the groups of tourists, the table reflects that except Kaziranga only three other wilderness areas (among 20 nos. of such areas) viz. *Manas, Bhalukpung* (Nameri National Park) and Orang (Orang National Park) attract some tourists. For example Manas National Park, the only tiger reserve of Assam, continues to attract only 11 percent of foreign and 3.4 percent of domestic tourists, due to negative media publicity both at national and international levels (deterioration of law and order situation and poor tourism infrastructural base). *Nameri National Park* (Bhalukpung) continues to attract only 5 percent of foreign and 1.8 percent of domestic tourists due to lack of adequate infrastructure along with poor publicity campaign at national and international levels regarding Assam. Similarly, *Orang* (Orang National Park), the only stronghold of rhinoceros, on the north bank of river Brahmaputra and the second largest pocket of one horned rhino population of the world, attract only 0.6 percent of domestic tourists due to lack of exposure and inadequate tourism infrastructure. The presence of foreign tourists could not be traced here in the survey period. Other destinations like *Sibsagar* (Historical town, famous for ancient monuments, tank-sagar, etc.), *Tezpur* (one of the beautiful towns of Assam with archaeological ruins, monuments, airport facility), *Jorhat* (important tea-town of upper Assam, major break-point of journey to the river island Majuli and airport facility), *Dibrugarh* (important city of upper Assam, with tea gardens around, airport facility), *Moriani* (important rail head, tea gardens), *Lumding* (important rail junction, journey break point for Lumding-Badarpur hill section railway), Hajo (pilgrimage site, monuments and handicrafts), Sualkuchi (famous for Assam silk and handloom), *Lakhimpur* (district headquarters, important gateway to Arunachal Pradesh, airport facility), *Majuli* (largest river island, existence of traditional Vaishnavite religious institutions 'satra', performing art and handicraft), *Madan Kamdev* (important ruins of ancient temples) attract merely 3 to 9 percent of foreign tourists. Rest of the destinations, viz. *Dhemaji* (district headquarters of *Dhemaji* district), *Dhubri* (district headquarters of *Dhubri* district) famous for craft and monuments, *Duliajan* (oil town of upper Assam), *Doomdooma* (tea town) and *Digboi* (the oldest oil field and refinery of the Asia) attract only 1 to 2 percent of tourists coming to the state.

Among the domestic tourists *Tezpur* continues to attract 8 percent followed by *Sibsagar* and *Haflong* (only hill station of Assam in N.C. Hills district) with 4.6% and 4 percent respectively. Destinations like *Madan Kamdev, Dibrugarh, Sualkuchi, Hajo, Tinsukia* (district headquarters, focal point of business in upper Assam, proximity to Dibru-Saikhowa National Park), and *Silchar* (important town of the Barak valley, airport facility, major journey break point to nearby three states viz Mizoram, Manipur and Tripura) attract merely 3 to 1.5 percent of tourists. Rest of the destinations viz. *Jorhat, Margherita* (mining town), *Naharkatia* and *Namrup* (industrial towns) can attract only a feeble flow of tourists ranging from 0.3 percent to 0.9 percent only.

As revealed by the table a highly polarized situation of the demands of the tourists is found in pockets like Guwahati and Kaziranga. Rest of the destinations have witnessed a very negligible share of demand due to lack of adequate infrastructure and publicity. Interestingly out of the total 18 destinations visited by domestic tourists, 7 destinations (39%) are of essentially having rural attributes of attraction. However, among such destinations, except Kaziranga, presence of tourist is quite insignificant. Similarly out of 22 destinations of foreign tourist, 7 destinations (32%) are from rural background. In case of foreign tourist also, except Kaziranga, no other rural destinations felt the presence of sizable number of foreign tourist. Hence, tourist destinations of the marginal areas of the state are yet to get benefit out of tourism. For example, destinations like Hajo (having historic monuments, local craft of bell metal product and rich in terms of native life and culture), Sualkuchi (having the tradition of Assamese silk weaving and rich in terms of native culture) and Madan Kamdev (one of the important ruins site of the state), which are located within a distance of around 30 km from Guwahati, attract only 3 to 4 percent of the foreign tourists due to inadequate publicity and lack of proper projection of peripheral tourist resources by the concerned government and private agencies.

Assessment of Tourism Potentiality of Destinations

Potentiality of tourism in an area is a result of interaction of tourist demand and supply of tourist resources. Here tourists' demand has been judged through preference pattern of the tourists in a purposefully designed resource inventory of seventeen appeal elements (Table 3). Percentage of preference received for each attraction category is taken as an index of tourist demand (both for domestic and foreign tourist-by considering average value) after being reduced to a scale of 1 to 10. Attempt has been made to evaluate the 'supply component' through the assessment of availability of tourist resources locally with the help of field survey. It is observed that, an assessment of existing tourist resource base can provide an ideal framework to identify relative importance of tourist resources of different areas of Assam.[1]

Assessment of Local Availability or Supply Component of Tourist Resource Base

There are some important aspects and requirements that make a place important as a tourist destination. Hence five such aspects, viz. importance, popularity, accessibility, seasonality and fragility of existing tourist resource base of Assam have been considered to judge the local availability or the supply of tourist resources[2]. These elements (seasonality, Fragility, etc.) of an area were assessed by ranking them in a nominal scale (i.e. good, moderate, bad, etc.) to get a relative rating[3]. The following scheme (Table 4) of ranking has been adopted to evaluate the local availability of tourist resources through the five selected criteria. Assessment has been made on the basis of author's practical acquaintance of the destinations.

In this process of ranking a destination identified as one of the best attractions (marks awarded 2) with excellent accessibility (2), having a comparatively long tourist season of more than six months (2), having a large development potential (2) and witnessing more than 50% of incoming foreign tourists of the state (2), receives an aggregate value of 10[4].

To understand the supply component of the available tourist resources of the state a statewide field survey was conducted by this author. Now each of the tourist destinations has two comparable numerical values representing a demand or appeal component (A), calculated on the basis of tourist preference pattern (already reduced to base 10 in Table 3) and a local availability or supply component (B) of resources as ranked by the author on the basis of field experience. A meaningful tourist potential index (T.P.) can be calculated with the

Table 3: Nature of Demand of Tourists, Assam (1995-96)

Sl. No.	Attraction category	% of domestic tourists	% of foreign tourists	Conversion to scale 1-10		Average of Domestic & Foreign tourists	Rounded value scale (1-10)
				Domestic	Foreign		
1	Wildlife	76.31	74	7.63	7.4	7.51	8
2	Visit to National Park and sanctuary	62.77	71	6.27	7.1	6.69	7
3	Scenery & Natural landscape	56.66	66	5.66	6.6	6.13	6
4	Pilgrimage places	53.23	18	5.32	1.8	3.56	4
5	A stay at hill resort	52	31	5.2	3.1	4.15	4
6	Zoo visit	44.31	14	4.43	1.4	2.92	3
7	Visit to monuments	37.23	36	3.72	3.6	3.66	4
8	Visit to museum	34.46	26	3.44	2.6	3.02	3
9	Archaeological spots	33.54	32	3.35	3.2	3.28	3
10	Native life & culture	32.92	66	3.29	6.6	4.95	5
11	Local art and handicraft	30.77	48	3.07	4.8	3.94	4
12	Flora and fauna	30.46	57	3.05	5.7	4.38	4
13	Dance & festivals/ performing art	25.54	33	2.55	3.3	2.93	3
14	Recreation & Entertainment	22.46	11	2.25	1.1	1.68	2
15	Water sports	21.23	12	2.12	1.2	1.66	2
16	Trekking, Mountaineering and cycling	16	38	1.6	3.8	2.7	3
17	Angling	4.62	6	0.46	0.6	0,53	1

Source: Based on tourist's preference pattern from tourist survey (1995-96), conducted by the author.

help of numerical values of demand (A) and supply (B) of tourist resources of an area[5]. The tourist potential index (IT) of an area so calculated is TP =A+B/2

Table 4: Ranking Scheme of 'Local Availability' of Tourist Resource in Assam

Criteria selected	Scale	Weightage
Among best attractions Importance	Good standard	2
	Moderate standard	1.5
	Less appeal	0.5
Accessibility	Excellent	2
	Adequate	1.5
	Limited	1
	Difficult	0.5
Seasonality	Over six months	2
	Over three months	1.5
	Less than three months	I
	Less than one months	0.5
Fragility	Large development potential	2
	Moderate development potential	1.5
	Controlled development potential	1
	No development potential	0.5
Popularity	More than 50% foreign visitor	2
	20% to 50% foreign visitor	1.5
	2 to 20% foreign visitor	1
	Rarely any foreign visitor	0.5

Source: Designed by die author and adopted from Ferrario. F.F.

Tourist Potentiality of Destinations

As per the formula stated above, the tourist potentiality of as many as 58 destination of the study have been assessed and shown in the table 5. The values are tabulated in a descending order. It is clear from the table that, tourist potential index values for destinations range from 10 to 26.75. For the purpose of prioritization of destinations for future tourism promotional venture, all the associated tourist potential index values are grouped together under a fivefold scheme, viz. very high potential area. (index value >21), high potential area (index value 18-21), high moderate potential area (index value 15-18), low moderate potential area (index value 12-15) and low potential area (index value 9-12). These priority groups of tourist potential areas are plotted on map to visualize their distribution throughout the state (Fig. 1). The table and the map reveal that only one destination belongs to very high potential group,

8 destinations belong to high potential group, 39 destinations belong to moderate potential group and 10 destinations belong to low potential category, in the perspective of tourism promotional venture. Among the very high and high potential destinations, Majuli, North-Lakhim Pur and Umrangso are yet to have development activities undertaken for basic tourism infrastructure by two Government agencies viz. Department of Tourism, Govt. of Assam, and Assam Tourism Development Corporation, which are entrusted with the task of tourism development in the state. Between these two groups of destination, only Guwahati and Kaziranga continue to get good response from both domestic and foreign tourists. It is, however, observed that potentiality of these two destinations are not yet properly utilized by the tourism development agencies, either government or private. A high tourist potential index of an area reflects its high weightage of 'appeal' and 'supply' elements of tourist resources. So, such areas provide larger choices of things to see and to do by the tourists themselves and deserve associated promotional activities to tap such potentialities. It is believed that such scheme of prioritization of potential pockets of tourism development may certainly provide an ideal framework for future tourism development strategies in Assam. Moreover the scheme also reflects the significance of rural pockets as tourist destination. Among the 8 high potential tourist destinations, 4 (50%) continue to be from rural areas. Similarly among high moderate potential groups (17 number), rural destination continues to share 71% (12 number). Out of 22 low moderate potential destinations of the state, rural pocket shared 77% with 17 potential destinations. Among low potential tourist areas (10 number), 'share of rural pockets constitute 50% (5 number). As a whole out of the 58 tourist potential areas, 38 (66%) belong to the peripheral pockets of the state. Hence the evaluation of tourist potential pockets also advocates for the need of exploring the future possibilities of development of rural areas with the help of tourism. Dearth of infrastructure may be a cause of concern in this regard. But as the state has a well-developed transport infrastructure in private sector, it can be easily oriented towards tourism promotion in rural areas. Similarly, as the tourist demand in the state is seasonal in nature (68% of foreign and 77% of domestic tourist come to the state within a six month span, from September to February), hence instead of permanent accommodation unit, provisions of' alternative accommodation like tented accommodation, tree house, paying guest system, etc. may go a long way to support accommodation sector in exploring tourist potentiality in marginal areas.[6]

Table 5: Tourist Potentiality of Assam, based on Tourist Potential Index

Sl. No.	Destination	Weightage of appeal or demand element(A)	Weightage of supply B element(B)	Potentiality index TP =A+B/2	Remarks
1	2	3	4	5	6
1	Guwahati south	48	8.5	26.75	–
2	Haflong	34	6.5	20.25	Including Jatinga
3*	Kaziranga	32	8	20	–
4*	Majuli	34	5.5	19.75	–
5	N. Lakhimpur	33	6.5	19.75	–
6*	Mahur	32	6	19	Including Maibang
7	Diphu	31	6	18.5	–
8*	Umrangso	30	6	18	Including Panlmur
9	Tezpur	27	9	18	–
10	Orang	30	5.5	17.75	Including Sonipura & Singri
11	Hamren	29	6	17.5	–
12*	Chandubi	29	6	17.5	–
13*	Pabitara	28	6	17	Including Mayang
14	Biswanath	27	6.5	16.75	–
15	Sibsagar central	25	8.5	16.75	–
16*	Hajo	25	8	16.5	Including Sualkuchi
17*	Sibsagar central	25	8	16.5	–
18	Tinsukia	27	6	16.5	–
19*	Garampani	27	6	16.5	–
20*	Shree Surya	25	7.5	16.25	–
21*	Guwahati north	25	7.5	16.25	–
22	Dibrugarh	25	7.5	16.25	–
23*	Bhuban hill	27	5.5	16.25	–
24*	Dokmoka	26	5.5	15.75	–
25*	Khetri	25	6	15.50	–
26*	Akashiganga	23	7	15	–
27*	Chapanala	23	6.5	14.75	–

Contd. . .

Table 5: *(contd.)*

1	2	3	4	5	6
28*	Gohpur	23	6.5	14.75	–
29*	Bhairab Kunda	23	5.5	14.25	–
30	Dhemaji	23	5.5	14.25	Including Bordoibam
31*	Chakrasila	22	6	14	–
32*	Manas	21	7	14	–
33*	Bhalukpung	21	7	14	–
34	Digboi	22	6	14	–
35*	Silchar north	21	7	14	–
36*	Silghat	21	6.5	13.75	–
37*	Sibsagar north	22	5.5	13.75	Ajanpir, Disanmukh, Panidihing
38*	Hawazan	21	5.5	13.25	Including Maghnowa
39*	Bordowa	18	8	13	–
40	Lumding	20	6	13	–
41*	Tukreshwari	20	6	13	–
42*	Sadia	20	5.5	12.75	–
43*	Pancharanta	18	7	12.5	–
44*	Kalaigaon	18	7	12.5	–
45	Gauripur	18	6.5	12.25	–
46*	Bagaribari	18	6.5	12.25	–
47	Dergaon	17	7.5	12.25	–
48*	Chaigaon	17	7	12	–
49*	Darranga	18	5.5	11.75	–
50*	Bandardewa	17	6	11.5	–
51	Barpeta	15	7	11	–
52	Kokrajhar	15	6.5	10.75	–
53	Pathsala	15	6.5	10.75	–
54	Dhubri	15	6	10.5	–
55*	Rangapara	14	7	10.5	Including Balipara
56	Jorhat	13	7.5	10.25	–
57*	Lawkhowa	15	5	10	Including Burhachapari
58*	Numaligarh	12	8	10	–

Source: Based on Survey conducted by the author (1995-96). * Indicates rural pockets.

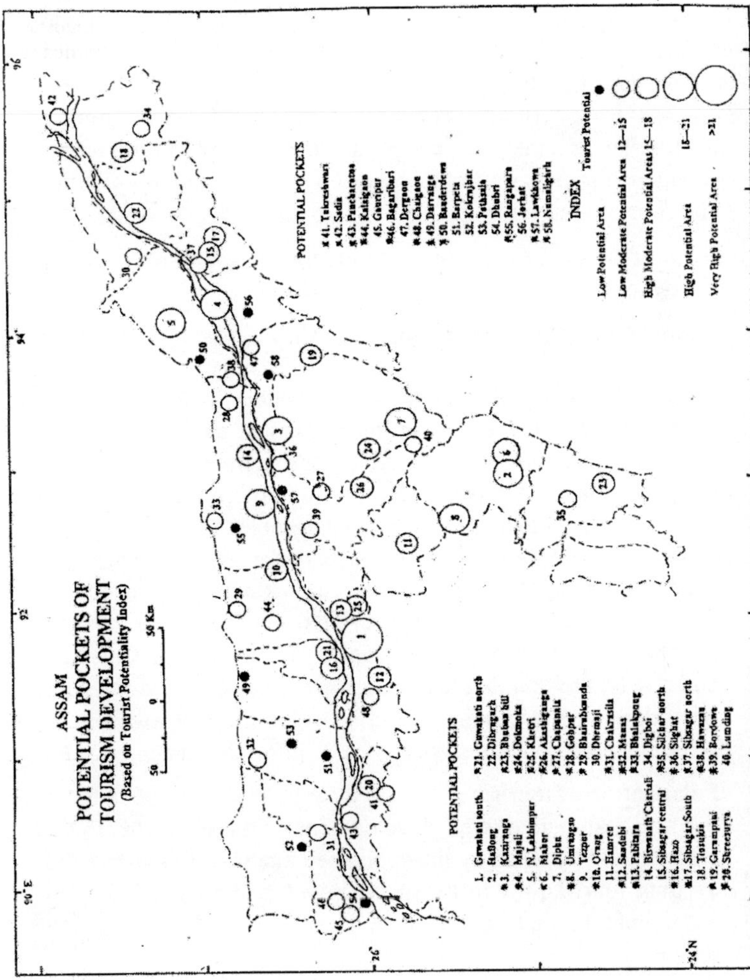

Based on survey conducted by the author * Indicates rural pockets

Fig.1

Conclusion and Suggestions

It is observed that there is no dearth of tourist attraction in the state, but they are not properly exploited. Up till now tourism ventures of the state are polarized in some pockets due to lack of evaluation of tourist demand and proper campaigning of resources as per demand. 'There is a wide gap between tourist demand and supply of recreational resources. Tourist's preference pattern towards recreational resources advocates for proper projection of both physical and cultural tourism assets, especially from peripheral areas. Hence, there is every possibility for utilizing tourism as a means of economic development in rural areas, as the assessment suggests that as many as 66% of the tourist potential pockets are from countryside.

On the basis of such observations following suggestions are made for future development of tourism in the state:

1. Formulation of a need-based tourism policy is must for promotion of tourism in Assam. Both the government and private agencies should give a serious thought in this matter. Both the sectors should join hands together in the process of tourism planning and policy making of the state. A task committee should be created with the active cooperation of both government and non-government tourism promotional agencies of the state. They should stress on four key areas: (a) Revenue generation through locally initiated fund rising, (b) Development of tourist products by evaluating all possible tourist resources, themes and preparation of calendar of local events, (c) Promotion of education and research by training local youth and service staff along with periodic market research and (d) Community awareness programmes through festivals, events, information centers, etc.
2. Polarization of tourism activities in some particular pockets of the state hampers overall development of tourism. Therefore, steps should be taken by the concerned agencies to redirect the existing tourist flow to the newly developed areas of tourism attractions, so that benefit of tourism spreads throughout the region.
3. As natural and wildlife attractions are the mainstay of tourism industry in Assam, hence forest policy of the state should have provision for promotion of wilderness by using tourism as a supporting means of it, in concerned areas. Considering the area's rich natural environment, eco-tourism (nature based tourism rooted on the idea of sustainability) should be initiated.

As eco-tourism requires less economic investment, it has economic and environmental gain. Hence it will be more suitable to the existing environmental setup.

4. All the existing tourist centers of the tourism department should be entrusted to prepare and execute micro-level tourism plans at grass root level. They can act as a catalyst between tourism department and local tourism promoters and can perform their role as a promoting unit for developing 'small scale' and 'local level' tourism ventures at village or panchayat level. Government should be flexible enough to encourage private entrepreneurs. In this context, provision should be made to introduce single window clearance of all the necessary formalities. Priority should be given to 'small-scale' tourism ventures, with the active participation of local people in this regard.

5. Tourism activity of the state is essentially seasonal in nature. Hence to meet the seasonal demand of accommodation, alternative accommodations like paying guest system, tented accommodation, tree- house, etc. should be made at the initiative of local people, tea garden management and other non-governmental organization especially in marginal areas.

NOTES AND REFERENCES

1. Bhattacharya, P. (2001) : *"Status and Potentiality of Tourism in Assam: A Geographical Analysis"* Project report under UGC, pp. 78-83.
2. Ferrario, FF. (1982): *"Method Approach for Evaluating Tourist Resources, case of South Africa", Study of Tourism Wildlife Parks Conservation,* (ed), Singh, TV. and others, Metropolitan Book Company, New Delhi, pp. 114-135.
3. Ferrario, FF. (1982) has done such assessment with the help of local authorities, pressure groups and other agencies, directly or indirectly interested in local tourist resources, to get a meaningful average opinion, so that possible personal bias can be eliminated. But in case of Assam, it cannot be done due to lack of awareness regarding tourism activity among local people. In some destinations 'tourism' is still a new term, which needs to be explained.
4. Bracketed figure indicates respective weightage of that category.
5. Partly adapted from Ferrario, FF. (1982): *"Method, Approach for Evaluating Tourist Resources: Case of South Africa", Study of Tourism Wildlife Parks Conservation,* Metropolitan Book Co., New Delhi, p. 129.
6. Bhattacharya, P. (2001), "Status and Potentiality of Tourism in Assam: A Geographical Analysis," Project Report under UGC, p. 72.

17

CO-OPERATIVE MOVEMENT IN MEGHALAYA
Its Growth, Performance and Weaknesses

Gurudas Das

BACKGROUND

Rise of Cooperative Movement: Historical Context

The modern cooperative movement began in the West European countries as a means to protect the interest of the marginalised members of society following the far-reaching economic, social and political consequences of industrial revolution and consequent disintegration of the feudal system during the eighteenth and nineteenth centuries. In fact, the modern coöperatives are indirect descendants of medieval European Guilds. These guilds were a kind of association of craftsmen which sprang up during the 16th century in England, France and Germany. The guilds, with a closed membership, sought to safeguard wages and conditions of employment, and to regulate supplies of goods and their prices through developing a common code of conduct. Their cooperative effort in a common pursuit makes the guilds the forerunners of the more advanced type of cooperatives which emerged in England, with the advent of the factory system, towards the beginning of eighteenth century (Namjoshi: 1977).

The rise of capitalism in the West not only brought material prosperity but also rising spectre of misery, destitution and poverty for the working class. Mixed by the sweated conditions of labour many a philanthropists tried to ameliorate them by organizing the labourers in mutual self-help societies for supplying credit.

In England, the Utopian Socialist thinker, Robert Owen (1771-1858) inspired the up spring of a consumer's movement which had its first success in the venture of Rochdale Pioneers, started in 1844, with 28 flannel weavers in Rochdale.

In fact the philosophy of the Utopian Socialists played a key role in the development of the doctrine of cooperation. The Utopian Socialists largely believed that the original constitution of human society was in essence communistic. The growth of private property system has destroyed the natural harmony of the society resulting into the rising spectre of poverty and unhappiness. They believed that the greed of human beings under competitive capitalism could be rectified through united action, and here lies the rationale of the doctrine of cooperation.

Thus the modern cooperative movement intended to help the small man. However, cooperatives are in no way welfare institutions to support the poor, but are self-help organizations. This unique form of economic organization can operate in societies irrespective of socio-political system - capitalist or socialist - without violating the basic socioeconomic norms and principles. It can be used to ameliorate the miseries of marginalised man under competitive capitalist social framework as well as miseries of man arising out of general economic underdevelopment, isolation, and market imperfections that are commonly seen in the third world countries.

It was this second consideration that led British colonial administration to introduce cooperation in India at the beginning of the present century. In fact, the colonial government became aware of the problems of rural indebtedness following the unrest in Deccan in 1875. The peasants of Poona and Ahmednagar rose against the money lending classes who were charging usurious rates of interest that kept them in perpetual indebtedness. The peasants forcibly snatched away their promissory notes and mortgage deeds from the money lenders and destroyed them (Tyagi: 1968: p.2). It was this incident that had prompted the British administration to think of cooperation as a structural instrument for lasting solution to the problems of small peasants. British followed the Raiffeisen and Luzzatti models of agricultural cooperatives that were developed in Germany by Friederich Wilhelm Raiffeisen (1818-88) and in Italy by Luigi Luzzatti (1841-1927). In 1892 Madras Government sent Frederick Nicholson, a civilian, to Germany to study the working of village banks organized there on cooperative lines for the benefit of small farmers. Nicholson in his report, submitted in two volumes in 1895 and 1897, made a strong plea for the introduction of cooperative credit societies. The Indian Famine Commission also substantiated the views of Nicholson in its report of 1901 by suggesting the formation of mutual credit associations. Another committee under the presidency of Sir Edward Law, set up by the Government of India in 1901, also recommended the organization of credit cooperative societies on the Raiffeisen model. Following all these recommendations of various committees, the British government finally enacted the Cooperative Credit Societies Act in 1904 which has been the milestone in the modern cooperative movement in India (Tyagi: 1968: pp. 2-3).

However, the Act of 1904 was greatly restricted in the sense that it only permitted the registration of primary credit societies and left non-credit institutions out of its purview. As a result; a new act was passed on 1912 known as Cooperative Societies Act of 1912 in order to remove the drawbacks of the Act of 1904. This Act of 1912 laid down the basic legal framework for the modern cooperative movement in India. In fact, this central act of 1912 was adopted with modifications by most of the Indian states following the Montagu-Chelmsford Constitutional Reforms of 1919, which made cooperation a transferred subject. The first provincial Act was passed in Bombay in 1925 and gradually the other provinces followed suit. The movement got momentum only after independence when the instrument of cooperation has been viewed to be a powerful means to develop the rural India and it has been accommodated into the programmes of planned development.

It is only after independence that Assam passed its own cooperative act in 1950 known as the Assam Cooperative Societies Act 1950. Meghalaya, after getting statehood on 1972, adapted this Assam Act of 1950 in 1976.

Before discussing the trend of growth of the cooperative movement in Meghalaya, a profile of the State has been outlined in the next section.

State Profile

Location: Meghalaya is situated in the north-east of India between 2511' and 2615' north latitudes and 85'49' and 92'52' east longitudes. The state was created on 21st January 1972 out of two hill districts of united Assam namely United Khasi and Jaintia Hills district and Garo Hills district. At present the state has seven districts, viz. East Khasi

Hills, West Khasi Hills, Ri-Bhoi, Jaintia Hills, East Garo Hills, West Garo Hills and South Garo Hills. Table 1 shows the details of area and population in the districts. The boundaries of Meghalaya consists of Brahmaputra Valley of Assam in the north and Surma Valley of Bangladesh in the south. The east and west are also bounded by Assam and Bangladesh respectively. The state has about 496 km international boundary with Bangladesh.

Table 1: District-wise Area, Population and District Headquarters of Meghalaya

Sl.No.	District	Headquarters	Area	Population*
1	East Khasi Hills	Shillong	2748	5,37,906
2	Ri-Bhoi	Nongpoh	2448	1,27,312
3	West Khasi Hills	Nongstoin	5247	2,20,157
4	East Garo Hills	Williamnagar	2603	1,88,830
5	West Garo Hills	Tura	3714	4,03,027
6	South Garo Hills	Baghmara	1850	77,073
7	Jaintia Hills	Jowai	3819	2,20,473
	Meghalaya		22,429	17,74,778

*Stands for provisional.
Source : Draft Proposals of Ninth Five Year Plan, vol. 1.

Physical Features : The state covers a land surface of about 22,429 sq. km. which consists predominantly of mountain terrain with narrow valleys in between and strips of plain land in the south-west and north bordering Bangladesh and Assam respectively. The western dissected hilly tract of the Garo Hills covers an area of 8180 sq.km. and has an average elevation of less than 600 metres. The central and eastern part of Meghalaya, i.e., the Khasi and Jaintia Hills region together covers an area of 14,249 sq.km.

Population : The state is predominantly inhabited by the Khasi, Jaintia and Garo tribes each having their distinct tradition, custom and culture. There are also a number of smaller tribes. As per 1991 census, a total of 17 tribal groups are there in Meghalaya. The total population of the state is 17,74,778 (1991). A little more than 81 percent lives in rural areas and tribal population constitutes about 86 percent of the total. The density of population in the state is 79. As per 1991 census, the state has a total of 5492 villages and only half of them are connected with roads (Draft Proposals, Vol. 1: p-4).

Natural Resources : The state is rich in natural resources. Occurrences of various mineral deposits like coal, limestone, kaolin, sillimanite, clay, fire-clay, glass sand, quartz, granite and uranium have been reported in the state. However commercial exploitation has been possible only of coal, limestone, sillimanite and very recently uranium deposits. As regards the distribution of minerals, it is observed that coal is available in the eastern part of Garo Hills, southern part of Khasi hills and Jaintia Hills, together accounting for 6,301 million tons of coal reserves (Draft Proposals, Vol. l: p. 2). Limestone, which is worth of 4.23 million tons, is distributed mainly in Cherrapunji-Dawki area. Sillimanite is extensively found in Sonapahar area of West Khasi Hills district, which accounts for almost 95 percent of country's total output (Dutta: 1996). Sillimanite reserves is estimated at 5 lakh tons and industrial clay 71 million tons. Besides mineral resources, the state has a total forest coverage of 8,510 sq.km. accounting for 37.5 percent of total geographical area. However, about 92 percent of total forest area is owned by private individual and only 8 percent by the Forest Department. The significant sources of forest revenue are sal, bamboos, timber lac and *tezpat*.

Agriculture : The economy of Meghalaya is basically agrarian. About 81 per cent of the total population of the state lives in the rural areas and mainly depends on agricultural activities for their livelihood. The cultivated area forms about 9 per cent of the total geographical area of the state. The gross cropped area is 2.39 lakh hectares (provisional) while the net cropped area was about 2.01 lakh hectares during 1994-95 (Draft Proposals, Vol. II, p. 1).

The *jhum* or shifting cultivation with reduced jhum cycle is still persistent and about 26 per cent of the net cropped area is under annual *jhumming* (State Focus Paper: 1997, p-8). Paddy is the main food crop grown all over the state. Maize, wheat, millet and pulses are some of the other food crops grown in different parts of the state. Potato, jute, mesta, short staple cotton, mustard, ginger, turmeric, arecanut, betel leaf are some of the main cash crops. The state has enough potential for growing a number of horticultural crops ranging from sub-tropical to temperate ones. Varieties of banana, pineapple and citrus fruits, mainly orange are grown in abundance in the medium and lower altitude regions and temperate fruits like plum, pear and peach are grown in the high altitude temperate region of the state. Vegetables cover a substantial area under cultivation particularly in the central plateau and are grown almost throughout the year.

The state is running in deficit in food grains by 1.14 lakh tonnes annually. However, horticultural crops have registered a significant increase in production of 2.15 lakh tonnes leading to a good marketable surplus (Draft Proposals, Vol. II: p-3).

As per 1991 census about 75 per cent of the total main workers in the state is engaged in the primary sector, and the share of the secondary and tertiary sectors is 3.73 and 21.46 per cent respectively (Census of India 1991, Series-1, Paper - 2 of 1992, p. 172). The contribution of the primary sector to total Net State Domestic Product was 33.58 per cent during 1990-91 and it has declined marginally to 32.13 per cent during 1995-96 (Quick Estimate) indicating thee stagnation of the economy of the state.

Industry : In spite of being rich in minerals, the industrial base of the state is very weak. There are only 7 units in the category of large and medium industries in the state as on 31 March, 1994, out of 166 in the north eastern region (Basic Statistics: 1995). A total of 58 factories have been registered in the state till 1995 employing together 2800 persons. Of them, 48 units are in Khasi Hills, 1 in Jaintia Hills and 9 in Garo Hills (Statistical Handbook: 1996). Up to 1996, a total of 202 companies have been registered in the state. Of them 39 are public and 163 are private. Of all the companies, 187 are in Khasi Hills, 3 in Jaintia Hills and 12 in Garo Hills (Statistical Handbook: 1996). Up to 1995-96, a total number of 2533 small scale units have been registered in Meghalaya and a total of 14,791 persons are employed in them. Of the total small scale units, 1702 units are in Khasi Hills, 327 in Jaintia Hills and 504 units in Garo Hills (Statistical Handbook: 1996).

However, the figures relating to factories, companies and small scale industries in Meghalaya hardly portray the actual picture of the industrial sector of the state, unless it is known as to how many of these registered units are actually functioning and how many are defunct. Moreover, cross-verification of the available statistics on the small scale industries in the state also provides conflicting trends of the growth of the small-scale sector. So far no empirical study has been made in order to assess the actual strength of the industrial sector in the state.

However, according to the 1991 Census, out of 715,587 main workers in the state, only 2,885 persons are engaged in the household manufacturing and 12,509 persons in other manufacturing activities, i.e., only 2.15 per cent of the main workers is engaged in the manufacturing sector. This no doubt indicates a very weak industrial base of the state.

In view of the resource potential of the state as well as conspicuously weak public and private initiatives, a wide space is left for the cooperative sector to grow and play a pivotal role in the development of the economy of Meghalaya. Before we evaluate the actual performance of the cooperative sector, the trend of growth of the cooperative movement in the state is presented in the next section.

Growth of Cooperative Movement in Meghalaya

The modern co-operative movement was formally launched in Meghalaya with the establishment of the regional office of the Assistant Registrar of Cooperative Societies in Shillong covering all the hill districts in 1948 (Khasi Hills District Gazetteers: 1991, p: 254). Even before 1948, during the second world war, when the prices of consumer goods rose very high, a consumers' cooperative was organized in Tura (Garo Hills District Gazetteer: 1996, p: 85). However, the movement took an organized shape only after the enactment of the Assam Cooperative Societies Act., 1950. Until 1971, Meghalaya was a part of united Assam. In 1972, the state of Meghalaya was carved out of erstwhile Assam districts of United Khasi and Jaintia Hills, and Garo Hills. During 1971-72, there were a total of 953 cooperative societies in Meghalaya having a total membership of about 57 thousand, Rs. 32 lakh of share capital and Rs. 133 lakh of working capital (Table 2).

However, records on the functioning, performance, type, viability and distribution of the cooperative societies in Meghalaya are not available while it was a part of Assam. For an assessment of the cooperative movement in Meghalaya prior to 1972, one has to consult the records with the Registrar of Cooperatives, Assam which needs a separate effort.

The number of cooperative societies in the state continued to rise steadily in the early years. From 904 during 1970-71, the number went up to 1,053 during 1975-76 (Table-2). For the same period, the total membership went up from 40 to 84 thousand, share capital from Rs. 32 lakh to Rs. 124 lakh and working capital from Rs. 120 lakh to Rs. 479 lakh (Table-2).

Table 2: Trend of Growth of Cooperative Societies in Meghalaya Since 1970-71 (including Apex Societies)

Year	*No. of Societies*	*Membership (in 000)*	*Share Capital (in Rs. Lakhs)*	*Working Capital (in Rs. Lakhs)*
1970-71	904	40	32.16	119.62
1971-72	953	57	34.74	132.99
1972 73	978	61	36.29	165.42
1973-74	990	63	36.84	148.54
1974-75	1,010	74	94.44	458.46
1975-76	1,053	84	123.88	479.34
1976-77	804	88	163.93	694.29
1977-78	899	72	267.01	969.65
1978-79	851	75	264.00	1,224.74
1979-80	782	79	295.00	1,497.83
1980-81	688	78	366.57	1,700.39
1981-82	707	87	260.51	1,541.73
1982-83	582	104	496.66	2,090.07
1983-84	NA	NA	NA	NA
1984-85	620	95	419.96	2,451.58
1985-86	646	111	512.45	5,283.52
1986-87	661	116	547.14	4,493.00
1987-88	678	117	408.30	4,242.69
1988-89	698	111	714.72	3,541.61
1989-90	708	126	1,968.51	8,813.64
1990-91	723	140	1,998.75	11,653.70
1991-92	763	163	2,240.03	12,192.70
1992-93	784	175	2,446.26	12,811.41
1993-94	763	166	2,446.31	13,949.48
1994-95	792	169	2,913.35	16597.35
1995-96	803	184	3,816.55	19,982.06

Source : Compiled from different Statistical Abstracts and Statistical Handbooks of Meghalaya.

During 1970-71, the averages for membership, share capital and working capital of the cooperative societies in Meghalaya were 44, Rs. 3.5 thousand and Rs. 13 thousand respectively. These figures rose up to 80, Rs. 1011.76 thousand and Rs. 45.52 thousand respectively during 1975-76 (Table-2). The appreciable increase in the average share capital and working capital during 1975-76 was largely because of government contribution to the two apex level societies. However, it may be noted that there were large number of small societies in the state having insignificant economic viability. There was hardly any vertical linkage between the primary and apex level societies and hence cooperative effects could not be felt. In fact, the primary societies grew mostly as part of the programme of target fulfilment on the part of the cooperative department rather than as peoples' cooperative efforts towards economic development.

With the achievement of statehood, the Government of Meghalaya took up the task of restructuring the cooperative sector. Emphasis has been laid upon the consolidation of the existing societies through horizontal integration of the primary societies as well as vertical integration by creating state level societies.

As the majority of the existing societies were Primary Agricultural Credit Societies (PACS), the Meghalaya Cooperative Apex Bank (MCAB) was incorporated on February 16, 1971, in order to cater the credit needs of the rural cooperative sector. MCAB started functioning from July 1, 1971. For providing marketing facilities to the produce of the PACS as well as to supply them essential inputs, the Meghalaya State Cooperative Marketing and Consumers' Federation (MECOFED) was established on July 1, 1975. Thus, the creation of these two apex level societies has provided the much needed infrastructural support to the PACS as well as other primary societies.

It has been felt that the strength of the cooperative movement depends much on the smooth functioning of the primary societies rather than their mushroom growth. As most of the primary societies were small, spread over far reaching areas, and unviable, the government took initiative to restructure them in the line of recommendations, of the Gorwala Committee, i.e., All-India Rural Credit Survey Committee 1954, as suggested by the RBI. The restructuring programme was initiated in 1974 under a Master Plan and largely completed by 1977. As per the Master Plan, the PACS were reorganized on the following line in order to make them economically viable: That every primary service cooperative society should have at least 500 membership. The size of the minimum population within which a PACS will be organized is 10,000. The area of operation of each of the PACS will be within a radius of 10 km. Contiguity of area is to be maintained. And a minimum business turn over of Rs.2 lakh will be required for the independent existence of a society. On the basis of these criteria, existing PACS were reorganized through amalgamation and liquidation.

On reorganization, the total number of PACS has reduced from 329 during 1976-77 to 180 in the subsequent years (Table-3). However, the membership of PACS has gone up from 52 thousand during 1976-77 to 71.5 thousand during 1982-83 and to 88.5 thousand during 1990-91 indicating a steady progress as far as membership is concerned. While the share of PACS to total number of primary societies in the state has declined from 41 per cent during 1976-77 to 25 per cent during 1990-91, the share of PACS membership has increased from 59 to 63 per cent during this period (Table-3).

Table 3: Growth of Primary Cooperative Societies in Meghalaya by Type

Sl.No.	Type of Society	1976-77		1982-83		1990-91	
		No. of societies	No. of members	No. of societies	No.of members	No.of societies	No. of members
01.	Primary Agricultural Credit Societies (PACS)	329	52000	180	71527	180	88495
02.	Marketing Coop. Socs.	73	2699	33	1513	33	470
03.	Consumers' coop. Socs.	57	6321	44	5596	54	7911
04.	Industrial Coop. Socs.	82	2053	67	2761	107	3035
05.	Weavers' Coop Socs	78	3103	38	2261	46	2689
06.	Cooperative Urban Banks	3	900	3	2649	3	5483
07.	Farming Coop. Socs.	24	911	30	1122	49	1756
08.	Milk Producers's Coop. Soc.	25	1742	39	2870	41	3185
09.	Fisheries coop. Socs.	35	1321	41	1678	51	2299
10.	Housing Coop. Socs.	17	679	29	1342	34	2835
11.	Thrift Coop. Socs.	30	6290	36	8545	48	14375
12.	Labour Contract Coop Soc.	8	437	13	329	24	717
13.	Piggery and Poultry Coop. Soc.	3	156	8	155*	9	270
14.	Multipurpose coop. Socs.	25	7331	Nil	Nil	2	70
15.	Others	12	1471	16	1413	39	5803
	Total	801	57414	577	103761	720	139393

Source : Constructed from various issues of Statistical Abstract and Statistical Handbook of Meghalaya.

* members of two societies in Jaintia Hills are not included.

However, unlike PACS,, other types of societies were not drawn into the reorganization programme. Except the marketing cooperative societies and the multipurpose societies, other societies like consumers', industrial, weavers', cooperative urban bank, farming, diary, fisheries, housing, thrift, labour contract and piggery made marginal progress since 1976-77 (Table-3).

Following the reorganization of the PACS and its effects on the marketing and consumers' societies, the total number of primary cooperative societies in the state declined from 801 during 1976-77 to 577 during 1982-83. But the total membership in the state went up from 87,414 to 1,03,761 indicating a 18.7 per cent growth during the 5 years (Table-3).

Along with the programme of reorganization, the government also established Meghalaya Cooperative Training Institute on August 2, 1976, in order to train the cooperators associated with the department of cooperation as well as the primary level cooperators. Another apex level society viz, Meghalaya Supervision and Cadre Management Cooperative Society was also established in 1976 in order to supervise the working of the primary level societies. In view of the fact that most of the primary level societies were run by non-trained part-timers who hardly could find time to work for the society, the government introduced a cadre scheme which intended to provide full time secretaries to the primary level societies at government expenditure. Initially, all the reorganized 180 PACS were brought under the scheme in 1976. Since 1986-87, another 29 weaving societies were also brought under the purview of the cadre scheme. The Cadre Management Society has been entrusted to look after the implementation of the scheme which has provided the much needed stability to the primary societies.

Another apex level society, viz., Meghalaya Cooperative Union, was established in 1978 in order to propagate the principles and ideology of cooperation for the healthy growth of the cooperative movement in the state. Besides the Meghalaya Cooperative Training Institute, Cooperative Union also conducts special training courses for the primary level cooperators. The Union undertakes the task of publication of periodicals, books, booklets, pamphlets, leaflets, etc., on cooperation.

Thus, the Training Institute, Cadre Management Society and Cooperative Union together have created an infrastructure for the healthy growth of the cooperative movement in the state.

Besides these training and managerial societies, another two apex level societies, viz., Meghalaya State Housing Financing Cooperative Society and Meghalaya Apex Hand loom Weavers & Handicraft Cooperative Federation (MEGHALOOM) were established in 1976 and

Table 4: Typewise and area-wise Distribution of Primary Cooperative Society in Meghalaya (As on 31.03.1997)

Sl.No.	Type of Societies	Khasi Hills			Jaintia Hills			Garo Hills			Meghalaya		
		Total	F	NF	Total	F	NF	Total	F	NF	Total	F	NF
01.	PACS	82	82	–	21	21	–	76	76	–	179	179	–
02.	Weaving	18	14	4	3	3	–	38	38	–	59	55	4
03.	Fisheries	25	20	5	3	2	1	37	23	14	65	45	20
04.	Housing	22	15	7	3	–	3	11	1	10	36	11	25
05.	Indusatrial	69	49	20	23	20	3	15	5	10	107	74	33
06.	Consumers'	44	35	9	4	4	–	10	7	3	58	46	12
07.	Thrift	37	34	3	1	1	–	23	18	5	61	53	8
08.	Dairy	44	16	28	5	4	1	11	10	1	60	30	30
09.	Horticulture	–	–	–	1	–	1	8	8	–	9	8	1
10.	Coop. Canteen	3	1	2	–	–	–	–	–	–	3	1	2
11.	Labour Contract	17	13	4	2	2	–	–	–	–	19	15	4
12.	Marketing	18	11	7	4	3	1	7	5	2	29	19	10
13.	Piggery	9	6	3	16	14	2	2	2	–	27	22	5
14.	Joint Farming	43	28	15	–	–	–	–	–	–	43	28	15
15.	Transport	18	12	6	16	15	1	1	–	1	35	27	8
16.	Processing	–	–	–	1	–	1	1	1	–	2	1	1
17.	Forest labours	3	2	1	-	-	-	-	-	-	3	2	1
18.	Poultry	2	1	1	-	-	-	-	-	-	2	1	1
19.	Coop. Urban bank	1	1	-	1	1	-	1	1	-	3	3	-
20.	Multipurpose	16	16	-	-	-	-	2	2	-	18	18	-
21.	Others	24	20	4	1	1	-	11	9	2	36	30	6
	Total	495	376	119	105	91	14	254	206	48	854	668	186

F = Functioning, NF = Not Functioning

Source : Office of the Registrar of Cooperatives, Meghalaya.

1989 respectively in order to assist and integrate the activities of the primary housing and weaving societies in the state.

Presently, as on 31 March, 1997, there are 6 state level and 854 primary level cooperative societies in the state. While all the apex societies are functioning, 78.22 per cent, i.e., 668 primary societies are reported to be functioning in the state and 21.78 per cent, i.e., 186 societies are non-functioning (Table-4).

The total membership during 1995-96, in all types of societies including the apex societies, amounts to 1,83,543 indicating a rise of about 32 per cent during the last five years, i.e., during 1990-91 to 1995-96. The number of primary societies had gone up from 720 during 1990-91 to 854 during 1996-97 thereby registering an increase of 18.61 per cent. For the same period, the share capital has increased from Rs.1998.75 lakh (1990-91) to Rs.3816.55 lakh, i.e., a rise by 90.95 per cent.

Thus the growth of the cooperative movement in the recent years in the state is not very impressive. While the annual average growth of the movement in terms of number of societies is only 3 per cent (1990-91 to 1996-97), the same for membership is accounted for 6.4 per cent (1990-91 to 1996-97). During the last six years (1990-91-1996-97), certain types of societies like PACS, joint farming, marketing, and labour contract societies have experienced negative growth. Both the industrial societies and urban cooperative banks have registered zero growth. While the consumers' and housing societies have grown marginally, significant progress has been made by the piggery, fishery, dairy, thrift and multi-purpose societies. Although the cooperative movement in the state has largely stuck at traditional lines, it had also broke fresh grounds in areas like transport, horticulture and processing.

The spatial distribution of the cooperative societies and the members associated with them reveal that the movement has always been relatively strong in the Khasi Hills region. Presently (1996-97) 58 per cent of the total primary cooperative societies in the state is located in the Khasi Hills region that consists of three districts of East Khasi Hills, West Khasi Hills and Ri-Bhoi. In this region the progress of the movement is largely concentrated in the lines of agricultural marketing, consumer, industrial, dairy, thrift, housing, joint farming and transport cooperatives. However, the region has the highest percentage of non-functional societies to the total number of registered societies in it. Of the 495 registered primary societies in Khasi Hills, 376 are functioning and 119 are defunct (Table-4).

Garo Hills ranks second in terms of number of primary societies as well as membership associated with them. Presently 30 per cent of the total primary societies in the state is located in Garo Hills. Here the movement has made considerable progress in agricultural, weaving, fisheries and horticultural lines. About 81 per cent of the total number of registered societies in Garo Hills (1996-97) is functional and 19 per cent is defunct (Table-4).

Since inception, the cooperative movement has remained weak in Jaintia Hills. Recently, of course, there has been a significant progress particularly in the lines of piggery and transport cooperatives. Out of a total of 105 primary level societies, 91 are functioning and 14 are defunct. The percentage of non-functioning societies in Jaintia Hills is the least i.e., 19 only (Table-4).

THE COOPERATIVE MOVEMENT IN MEGHALAYA: A VIEW FROM ABOVE

Altogether 860 cooperative societies, including the 6 apex level societies, are there in Meghalaya. This paper is written on the basis of the experience gained from survey of the apex societies as well as from the discussions held with the cooperators working for these societies and the cooperators associated with the department of cooperation, Meghalaya. As a result, the observations contained in this paper are the partial reflections of the ground reality as far as it is manifested from the state of functioning of the apex level societies. An attempt is made here to assess the performance of the apex level societies and their contribution to the growth of the cooperative movement in the state.

The Meghalaya Cooperative Apex bank (MCAB) and the Flow of Credit to the Cooperative Sector

The MCAB is the apex body in the cooperative credit-structure in Meghalaya. It was incorporated in 1971 in order to act as a balancing centre for all registered cooperative banks and societies in Meghalaya besides its normal banking functions. The objectives as they are laid down in the bye-laws of MCAB in relation to the cooperative movement are : (i) to provide loans to registered cooperative institutions, (ii) to provide long term loans for the development of agriculture and allied sector in the state, and (iii) to develop, assist and coordinate the work of affiliated societies and to arrange for their supervision as well as to establish, promote and maintain the cadre of key-personnel for the benefit of affiliated societies (Bye-Laws of MCAB, 1988).

Thus MCAB is viewed not merely as an apex credit organisation but as leader of the cooperative movement.

Starting with a share capital of Rs.6.97 lakh in 1971, the bank has made a considerable progress during the last 25 years. The share capital has gone up to Rs.214.38 lakh in 1996 (Table-5), of which the government share amounts to Rs.122.58 lakh i.e., 57.18 per cent, contribution of the affiliated societies accounts for Rs.91.74 lakh, i.e., 42.79 per cent and the rest comes from the individual members (Annual Report -1995-96, MCAB). There are 859 registered societies (excluding MCAB) in the state and of them 463 societies are affiliated to the MCAB. Although government contribution still forms a major chunk of the Bank's share capital, it has also succeeded to mobilize a considerable amount from the affiliated societies.

Starting with two branches - one at Shillong and the other at Tura - in 1971, presently the Bank has 37 branches spread all over the state. Of them 17 branches are in Khasi Hills, 15 in Garo Hills and 5 in Jaintia Hills.

The working capital of the Bank has steadily increased from Rs.7.01 lakh in 1971 to Rs.942.29 lakh in 1981, Rs.6829.57 lakh in 1991 and to Rs.14843.31 lakh in 1996 (Table-5). The deposit mobilization of the Bank and its capacity to advance loans have registered a steady rise over the years. During 1995-96, the Bank has mobilized deposits to the tune of Rs.12985.47 lakh and advanced loans to the tune of Rs.4349.60 lakh. The credit-deposit (C-D) ratio for the year, thus, amounts to 33.5 per cent. Although the Bank has the highest C-D ratio in the state compared to other nationalized banks, the C-D ratio of MCAB in recent years has declined substantially, while the average C-D ratio during 1971-80 was 43.86 per cent, it went up to 47 per cent during 1981-90 and then in recent years (1991-96) has declined to 33.59 per cent (Table-5). Although the MCAB is making marginal profits, the rate of return on capital is not significant. For the year 1995-96, the rate of return on share capital amounts to 4.90 per cent only.

The Bank has been extending short-term agricultural loans both under the Normal Credit Limit System and through Cash Credit System. As on June, 1997, the Bank has issued a sum of Rs. 987.27 lakh out of the sanctioned amount of Rs. 1297.70 lakh as short term agricultural loans to 157 PACS involving a total. of 58,933 borrowers. Out of the amount issued, a total of Rs. 583.55 lakh has been recovered indicating 59.14 per cent rate of recovery. Although the recovery rate may be considered as satisfactory while viewed from the overall repayment position of agricultural credit in the north-eastern region, it does not reflect the ground realities about the performance of the PACS in the state.

Table 5: Growth of Meghalaya Cooperative Apex Bank

(Rs. in lakhs)

Year	*Share Capital*	*Working Capital*	*Deposits*	*Loans & Advances*	*C–D Ratio*	*Profit (+) Loss(–)*
1971	6.97	7.01	0.02	–	–	–0.06
1972	17.27	129.52	108.89	25.60	23.50	+0.22
1973	22.96	268.05	197.04	86.48	43.89	+0.58
1974	33.03	258.30	214.78	110.18	51.30	+0.73
1975	37.71	297.00	240.70	136.39	56.66	+0.85
1976	42.98	366.98	281.81	147.96	52.50	+1.02
1977	51.46	417.17	325.16	175.12	53.86	+1.13
1978	64.29	536.70	425.52	223.00	52.41	–8.54
1979	72.27	688.38	530.84	290.67	54.76	–2.87
1980	75.22	885.77	700.00	347.81	49.69	+0.65
1981	82.84	942.29	739.42	340.91	46.10	+0.86
1982	87.77	1086.97	880.92	457.38	51.92	+12.68
1983	100.85	1317.34	1081.09	628.65	58.15	+2.76
1984	110.83	1720.75	1457.65	710.69	48.76	+1.48
1985	119.35	2024.05	1734.35	901.64	51.99	+3.58
1986	128.91	2351.56	2041.65	1051.23	51.49	+2.74
1987	135.08	2887.81	2521.58	1137.66	45.12	+2.82
1988	140.11	3426.32	3003.78	1261.34	41.99	+3.48
1989	144.09	4457.96	3895.59	1472.40	37.80	+3.78
1990	161.17	5518.27	4803.61	1761.20	36.66	+5.73
1991	171.77	6829.57	5834.05	2012.47	34.50	+9.52
1992	181.43	6959.23	5807.58	1999.37	34.43	+10.71
1993	192.23	8530.85	7163.47	2302.88	32.15	+11.50
1994	201.82	9794.32	8222.46	3058.24	37.19	+5.57
1995	204.58	12017.89	10168.10	3026.43	29.76	+7.49
1996	214.38	14843.31	12985.47	4349.60	33.50	+10.51

Source: Compiled and calculated from various issues of Annual Report of MCAB.

This high recovery rate is due to the intervention of both the state and central governments, who time to time come forward to rescue the small and marginal farmers from perpetual indebtedness by releasing fund. However, the fact that 94.15 per cent of the amount on demand

Table 6: Branch-wise (MCAB) Position of short Term Loan to Coop. Societies (as on June 1997)

(Rs. in lakhs)

Sl. No	Name of Branch	Amount Sanctioned	No. of SCS Involved	No. of borrowres Involved	Amount Issued	Amount Recovered	Amount Outstanding	Amount Overdue	Demand
KHASI HILLS									
1	Shillong	212.51	20	3,844	108.11	86.72	21.39	18.66	22.25
2	Cherrapunjee	8.02	2	365	6.55	3.19	3.36	3.36	3.36
3	Smit	67.65	5	1,496	57.99	34.83	23.16	17.35	20.45
4	Balat	102.99	6	2,616	100.93	68.39	32.54	32.54	32.54
5	Nongpoh	39.19	9	6,125	28.17	23.14	5.03	5.03	5.13
6	Umsning	50.03	5	1,763	42.93	22.49	20.44	16.22	16.65
7	Nongstoin	49.99	10	3,193	47.87	36.91	10.96	10.96	11.31
8	Mairang	69.21	6	2,051	47.63	37.35	10.28	5.43	6.92
9	Mawkyrwat	62.39	7	1,436	49.44	35.96	13.48	8.13	9.82
JAINTIA HILLS									
10	Jowai	24.43	3	1,021	19.34	17.99	1.35	1.35	1.39
11	Ladthalaboh	12.25	2	551	2.20	0.09	2.11	2.09	2.16
12	Dawki	1.75	2	129	1.69	1.44	0.25	0.25	0.26
13	Nartiang	14.70	2	739	6.97	6.97	-	-	-
14	Khliehriat	18.04	5	901	14.34	13.67	0.67	0.67	2.08

contd. . . .

Table 6: (contd.)

Sl. No	Name of Branch	Amount Sanctioned	No. of SCS Involved	No. of borrowres Involved	Amount Issued	Amount Recovered	Amount Outstanding	Amount Overdue	Demand
GARO HILLS									
15	Tura	12.90	4	961	9.65	7.86	1.79	1.23	1.27
16	Araimile	17.23	4	1,139	13.66	0.14	13.52	13.49	13.76
17	Phulbari	103.59	9	5,947	90.81	35.61	55.20	54.79	55.92
18	Garobadha	92.09	11	6,385	77.70	39.77	37.93	37.20	37.31
19	Dalu	33.48	8	2,295	31.81	15.55	16.26	15.69	17.95
20	Mahendraganj	55.66	4	1,819	28.86	12.82	16.04	12.12	14.39
21	Tikkrikilla	28.38	3	1,960	11.58	6.83	4.75	4.45	4.76
22	Chokpot	34.85	7	3,007	34.41	9.59	24.82	24.52	26.22
23	Baghmara	14.53	4	1,009	14.08	6.74	7.34	7.08	7.78
24	Williamnagar	23.90	4	1,789	17.91	10.87	7.04	7.04	8.21
25	Mendipathar	69.57	6	2,123	48.69	21.15	27.54	27.54	27.55
26	Rongjeng	22.27	5	1,677	21.70	13.69	7.71	7.42	7.51
27	Bajengdoba	56.20	4	2,592	52.25	13.79	38.76	38.36	39.25
	Total	1,297.70	157	58,933	907.27	583.55	403.72	372.97	396.14

Source: MCAB, Shillong.

(as on June, 1997) has become overdue (Table-6) reveals the dismal repayment capacity of the primary agricultural societies in the state. In spite of government subsidy, the total outstanding with the PACS against short term loans amounts to Rs.403.72 lakh and total overdue amounts to Rs.372.97 lakh (Table-6). This has substantially reduced the lending capacity of the MCAB as well as made the short-term agricultural credit through cooperative societies less rewarding.

The Bank has been providing financial assistance in the shape of overdraft facilities, Cash Credit Accommodation and Term Loans to state level cooperative institutions namely MECOFED, Meghalaya State Cooperative Housing Financing Society and Meghalaya State Cooperative Union. The amount outstanding against them as on 31.03.96 amounts to Rs. 300.48 lakh. This huge amount of outstanding has, no doubt, made the Bank handicapped.

The Bank has been catering to the credit needs of the farmers and growers for allied agricultural activities in the shape of medium, and long term loans through the Land Development Banking Division since 1977-78. Credit facilities are provided for a variety of allied agricultural purposes like land development, minor irrigation, farm-mechanization, piggery, poultry, goatery, dairy, horticulture and plantation schemes. Separate statistics relating to amount of loans issued for these activities through cooperative societies, recovery thereof and amount outstanding are not readily available. However, as on 31 March, 1996, total outstanding against loans issued to societies as well as individuals for allied activities amounts to Rs.610.31 lakh (Table-7).

The Bank has been providing cash credit accommodations to marketing, consumers, urban banks and other type of cooperative societies and the amount outstanding against them as on 31 March, 1996 amounts to Rs. 102.84 lakh. Similarly the total outstanding against loans given to the industrial and transport cooperatives and individuals as on 31 March, 1996 amounts to the tune of Rs.428.36 lakh.

This huge outstanding against loans to the cooperative sector has substantially blocked the Bank's loanable fund. In recent years the flow of credit to the cooperative sector has declined compared to that of the private sector. While during 1994-95, 47.41 per cent of the total loans has gone to the cooperative sector and 52.59 per cent to the sectors other than co-operatives, the same for the year 1995-96 have been 40.63 and 59.37 per cent respectively,

Table 7: Outstanding Position of Loans Issued to Allied Activities (As on 31.03.1996)

(Rs. in Lakhs)

Activities	*Loan issued During 1995-96*	*Recovered During 1995-96*	*Outstanding at the end of 1996*
Piggery	7.44	1.34	157.20
Dairy	1.30	0.30	28.01
Fishery	3.49	0.44	37.42
Land Reclamation	-	0.16	9.77
Poultry	0.64	0.05	2.93
Plough Cattle	1.17	0.33	17.32
Tractor	-	-	20.30
Horticulture	13.48	2.07	111.27
Goatery	2.42	0.49	49.44
Power Tiller	1.34	2.58	11.06
Others	24.30	1.39	165.59
Total	55.58	9.15	610.31

Source : Annual Report, 1995-96, MCAB.

Meghalaya Supervision and Cadre-Management Cooperative Society and the Primary Agricultural Cooperative Societies

The Meghalaya Supervision and Cadre Management Cooperative Society was registered in 1976 in order to create and maintain a cadre for secretaries, managers and other paid employees of the primary cooperative credit societies. In 1976, the state government initiated a cadre scheme as part of the programme of reorganization of the Primary Agricultural Cooperative Societies (PACS) also known as, Service Cooperative Societies (SCS) in order to make them viable, functional and efficient. After reorganization, the total number of PACS in the state reduced from 548 in 1975 to 180 in 1979. All these 180 PACS were brought under the supervision of the Cadre Management Society. The managing committee of each society selected its secretary and referred the name to The Cadre Management Society for approval. The secretaries of the PACS appointed under the cadre scheme are paid from the fund of the Cadre-Management Society that has been created out of contribution from government, MCAB and other beneficiaries of the scheme. During 1986-87, another 29 primary weaving societies are also brought under the scheme. Presently, the cadre management society deals with 209 primary societies - 179 PACS (1 PACS is not functioning) and 29 weaving societies.

More than 80 per cent of society's fund comes from the state government and the whole fund is used to pay the salary bill of the 209 primary societies as well as its own staff (Table 8).

Table 8: Annual Financial Position of Meghalaya Supervision & Cadre Management Cooperative society (1991-92 – 1996-97)

(Rs. in Lakhs)

Particulars	*1991-92*	*92-93*	*93-94*	*94-95*	*95-96*	*96-97*
Contribution from:						
(i) Government	22.00	19.75	21.00	22.00	20.00	20.00
(ii) MCAB	1.00	1.00	1.25	1.25	1.25	1.25
(iii) SCS	2.63	2.23	2.39	1.66	2.11	1.93
(iv) HWCS	0.37	0.19	0.49	0.30	0.36	0.48
(v) Meghaloom	0.15	0.15	0.25	0.30	0.30	0.30
Total Income (i to v)	26.15	23.32	25.38	25.51	24.02	23.96
Expenditure on Salary	26.51	23.16	24.80	25.14	24.68	25.36

Source : Meghalaya Supervision & Cadre Management Coop. Society

Note : MCAB = Meghalaya Cooperative Apex Bank
SCS = Service Cooperative Society
HWCS = Handloom and Weaving Cooperative Society

Contribution of the primary societies to the annual fund of the cadre management society amounts to only 9.5 per cent indicating their very weak financial base.

The Managing Committee of the society consists of 7 members. The Registrar of Cooperatives acts as Chairman and Managing Director of MCAB as secretary. Besides them, the Secretary to Government of Meghalaya, Agricultural Department or his nominee, three members from PACS nominated by the Registrar of Cooperatives and one representative from Meghalaya Cooperative Union act as members.

The Society is thus mainly controlled and financed by the government. The day-to-day business of the society is managed by the two Deputy Secretaries - one posted in Shillong and the other at Tura - and one Assistant Secretary posted in Shillong. Both the Deputy Secretaries are retired officials of the Department of Cooperation.

The activities of the Society, like any other government department, has become mechanical and routinized. Since its inception, the Society is only acting as a via medium between the government and the primary societies - receiving annual government grants and disbursing it through local branches of MCAB to the secretaries of primary societies. It does not have adequately efficient manpower to motivate the primary societies to conduct their business with professional spirit and to reorient the cooperative movement based on the principle of self help by reducing its dependence on the government. It is learnt that out of the 197 functioning PACS, only about one third of them are making marginal profit. About 39 PACS are almost defunct. However, a detail survey of the primary societies can only reveal the actual position of their operation.

The statistics relating to PACS released time to time by the office of the Registrar of Cooperation, Meghalaya, hardly useful for any sort of trend analysis. Because, in the first place, it is not known as to how they are arrived at, and secondly the wild variations in them are left unexplained. However, an analysis of the performance of the PACS for the last decade exhibits a slow growth in their performance.

Table 9: Position of the PACS/SCS* for the period 1986-87 – 1995-96

(Rs. in Lakhs)

Year	*Membership (Nos.)*	*Share Capital*	*Working Capital*
1986-87	73,790	124.65	807.25
1987-88	79,414	130.75	894.89
1988-89	95,406	160.56	1084.14
1989-90	79,054	122.77	2068.79
1990-91	88,495	135.14	1002.08
1991-92	90,495	138.00	906.68
1992-93	97,822	226.36	973.52
1993-94	98,109	230.49	653.11
1994-95	98,493	296.57	524.80
1995-96	1,13,050	517.04	700.38

Source : Different issues of Statistical Handbook of Meghalaya.
*For all these years there were 180 PACS/SCS in the state.

During 1970-71, a total of 1970 persons (members) were organized under 508 PACS. These figures went up to 33,147 persons under 548

PACS during 1974-75, just before the initiation of the reorganization scheme in 1976. During 1990-91, 88,495 members were there under 180 PACS, i.e., 18.24 per cent of the agriculturists (cultivators and agricultural labourers) had been brought into the cooperation movement. During 1995-96, the total membership of the PACS has gone up to 1, 13,050. Calculated on the basis of 1991 population figures, 23.30 per cent of the agriculturists have been brought into the movement during 1995-96. Although a comparison between 1990-91 and 1995-96 positions provides only an approximation, it however shows a positive trend about the performance of the PACS in the state as far as membership is concerned. The average annual rate of growth of membership during 1986-96 has been only 5.37 per cent (Table-9). This, no doubt, indicates very slow progress of the movement during the last decade.

Table 10: Year-wise position of loans and advances issued by the PACS/ SCS during 1986-87 - 1995-96

(Rs. in Lakhs)

Year	*No. of Societies (Nos.)*	*Loans & Advances During the Year*	*Amount Outstanding at the end of the year*
1986-87	180	198.06	432.06
1987-88	180	61.36	201.02
1988-89	180	58.67	209.66
1989-90	180	391.53	995.00
1990-91	180	136.15	664.46
1991-92	180	378.20	991.74
1992-93	180	353.23	662.33
1993-94	180	224.64	985.70
1994-95	180	280.61	1013.51
1995-96	180	340.96	687.61

Source : Different issues of Statistical Handbook of Meghalaya.

Besides membership, the share capital of the PACS has grown annually at the rate of 20.56 per cent on an average (Table-9) and the average annual rate of growth of the working capital amounts to only 5.56 per cent (Table-9). The average annual rate of growth of sales turnover during the decade 1986-96 has been 19.16 per cent (Table-11) and that of loans and advances has been 67.75 per cent (Table-10). All these indicate a tardy progress of the PACS in the state.

Table 11: Sales Turnover of the PACS/SCS During 1986-87 – 1995-96

(Rs. in Lakhs)

Year	Sales Turnover from			Total
	Agricultural Produce	Consumer Goods	Others	
1986-87	13.97	43.92	40.31	98.20
1987-88	12.76	129.35	2.81	144.92
1988-89	18.68	98.48	14.57	131.73
1989-90	4.70	73.11	2.61	80.12
1990-91	5.44	106.14	3.35	114.93
1991-92	34.20	142.13	-	176.33
1992-93	51.68	326.93	-	378.61
1993-94	143.60	337.60	-	481.20
1994-95	163.60	184.20	-	347.80
1995-96	102.00	70.00	45.20	217.20

Source : Different issues of Statistical Handbook of Meghalaya.

The credit activity of the societies went on smoothly for few years after reorganization. But with the gradual accumulation of overdues at the ultimate borrowers level the flow of credit to the farmers through the societies came to a halt. The government then came up with debt relief scheme and waved the loans. This has helped in reopening the line of fresh credit flow. But again after few years the line of credit flow got choked due to accumulation of overdues. Again government intervention was sought to reopen the line. This has now become a perennial problem and has entangled with the interest of electoral politics. Political parties and aspirant politicians have largely contributed to the growing indiscipline in loan repayment by making promises to help in waving loans on their election.

Meghalaya State Cooperative Union: Its Role in the Progress of Cooperative Movement in the state

The Meghalaya State Cooperative Union was registered in 1978 with the following objectives:

(i) to propagate cooperative principles and ideology for healthy growth of the cooperative movement in the state,

(ii) to serve as exponent of cooperative opinion and render advice to the government on all matters effecting the movement,

(iii) to promote different types of cooperative societies as per the need of the people of the state,

(iv) to promote and strengthen inter-cooperative relationship and discipline within the same sector of the movement and among different sectors,

(v) to plan, implement and review education and training activities in the state,

(vi) to promote studies on cooperation and allied subjects and to carry on research activities relating to the movement;

(vii) to arrange for the mass education programmes,

(viii) to publish periodicals, books, booklets, pamphlets, leaflets, teaching aids, educational material and other literature on cooperative and allied subjects,

(ix) to organize exhibitions, study tours for the promotion and development of the cooperative movement

(x) to act as information bureau for and on cooperative matters,

(xi) to run training centres, schools and colleges for cooperative personnel,

(xii) to convene conferences, seminars, meetings, workshops, fairs, etc.,

(xiii) to organize cooperative union at the district as well as sub divisional level and to coordinate their activities.

Thus, the Union is viewed to be the brain of the movement - the mind of the mass of cooperators working both at primary and state levels. It is expected to act as the watchdog which will always keep an eye on the day to day running of the movement. The Union is supposed to inject fresh blood into the movement through constant interaction with the cooperators in the field - identifying the drawbacks, searching the means to solve them and prescribing the solutions to the government as well as concerned societies.

Although the Union was registered in 1978, it started functioning only in 1983. All types of cooperative societies in the state are supposed to be the members of the Union. But till now, only 131 members (including 24 individual members) are there in the Union. It has only two zonal offices - one at Shillong and the other at Tura. Apart from publication of a journal, organizing one or two training courses for the cooperators at the primary level, a few study tours - the Union has largely remained defunct.

It is learnt that the Union receives about Rs.20 lakh annually from the state government under different heads but it has to pay a salary bill to the tune of Rs.27 lakh annually to its more than 50 staffs. It has utterly failed to generate resources by extending its base among the cooperative societies in the state. Since its inception, the Union is running under perpetual financial crisis. While the author visited the office of the Union, it was almost deserted. As the employees are not getting their salaries for last eight months, they hardly have any interest in attending to their duties.

Thus the Union, which is supposed to lead the movement in the state, itself is struggling for its survival.

Meghalaya State Cooperative Marketing and Consumers Federation (Mecofed): Its Role in Marketing Agro-Horticultural Produce of the State

The Meghalaya State Cooperative Marketing and Consumers Federation Ltd. (MECOFED) was established on 1st July, 1975, after taking over all the assets and liabilities of the erstwhile Assam Hills Cooperative Development Corporation. The main objectives of MECOFED are to organize, promote and develop marketing, processing, storage and sale of agricultural and minor forest produce, and to produce and distribute by sale of consumer goods, agricultural inputs and to assist, aid, guide its affiliated member societies in the state.

The Federation is run by an elected Board of Directors consisting of members of different types of cooperative societies and government nominees. The Chief Executive of the Federation is the Managing Director and till date all Managing Directors were appointed by the state government on deputation and drawn from the I.A.S. cadre.

The Federation started with initial authorized capital of Rs.5 crore and subsequently enhanced it to Rs.8 crore during 1990-91. The paid up share capital, as on 31 March, 1997, is Rs.688.52 lakh and 99.63 per cent of total share capital is contributed by the state government.

The membership of the Federation consists of state government, PACS, primary and sub-area marketing cooperative societies, consumers and industrial societies, individuals of erstwhile Assam Hills Cooperative

Development Corporation and other types of societies. As on 31 March, 1997, the Federation has a total of 195 members. Besides state government, there are 134 PACS, 25 marketing societies, 15 individual members and 20 other types of societies. All the societies together have contributed only 0.28 per cent of the share capital of the Federation. This, no doubt, indicates a very weak base of the Federation.

At present the activities of the Federation are basically confined to (i) procurement and disposal of agricultural and minor forest produce, (ii) procurement and distribution of inputs like chemical fertilizers and potato seeds, and (iii) procurement and sale of consumer goods.

To undertake the above business, the Federation has set up 6 branch offices and 12 retail outlets throughout the state. It also runs one emporium at Kolkata. It has also constructed storage godowns with financial assistance from National Cooperative Development Corporation (NCDC) at different points with a total capacity of 24,250 M.T.

As far as procurement and sale of agricultural produce are concerned, MECOFED mainly deals in potato, ginger, *tez patta*, broom sticks, jute and mesta, cotton and mustard seeds. Jute and mesta mostly grow in Garo Hills and the Federation has established Jute Bailing Plant at Phulbari, Ampati, Zikzak and Dalu where the raw jute and mesta are bailed before dispatching to the mills outside the state. The cotton and mustard seeds procured by the Federation are ginned and crushed for mustard oil extraction at the Garo Hills Cooperative Cotton Ginning and Oil Mills Ltd., Phulbari. The Federation procures most of the agricultural produce directly from the farmers as well as through the PACS at the village level. It also takes up price support operation for agricultural produces on behalf of the state government in case the market price goes down abnormally below the cost of production level.

However, the procurement capacity of the Federation is far below the amount of marketable surplus of agricultural produce. Moreover, a number of agri-products having marketable surplus are not marketed by the Federation (Table-12). Generally it markets the agri-products through national level cooperatives like National Agricultural Cooperative Marketing Federation (NAFED) and Tribal Cooperative Marketing Development Federation (TRIFED). Since the national marketing cooperatives do not have sustained demand, MECOFED finds it difficult to market the agri-products outside the state.

Table 12: Production and marketing Surplus of Important Agro-Horticultural Crops in Meghalaya During 1994-95

Sl. No.	*Crops*	*Units*	*Production*	*Estimated Marketable surplus*
1.	Cotton	Bales*	5,317	5,100
2.	Jute & Mesta	Bales*	56,694	53,900
3.	Turmeric	M.T.	1,756	1,400
4.	Ginger	M.T.	43,337	39,000
5.	Potato	M.T.	1,21,240	84,900
6.	Pineapple	M.T.	76,888	53,800
7.	Banana	M.T.	60,549	30,349
8.	Misc. Fruits	M.T.	37,124	27,800
9.	Citrus Fruits	M.T.	32,838	26,300
10.	Vegetables	M.T.	68,000	27,200

Source : Draft Proposals, Ninth Five Year Plan, Vol. II, Planning deptt. Govt. of Meghalaya.
*Cotton in Bales of 170 kg each and Jute and Mesta in Bales of 180 kg. each.

Although agricultural marketing is one of the main objectives of the MECOFED, its performance in this area is not very commendable. Sale of agricultural produce constituted only 6 per cent of the total turnover of the Federation during 1991-95. The same for the year 1995-96 has been about 18 per cent and about 15 per cent during 1996-97 (Table-13).

Table 13: Type-wise Sales Turnover of MECOFED

(Rs. in lakh)

Particulars	*1994-95*	*1995-96*	*1996-97*
Chemical fertilizers	258.25	347.71	410.90
Agricultural Produce	36.06	152.31	121.07
Consumer Goods	270.88	327.31	294.08
Total	565.19	827.33	826.05

Source : MECOFED.

Instead of emphasizing the agricultural marketing, the Federation is increasingly involving itself in consumer goods and fertilizer business.

Fertilizers are procured by the Federation directly from the manufacturers and distributed to the farmers through the PACS, private retailers possessing licenses from the agricultural department and through its own retail outlets.

As far as consumer goods business is concerned, the Federation deals in groceries, toiletries, plastic goods exercise books and stationeries. Most of these goods are procured locally from the distributors of different companies and from local traders. Sale of fertilizers and consumer goods contributed 94 per cent of the total turnover of the Federation during 1994-95 and the same has been 82 and 85 per cent for the years 1995-96 and 1996-97 respectively.

The average annual rate of growth of turnover of the Federation during 1993-97 has been only about 7 per cent and that of purchase has been only 6 per cent. This indicates almost a stagnant position in its business. The accumulated loss of the Federation during 1996-97 amounts to more than 12 crore (Table 14). Whatever gross profit the Federation makes in its annual transaction, it has to pay more than double the amount as salary bill to its 193 employees that comes to Rs. 118.89 lakh (1996-97).

Table 14: Financial Position of Mecofed (1992-93–1996-97)

(Rs in Lakhs)

Particulars	*1992-93*	*1993-94*	*1994-95 (9 months)*	*1995-96*	*1996-97*
Sales turnover	682.01	705.83	565.19	827.33	826.05
Purchase	601.60	587.39	526.29	753.95	708.70
Gross Profit	71.74	80.85	49.14	73.74	71.65
Net Loss	78.52	70.08	39.67	85.15	150.51
Accumulated Loss	858.11	928.19	967.87	1053.02	1203.54
Storage Subsidy received from Govt.	3.25	3.50	3.50	3.50	3.50
Managerial Subsidy from Govt.	13.75	22.37	16.00	23.74	20.00
Godown Subsidy	7.31	-	-	-	-
Govt. Share Capital	22.45	24.51	-	26.50	27.40

Source : MECOFED.

Because of this perpetual financial crisis, the Federation has to frequently fall back upon its working capital in order to pay the employees which in turn adversely affects its business turnover. As a result, it failed to instill business confidence among its members.

There is hardly any vertical integration between the Federation and the affiliated primary societies. It is learnt that out of 179 affiliated primary societies, only 10 to 12 societies are having regular business with the Federation. Usually the Federation runs its business through its branch offices and retail outlets. As a whole, MECOFED has failed to generate any significant positive cooperative effects in the economy of the state and agricultural marketing through cooperatives still poses to be the most serious problem in the state.

Meghalaya Apex Handloom Weavers and Handicrafts Cooperative Federation (Meghaloom)

The Meghalaya Apex Handloom Weavers and Handicrafts Cooperative Federation (Meghaloom) was registered in 1982 in order to organize, promote, aid and guide the primary handloom and handicraft societies in the state by way of producing raw materials such as yarns, dyes, chemicals, etc. and supplying them to the affiliated primary societies, purchasing weaving appliances such as looms and accessories for and buying the finished products from the member societies, carrying out inter-state trade in raw materials, undertaking processing activities connected with handloom activities, acting as the central marketing centre of the affiliated societies and render technical guidance and assistance to them to implement improved methods, qualities and design.

The Federation is run by a board of directors, consisting of 15 members. Of them, 5 members are from the primary weaving societies, 3 from other societies, 2 from individual promoters, 3 government officials including the Registrar of Cooperatives or his nominee and the Managing Director of MCAB as well as Meghaloom. Till now, all the office bearers are nominated by the state government.

As on 31 March, 1997, 42 primary weaving societies are affiliated to Meghaloom out of 55 functioning societies in the state. Out of the total number of affiliated societies, 34 are functioning and 8 societies are defunct. However, the figures released by the office of the Registrar of Cooperatives relating to defunct weaving societies does not tally to that collected from Meghaloom. This is indeed a serious problem that a researcher has to face in making an objective assessment of the movement based on data released by the government departments. In most cases, the reliability of' such data is not beyond the doubt.

However, besides the weaving societies, 3 primary handicraft societies are also affiliated to Meghaloom.

The paid up share capital of Meghaloom during 1995-96 has been Rs.44.40 lakh. The government contribution to total share capital amounts to 99.54 per cent. This indicates its complete dependence on government. All the affiliated societies together have contributed only 0.42 per cent of the total share capital of Meghaloom which shows their abjectly poor financial base.

Meghaloom is basically dealing with buying and selling business. It purchases yarns in bulk and sells them to the affiliated societies and in turn buys a portion of the produce of the affiliated societies and sells them. For conducting this business, Meghaloom maintains 3 godowns one each at Guwahati, Nongpoh and Tura and runs two sale counters one each at Shillong and Tura.

Although buying and selling of yarns is the major activity of Meghaloom, the volume of this business carried out annually is also not very significant (Table-15). As a result it hardly generates any substantial economies of scale that can make the produce of primary societies competitive in the market.

Table 15: Trading Position of Meghaloom

(Rs. in Lakh)

Year	*Purchase of Yarn*	*Sale of Yarn*	*Net Profit During the year*
1990-91	0.23	0.090	0.13
1991-92	0.03	0.005	0.04
1992-93	1.10	0.060	0.10
1993-94	2.77	1.850	0.07
1994-95	2.33	1.460	0.01
1995-96	4.74	3.390	0.09

Source : Meghaloom.

Most of the weavers associated with the primary societies are accustomed with the traditional looms and produce traditional ethno-cultural products like shawl, *gamocha*, bed sheet, curtain, clothes, table mat, *dakmanda* (a piece of cloth used as traditional ladies ware by the Garo women), *jainkyrsha* (traditional ladies ware used by Khasi women) etc. Similarly, the craftsmen associated with the primary handicrafts societies use to produce traditional craft-goods like bamboo basketry, wood carving products, wooden pipes, spoons, etc. These traditional goods are losing their market with the fast changing consumer's taste and preferences even within the state. Meghaloom neither has the financial strength nor adequate trained manpower to modernize the handloom and handicraft sector so that it can keep pace with the changing market taste and preferences.

Although Meghaloom is making a marginal profit (Table- 15), its rate of return on share capital is almost insignificant.

Meghalaya State Housing Financing Cooperative Society

The Meghalaya State Housing Financing Cooperative Society was established in 1976. The society started functioning since 1980. The prime objective of the society is to provide financial assistance in the form of loans and advances to primary housing cooperative societies for construction, repair, addition and alteration of houses. The membership of the society is also open to other registered cooperative societies.

The society is managed by a Board of Directors drawn from the primary housing societies, other societies, government officials as well as financing agencies. The Chief Executive, i.e., the Managing Director is a government nominee.

As on 31 March, 1997, 30 primary housing societies are affiliated to this organization. Of them 17 societies are from Khasi Hills, 4 from Jaintia Hills and the rest 9 from Garo Hills. Out of these 30 affiliated societies, 15 are not functioning. All the four societies in Jaintia Hills are defunct. In Khasi Hills, out of 13, 6 societies are not functioning and another 5 societies in Garo Hills are not functioning. This indicates the very weak base of the apex housing society. However, the figures relating to primary societies released by the office of the Registrar of Cooperatives and the same collected from Housing Financing Society do not tally.

At present the authorized capital of the society is fixed at Rs.5 crore. As on 31 July, 1997, the paid up share capital amounts to Rs.72.32 lakh. The contribution of the state government to the total share capital comes to 96. 10 per cent indicating society's complete dependence on the government. Besides share capital participation, the society annually receives some amount from the government by way of managerial subsidy. Since inception, the society has received Rs. 57.65 lakh as managerial subsidy.

As on 31 July, 1997, the society has a working capital of Rs. 136.77 lakh. As of now, the society has issued loans to the tune of Rs.77.18 lakh to the 14 primary societies involving 263 members. As far as the repayment is concerned, the society could realize 54 per cent of the principal amount and the lion's share of the rest 46 per cent is long overdue. The lack of regular communication between the apex body and the primary societies is acting as a big hurdle against the timely realization of the society's fund. Although the society is making a marginal profit, the rate of return on capital is almost insignificant.

WEAKNESSES OF THE MOVEMENT

The foregoing discussion although not exhaustive, unfailingly indicates that even after 25 years of planned efforts cooperative movement in the state has failed to take off. At this stage of enquiry, it is neither possible to make an in-depth analysis of the causes of failure of the movement nor it is desirable to make too many inferences about them. A detail survey of the primary societies at the village level can only enable us to make a critical assessment of the movement and in-depth analysis of the causes of its failure.

However, the experience gained from the study of the apex level societies in the state and the trend analysis of the available statistics relating to primary societies reveal certain major trends of weaknesses of the movement. While some of them are part of the general weaknesses of the movement in the country, i.e., they are not in any way unique to the state alone rather unique to the movement across the country, some other, of course, are specific to the state. However, the specificities of general weaknesses are more important and an attempt is made here to outline some of them. The observations made here are tentative in nature and need to be substantiated by further studies.

1. Lack of spontaneity : Although cooperation at the social and community level has always been a unique feature of the tribal societies in the state, the modern cooperative movement did not spring from the traditional values of cooperation. While the traditional values of cooperation among the different tribal communities are based on informal reciprocity at the household level, the legal framework of modern cooperative movement is based on the reciprocity at the institutional level. The spontaneity of the movement is, perhaps, lost due to the failure of the general legal framework in codifying the traditional principles of reciprocity. As a result the movement has been superimposed by the state and it is yet to be internalized by the people. The excessive dependence of the movement on the government is thus obvious.

2. Excessive Dependence on the Government: The movement has not only been initiated by the government but it has taken the form of a government department. The cooperators both at the village and apex level always look for government assistance in running their business. The government officials working for the promotion of the movement have utterly failed to propagate the self-help principle of cooperation. The chief executives of most of the state level societies are appointed by the government and all of them exclusively depend on the government contribution to their share capital. As a result, these societies function as almost extended government departments, even in case of the primary societies, which have been brought under the cadre scheme controlled by the department of cooperation the secretaries of these societies are paid from the government coffer, they feel themselves to be the most deprived government employees having very low basic salary scale. This has largely frustrated the cadre scheme which was devised to improve the conditions of the primary societies.

3. Lack of Funds : The financial base of both the primary as well as state level societies is very weak. Because of the principle of unlimited liability, the rural rich class hardly associate itself in the primary credit societies. As most of the state level societies completely depend on the government contribution to their share as well as working capital, the financial base of the state and its attitude to cooperation largely determine the flow of fund into this sector. The revenue base of the state is very narrow. About 85 per cent of the budgetary expenditure of the state comes from the centre in the form of grants-in-aid and the state can only cover about 15 per cent from its own revenue. The sectoral allocation of plan outlays shows that cooperative sector has never been treated as priority sector in the state. Four five years plans have been completed since Meghalaya got its statehood. None of the plan has given much importance to the cooperative sector. The share of the cooperative sector to the total plan outlay has steadily declined from 2.43 per cent in the Fifth Plan (1974-79) to 2 per cent in the Sixth Plan (1980-85), 1.24 per cent in the Seventh Plan (1985-90) and to 1.02 per cent in the Eighth (1992-97). In the proposed Ninth Plan (1997-2002) this share is fixed to 0.89 per cent (Table-16). Thus, in a state like Meghalaya, where the cooperative movement gets its sustenance from the government resources, gradual withdrawal of government support long before the movement takes off may result in the ultimate collapse of the movement.

Table 16: Sector-wise distribution of Plan Outlays of Meghalaya(%)

Sl. No.	Sectors	Fifth Plan (1974-79)	Sixth Plan (1980-85)	Seventh Plan (1985-90)	Eighth Plan (1992-97)	Ninth Plan (1997-2002)
1.	Agriculture and allied service	22.10	20.70	18.54	8.63	9.43
2.	Cooperation	2.43	2.00	1.24	1.02	0.89
3.	Irrigation, Flood Control & Power	18.34	18.60	18.89	15.79	15.59
4.	Industry & Minerals	6.10	4.80	4.40	4.57	3.78
5.	Transport and Communications	21.04	21.20	18.18	24.30	21.52
6.	Social & Community Services including Rural Development	17.09	29.20	27.89	31.17	4.16
7.	Economic Services	6.37	0.30	1.72	2.92	2.68
8.	General Services	2.43	3.20	6.49	5.82	2.70
9.	Others	4.10	-	2.65	5.78	3.25
	Total	100.00	100.00	100.00	100.00	100.00

Source : Basic Statistics, 1995, and Draft Proposals for Ninth Plan, Vol. I, Govt. of Meghalaya.

4. Lack of Management Efficiency and Professionalism : The chief executives of most of the state level societies are appointed by the state government. They are mainly drawn from the retired officials of the department of cooperation as well as from retired government bureaucrats. At times, political considerations in such appointments undermine the efficiency criteria. Of course, the appointment of retired personnel involves less expenditure as far as salary head is concerned, but simultaneously such appointments often fail to bring the necessary drive, innovation, initiative and professionalism without which the societies become handicap to face the tremendous challenge in building up the movement. Moreover, the *ad hoc* nature of such appointments and consequent frequent change of the chief executives have largely engulfed the movement into *ad hocism.*

As far as the primary societies are concerned, the secretaries of the societies under the cadre scheme have to undergo training programme conducted by the government run Cooperative Training Institute in order to improve their managerial efficiency. The Training Institute conducts Junior Basic Certificate Course of 6 months' duration for the cooperators associated with the department of cooperation, Certificate Course for cadre secretaries of 3 months, duration and Management Course for office bearers of the primary level societies of 2 weeks' duration. The Institute has adapted the curricula of the National Cooperative Union of India for all these courses. The course materials of these training mainly deal with the legal aspects of the cooperative societies. The Institute does not have trained manpower to conduct business specific training to the cooperators associated with different business specific societies. As a result, the training imparted to the secretaries hardly helps them in the promotion of their business conditions as well as market competitiveness.

5. Very Weak Vertical Linkage : The weak vertical linkage between the state level societies and the primary level societies affiliated to them seems to be a major structural problem for the healthy growth of the movement in the state. As far as the societies under cadre scheme are concerned, their performance is supervised by the Cadre Management Society but they do not have any business dealings with it. The PACS are affiliated to MECOFED and they buy agricultural inputs and consumer-goods from it and market their produce through it. But MECOFED has no control over the PACS and it cannot take any measures against the non-performing primary societies. Similarly, the primary weaving societies under the cadre scheme are controlled by the Cadre Management Society but they do business with Meghaloom. Meghaloom without any controlling power, hardly can do anything against the non-performing primary weaving societies. Thus there is a need to link the cadre scheme with the level of performance. Moreover, most of the affiliated societies hardly take any interest in running the business of their respective apex bodies. The organic vertical linkage between them is a necessary condition for the growth of the movement which is yet to be established.

6. Faulty Re-organization : The programme of re-organization of the PACS undertaken during 1976-77 had laid too much emphasis on the viability criteria that appeared to have undermined the principle of homogeneity in forming the co-operative society. Customs, traditions, clan lineage, etc., vary from village to village among the tribal communities in the state. Fixation of a minimum 500 members criterion for a viable society and consequent amalgamation of a number of small societies into one have drawn different villages under one society irrespective of their differences at the cultural plane and clan loyalty. This has led to the growth of diversity of interest and heterogeneity of purpose and thereby has shaken the mutual confidence among the members. As a result the re-organization could hardly improve the overall functioning of the PACS. Many of them do exist only on paper.

7. **Weak Forward Linkage :** The softest point of the cooperation movement in the state is very weak forward linkage between production and marketing. While a considerable amount of marketable surplus is generated in agro-horticultural produce, the problem of marketing of such produce is acting as a disincentive to the growers. The failure of MECOFED as well as other primary marketing societies to market them is ultimately helping the private traders to appropriate large part of surplus by way of unequal exchange. This in turn substantially reduces the loan repayment capacity of the members of primary societies leading to the ever mounting volume of outstanding against the society loans to this sector.

8. **Traditional Land Tenure System :** The traditional land tenure systems of the different tribal groups in the state are full of ambiguities in relation to ownership, control and occupancy rights over land. So far neither any cadastral survey has been undertaken nor any effective attempt has been made in order to codify the traditional customs in order to clearly define the concepts of ownership, control and occupancy rights. There exists multiple authority of public land. Private land is largely owned clan-wise where individual occupancy is recognized. Because of the complicated land tenure system, most of the cultivators do not have any legal land ownership documents. As a result, it is very difficult to use land as mortgage for getting loans from banks. In fact, the security structure of banks does not correspond to the traditional land ownership pattern of the tribal societies that stands on the way of free credit flow to agriculture and allied sectors.

9. **Non-Correspondence Between Cooperative Democracy and Tribal Democracy:** The principles of cooperative democracy hardly take into confidence the institutions of tribal democracy that mobilize and control peoples' initiative at different levels. In the Khasi society, the institutions like village Durbar and village headman, Durbar Raid and

the office of Basan or Lyngdoh or Sirdar, Durbar Hima and the office of the Syiem play the pivotal role in the management of community life at village, Raid and Syiemship levels respectively. Similarly, among the Jaintias, the office of the village headman and Doloi and among the Garos the office of the Nokma use to play crucial roles in the management of the Jaintia and Garo societies respectively. These traditional institutions use to mobilize resources in order to undertake activities of common interest like village sanitation, water supply, health, roads, education, etc. They lead the people at the local level, speak for their people and protect the collective interest of the people. Unless these traditional institutions are accommodated and allowed to play their due role in the cooperative movement, the spontaneity will remain a far cry.

REFERENCES

Census of India, 1991, Series-1, India, Final Population Totals: Brief Analysis of Primary Census Abstract, Paper-2 of 1992, Registrar General and Census Commissioner, New Delhi.

Government of Meghalaya, 1997, Ninth Five Year Plan 1997-2002 and Annual Plan 1997-98, Draft Proposals, Planning Department, Shillong.

Government of Meghalaya, 1991, Meghalaya District Gazetteers, Khasi Hills District I.M. Simon, (ed.), Directorate of Arts and Culture, Shillong.

Government of Meghalaya, 1996, Meghalaya District Gazetteers, Garo Hills District, Directorate of Arts and Culture, Shillong.

Meghalaya Cooperative Apex Bank, 1995-96, Annual Report, MCAB, Shillong.

Namjoshi, M.V., 1977, "Cooperation and Welfare", in P.Y. Chinchankar and M.V. Namjoshi, (ed), *Cooperation and Dynamics of Change*, Somaiya Publications, Bombay.

National Bank for Agriculture and Rural Development 1997, State Focus Paper, Meghalaya, 1997-98, Shillong.

North Eastern Council, 1995, Basic Statistics NEC, Shillong.

Tyagi, R.B., 1968, *Recent Trends in the Cooperative Movement in India*, Asia Publishing House, Bombay.

18

PEOPLES' PARTICIPATION AND THE FUNCTIONING OF GAON PANCHAYAT SAMABAY SAMITIES IN ASSAM

Nripendra N. Sarma

The first Prime Minister of India, late Pt. Jawaharlal Nehru, in his address to the Indian Cooperative Congress at New Delhi in April 1958, observed, "The three pillars of India at the base should be the village panchayat, the village cooperative and the village school. It is on these that the whole structure of India, politically, economically and socially, should be built up. If cooperation in India succeeds in bringing the people of different casts and creeds to a common platform and creates in them an urge for cooperative working and living, it will usher in an era a of peace and pentry" .

The concept of cooperation and the utility of cooperatives as a development tool remain as valued as ever and wherever the cooperative structure have been properly established upon a strong membership base, they have demonstrated to the world that there is no better means for promoting economic and social progress.

The genesis of the term 'cooperation' can be found in the Latin word 'co-operai', 'co' means with and 'operari' means working together with others for a common purpose. There is no universally accepted definition on "Cooperation", mainly because of two reasons :

(i) First, the term has assumed different connotation according to the environments and circumstances prevailing in different countries giving birth to the movement.

(ii) Second, in some countries, cooperatives are state partnered, in others they are aided and controlled by the state and in still some others they are either state organisations or used as instrument of state planning.

The essence of cooperation is the spirit of team. Cooperation is a philosophy which can permeate every aspect of human activity. The term can be applied to any field of activity where people work, not in isolation, but in combination for a common end. In the more restricted economic sense, it may conveniently be defined as a system of organised work in which people voluntarily associate on the basis of equality and act in harmony for mutual economic benefit. The underlying principle is "self-help" and "mutual' help" and the coworkers are inspired by the noble ideal of "each for all and all for each".

Cooperation was introduced in India in the early years of this century as a means of providing credit on easy terms to help the farmers to fight indebtedness and poverty. Cooperatives have over the years significantly diversified their activities to include credit, banking, agri-input distribution, agro-processing, storage and warehousing etc. In dairying and oil processing activities, cooperative sector has emerged as an important countervailing factor to the private traders for the benefit of both producers and consumers. In terms of its institutionalization, membership, area of operation, the cooperative movement of India does not have its parallel in the world.

Cooperative movement in Assam made its formal appearance in an organised manner under the patronage of the government in the year 1904 under the Cooperative Societies Act. The Shillong Cooperative Town Bank Ltd. was the first cooperative credit societies of the North East, registered on 3rd September 1904. Since then, the cooperative movement has gradually gained momentum in the region particularly after independence. The cooperative movement in Assam has attained an impressive status in terms of the members of societies, membership, working capital, volume of business transacted etc. The movement has diversified into new fields of activities, the multipurpose Gaon Panchayat Samabay Samities, consumer cooperatives, as well as major industries like spinning mills etc.

To provide an institutional infrastructure at the grass-root level for bringing about all-around development with the active participation of the people, in Assam GPSS were set up in the year 1973 with an area of operation coterminous with that of a gaon panchayat to cater to the needs of 15 to 20 thousand population under each society in the plain districts of Assam more or less in the lines of Farmer Service Societies as recommended by the National Commission on Agriculture under the Chairmanship of Nathu Ram Mirdha. The objectives of these societies as stated in the model bye-laws are not only to provide credit but also a package of services such as supply of agricultural input, sale of essential commodities etc. Based on these objectives the function of these societies can be so vast that hardly any aspect of rural development remains untouched. In order to bring all the villages under the GPSS, enrolment drive was made and more than four lakhs members were enrolled up to 1974-75.

In Assam GPSS with universal coverage of rural population are expected to serve as a limb of the cooperative movement of the state and rendering multifarious services to about 20 lakhs rural families of the state by distribution of essentials and other consumers articles as agents of the government. Now the GPSS can provide the basic infrastructure for the marketing of agricultural produces, supply of credit and distribution of essential commodities at fair price shops. Some of the GPSS have taken up business of other necessary items such as non-controlled articles, confiscated goods, general merchandise, tea, fertilizer, seeds, pesticides etc.

The growth particulars and performance of GPSS have been studied for the period from 1984-85 to 1994-95. From this study the followings can be observed:

(i) The number of GPSS went up from 701 in 1984-85 to 707 in 1992-93.

(ii) The number of villages covered went up from 20, 901 in 1984-85 to 28,379 in 1994-95.

(iii) The percent of government share capital to total share capital increased from 68.62 in 1984-85 to 71.45 in 1994-95.

(iv) During the period 48 percent growth in sales was observed.

(v) Profit for the GPSS went up from Rs. 31.1 lakhs in 1984-85 to Rs. 105.85 lakhs in 1994-95. Maximum amount of profit was earned in

1990-91 (Rs.249.16 lakhs) while the maximum amount of loss was incurred in 1989-90 (Rs. 185.18 lakhs)

The government share capital contribution is the most important constituent of the capital structure of GPSS. Corresponding to the growth in age, there were not growth in the volume of sales, working capital and recovery of loans. The high percentage of government share capital to total share capital proves that the societies are heavily dependent on government subscription for their survival. Thus it may be inferred that it will be very difficult on the part of the societies to survive if the subscription from government is withdrawn. Thus the heavy losses, low level of profit, lower amount of loans issued, higher amount of outstanding loans with poor possibility of recovery, heavy dependence on government for working capital all these present a dismal picture of the GPSS. In most of the societies, sale proceeds mainly come from the sale of consumer goods, that too in a wide majority of cases in PDS items. Even after 25 years of formation, these societies have not been able to project themselves as the saviours of the rural people. Rather they are languishing under heavy burden of losses. Some causes which are attributed for the under performance of these societies are:

(i) lack of loyalty of members

(ii) lack of mutual understanding

(iii) procedural delays as far as supply arrangement, purchase matters etc. are concerned

(iv) absence of regular supply system; and

(v) heavy transportation cost

The weaknesses inflicting the cooperative institutions, such as structural weaknesses, lack of professionalism in management, poor resource base and over dependence on government support and patronage are to be removed. Today cooperative movement is at the crossroad and is passing through a critical phase. Many cooperators have a feeling that new economic reforms will cripple the whole system built over the years because new economic policy is perceived for total removal or slashing down of subsidies and other assistance extended to the various sectors. In the year 1992-93, the government of India discontinued the central sector scheme and centrally sponsored schemes for the development of cooperative sector.

The state government is also financially starving and is not providing adequate funds to this sector. In context of the contemporary changes, the overriding need for cooperative movement is to increase their efficiency and competitive power in the face of emerging competition. The developments make it imperative that collaboration between the cooperatives intensifies.

The kind of competition envisaged during the days ahead, the GPSS have to reorient and gear themselves in terms of professional competencies and strengthening cooperative business. Members would be required to increasingly share a major responsibility in garnering funds to support cooperative programmes. Intensified efforts are required from Assam State Cooperative Union and other member developmental organisations. The task is gigantic and requires measures for plugging the credibility crisis of the GPSS. Since the government of Assam is still enjoying the control over the majority of the GPSS and the cooperative promotional organization the primary initiative has to be originated from there itself to project the cooperatives and their performance in the right perspective.

As a, basic policy, the GPSS should be treated as member driven, member controlled and member responsive organization efficiently managed by trained professional staff.

EDUCATION, GENDER AND POVERTY

19

RURAL DEVELOPMENT
An Educational Perspective

B. Lynden
M.P. Khonglah

The World Bank had defined rural development as a strategy designed to improve the economic and social life of a specific group of people - the rural poor. It involves extending the benefits of development to the poorest among those who seek a livelihood in the rural areas. The group includes small farmers, tenants and the landless.

Rural development has been identified variously with economic growth, with modernization, with increased agricultural productivity, with socialist form of organization and with services of basic needs such as health, education, transport and water supply. It is now widely recognized that rural development is by no means an agricultural or productivity problem alone, nor is it a technical problem.

Poverty is spreading, while constraints seem to multiply and continue to hold progress. It is on the removal of these constraints and the identification of gaps in rural development policy, and research that there is a real need to focus attention. Rural development must be looked upon as a process of change in societies whereby poverty will be reduced, if not totally, eliminated, and the creativity and existing knowledge of the poor fully utilised. The poor must be enabled access to the resources in order to make available resources more productive of amenities, services and goods required and wanted by the poor and their government.

Much have been talked about eradication of rural poverty. A number of different schemes and policies have been formulated and implemented by different agencies. Crores of rupees have been spend, in the name of rural development, however the mute question is, have we really achieve our objectives to develop the rural poor? It is disheartening to note that poverty still reigns supreme and almost half of India's population are still deprived of basic amenities of life such as education, health, safe drinking water, food and shelter etc. This indicates that the various developmental schemes and policies have not really percolate down to the grassroot level and this invites serious and sincere introspection on the part of the policy maker, planners and the implementing agencies. Hence there is a need for new policy and new institutional settings and forms that would enable local control and initiative. As of now the Participatory Rural Appraisal (PRA) method is widely acknowledged as the best approach i.e. bottom-up-approach. Such strategies can help to achieve social transformation based on peoples centred development values and the potentials of advanced, information based technology.

It is generally realized that the relationship between education and poverty is two directional. The effect of poverty on education is easy to appreciate. A poor parent may not be able to afford much education for his children. Free education even in primary schools is not really that free. On account of limited impact a poor person may not be able to improve his own educational level also.

On the other hand, the effect of education on poverty is less direct and involves time lag also. As our education mostly lacks vocational bias, its utility may not be easily reflected in higher earnings for the lower income groups. This possibly true on early childhood education as well as adult education.

The importance of education in terms of investment in human capital to enhance human capabilities and its role in enhancing productivity, income and welfare has been recognised as crucial factor for poverty alleviation. Inadequacies in human resources are often considered to be manifestation of poverty. However in most of the developing countries, high priority for education in the allocation of resources is not forthcoming. Though the effects of investment on education may not be felt immediately, it has long term effects especially in improving the human capabilities of skills or entreprenurial abilities which in turn enhanced the productivity of human endeavours. Therefore, there appears to be major ties between quality of human resources and poverty. Further there may be important interactions among investments (like health) in various human resources with education in particular which will improve the results of investments in other human resources.

Rohini Nayyar in her study on inter-state-differences in rural poverties (excluding Kerala) used data and found no correlation between the incidence of rural poverty and the level of literacy. T.L. Jain considered the same data and reported that literacy rate had to be dropped at a preliminary stage in the analysis on account of which low correlation with poverty. However, education index was found to be positively related to poverty. He concluded that education does not help in poverty elimination. P.K. Bhardhan cited data from West Bengal for agricultural households as well as primarily cultivator households. The variable on education was in terms of numbers of men with above primary education level in the 15-60 age group in the household. It was found that the probability of falling below the poverty line is lower for an agricultural labour household with some characteristics which included a higher educational level which is an immediate relation between literacy rate and income generation.

In the international context, a review of the literature on the relationship between poverty and education has been made, and it was mentioned to the conclusion that in each of the countries studied the incidence of poverty decreased with educational attainment, and it was found that the correlation between education and poverty was significant and negative.

Education has been considered to be the most important instrument of change be it social, economic, political. Sadly enough, while almost half of the country's population remains illiterate, it is still a far cry to talk about rural development in its true sense. It is through education that the rural masses could become aware of various information relating to developmental schemes and policies provided by different agencies. At the same time a literate person can become aware of his deprivation and moves towards amelioration of his conditions through organizations and participation in the process of development. He could also acquire skill to improve economic status and general well being. In order to accelerate the process of rural development, it is imperative that more stress should be given on education of rural masses so that they can participate more efficiently at all levels of developmental activities and acquire the benefits.

Education is thus a prior variable and income/poverty a consequential variable. On account of the generally low impact of adult education in later years it may be noted that education may , in several ways ,be affecting income/poverty.

In conclusion, in order to achieve a real development, it is suggested that the rural people must be involved in planning, implementation of various schemes on rural development. This will infuse a sense of responsibility to them to manage, control and access the development schemes and ensure transparency and accountability on the part of the implementing agencies.

REFERENCES

Bardhan, P.K., 1987, Poverty and "Trickle Down" in Rural India: A Quantitative Analysis, in: Jain, T.L. (ed), *Poverty in India*, New Delhi, Ess Ess Publications, pp. 76-94.

Jain, T.L., 1987, *Poverty in India*, New Delhi, Ess Ess Publications, pp. 9-4, 101.

Jandhyala, B.G. Tilak, 1996, How Free is 'Free' Primary Education in India? *Economic and Political Weekly*, Vol XXXI, No. 5, February 3.

Nayyar, Rohini, 1991, *Rural Poverty in India*, Bombay: Oxford University Press.

20

EDUCATION AND SOCIAL ENVIRONMENT AMONG THE TEA TRIBES IN ASSAM

Bolin Hazarika

Of all the forms of government, the democratic form provides maximum scope for people's participation in various governmental activities. Effective people's participation demands prior development of people's thinking faculty and their capacity to judge as social being. No other single factor can impart proper thinking and behaviour to the citizen to the extent that education does. While talking about education we are however, not restricting ourselves to only educational institutions due to the simple reason that these institutions are not isolated centres of learning. Rather they are a part of the whole which very often finds expression in the term general environment. Any attempt to analyse the role of education in the development of' a particular social group must, therefore, entail the part played by both the educational institutions where the group in question send their wards and the broad socio-political environment of the group. The present paper endeavours to analyse the role of education in the development of an important social group in Assam, namely the Tea Tribes.[1] Although the term Tea Tribes broadly covers the working as well as the ex-tea garden labours, the paper intends to discuss about the role of education in the development of only the working tea garden labourers of the Tea Tribes. Development in case of human resource is understood here as enhancement of inner qualities of a person which aims at overall improvement of himself and the society in which he lives in.

The tea gardens of Assam are situated mostly in rural areas. Housing, sanitation, health, education and such other welfare provisions in tea gardens are looked after on the basis of the provision of Plantation Labour Act 1951 (hereafter mentioned as PLA). Section 14 of the PLA provides for a primary school in each tea garden where number of children of 6 - 12 years age group is more than 25. This is endorsed in Rules 52-57A of Assam Plantation Labour Rules, 1956 (hereafter mentioned as PLR). Rule 52 however states that the management may not establish a school in the garden in case there is a school within one mile from the garden where free tuition is provided and where sufficient seats are available to enrol the students of the garden. According to Rule 53 (1) all schools have to be established in the mid-position of the gardens. Rule 54 demands that garden schools must possess all the required learning equipments. An important (Rule 55) Rule of this Act provides that there must be one teacher for every 40 students or fraction thereof in such schools. The teacher must posses equal educational qualification with the teachers of "non-tea garden area school teachers". Article 56 provides that the curriculum, teaching hour, text books and teaching standard of garden schools must be approved by the State Education Department. Article 57 states that education in tea garden schools must be free.

But these provisions of PLR are often violated in the tea gardens. For example, 40: 1 student teacher ratio is not maintained in majority number of tea garden schools. This is revealed in the report of a field survey of the tea garden schools of Nagaon district by a team of Assam Tea Tribes Students Association, headed by its president Simanchal Dighal in early 1999.[2] The Field Report can be presented in the form of a table in the following manner.

Table 1 : Teacher-student Ratio in some schools of Nagaon District

Sl. No.	*Name of the School*	*No.of Teacher*	*No. of Student*
1.	Kaliabor Tea Garden School	1	140
2.	Barghat Tea Garden School	1	85
3	Salona Tea Garden School	1	87
4	Barghat Lusai Line L.P.School	1	81
5.	Chikbai T.G. School	3	280
6.	Kelydon Tea Garden School	2	115
7.	Burapahar Tea Garden School	2	130
8.	Lengteng Tea Garden School	2	110

Source : Assam Tribune, 6.3.99.

Moreover teaching in most of the garden schools is not a full time job. The teachers are required to look after other garden works as well.[3] In some cases a garden Mohori, or a factory employee is often transferred to the work of teaching in the garden school.[4] Sometimes the garden Mohori has to manage both the works of garden Mohori and school teacher.[5]

In all such cases the qualification of the Mohori or the factory employee is not given adequate importance. A different kind of violation of the education provision of the PLR is found in Macneill and Magor group of gardens of Sonitpur district where due to increase in student enrolment in 1999, the management forced the teachers to teach the students by making separate groups and shifts.[6] In this way the management evaded the responsibility of appointing additional teacher to maintain 40:1 student teacher ratio in their schools.

Although the PLR demands that schools should be situated at centre place, in practice most of the garden schools are situated at outskirts of the garden with an average distance of 2 to 3 km from the lines. Many parents hesitate to send their children to school for the distance that they have to cover, in most cases through lonely places.[7]

Non-Institutional or General Environment : It is rightly said that family is the original starting point of education and mother is the first teacher of the children. In a tea garden, a student remains at school for limited hours of the day. The rest of the hours they spend either in their family or in the lines. Unfortunately the environment of these two sectors presents only a dismal picture.

The nature of garden work for tea garden labourers allows practically no time for parents to look after their wards properly They leave for work early in the morning and return home tired in the evening. Being completely exhausted, they cannot think of re-engaging themselves in any matter other than doing necessary preparation for their supper and going to bed early. In such a situation child's study gets only secondary importance even in case of those parents having a learning towards the matter of their child's education.[8] The parents cannot afford for the habit of going to bed late as it will necessitate more money in buying kerosene oil for lightening their houses.[9] But what is unfortunate in their life is that they find both money and time for regular purchasing of alcohol and for gossiping - often leading to quarreling and polluting the healthy social environment.[10] Although primarily the male folk is addicted to suchpractices of drinking, in many cases the female folk is also engulfed by this evil habit.[11]

It is true that the tea garden labourers of Assam use to receive less amount of wage than their counterparts in West Bengal and Kerala.[12] But the more conscious section of the Tea Tribes themselves believe that with that amount of wage the expenditure of a family can be managed.[13] Difficulty arises in this respect only because they misuse their money and are extravagant in nature. They spend lavishly whenever a good amount of money comes to their hand either by way of bonus payment or by some other ways.[14] Very often they purchase luxury items of low standards. They will prefer purchasing a radio, a tape-recorder or even a battery run TV set to a mosquito net and sleep on floor laying a sack over it.[15] For such purposes they also take loan against exorbitant rate of interest from local money lenders.[16] The practice of gambling is also quite common in them.

In order to fight against such a deplorable plight of this section of the Tea Tribes, the nascent elite section from among them have formed a number of socio-economic organizations. Special mention may be made in this regard to the Assam Chah Mazdur Sangha and the Cachar Chah Shramik Union, the leading trade unions of the tea garden labourers of the Brahmaputra and the Barak Valley respectively and the Assam Tea Tribes Students Association, the pioneer student association of the Tea Tribes. But due to some or other reason these organizations have not been able to see much success in this respect. The loopholes in the PLA, 1951 also make the Act weaker. For example, the PLA and the Rules thereof provide that a charge of violation of any of the Act provisions can be brought by only the Chief Inspector of Plantations. No labourer or trade union or any other individual or organisation is authorised to file a case against the garden authority for violation of the welfare provisions. Even the inspectors are not empowered to do so.[17] It simply means that the Chief Inspector of Plantations may prohibit a charge of violation of welfare provisions being brought to the court, if he, so desires. In case of conviction too, the Act provides for a punishment of three years imprisonment or a fine of Rs.500/- or both.[18] Compared to the gravity of offense such a punishment is treated as light even by the garden authority. Although the Parliament has passed the 93rd Amendment to the constitution (on 28th November, 2001) to make education compulsory for the children of 6-14 age group, the same has no provision for correcting the evil environment of the rural and urban sectors of the country. The parents of the Tea Tribes children are less likely to receive any impetus from the Amendment. It is rightly mentioned that if the compulsory education is enforced in the present form, one may find more parents in jail than more children at school.[19] This may come true particularly in the tea garden areas of Assam.

REFERENCES

1. The Tea Tribes are known by several names in Assam. A particular group is in favour of identifying them as "Jharkhondi". Another group likes to call them "Adivasi". But no single term can claim to cover them all to the extent covered by the term "Tea Tribes", Bolin Hazarika, "In Search of An Identity For an Ethnic Group: The case of Tea and Ex-Tea Garden Labourers of Assam", paper presented at a Seminar on *Ethnicity in Assam Today,* held at Dibrugarh University on 12-13 March, 2001.
2. *Assam Tribune,* 6.3.99.
3. Prahlad Ch. Tasa, *Chah Bagisat Sikhar Prasar,* (Dibrugarh, 1991) p. 37.
4. *Ibid,* p. 36.
5. Guneswar Sonowal, *"Chah Asomia Sokolor Artha Samajik Potobhumi",* in *Juhar,* ATTSA Souvenir (1998)
6. *Assam Tribune* 6.3.99.
7. Dimbeswar Tasa, *"Chah Mazdoor Samaj Aru Samajik Riti Niti",* in Rajen Gogoi, (ed), *Chah Jonogosthir Chinta Setona,* (Asom Sahitya Sabha, Jorhat, 2001).
8. Abhiram Tasa, "Asomor Chah Jonojati Aru Prapta Bayaska sikha", in *Kochasona* (ATTSA Souvenir, 2000), p.100.
9. Meghraj Karmakar, "Chah Bonua Samajar Saikhik Obostha", in *Kochasona* (ATTSA Souvenir, 2000) p.73.
10. *Ibid,* p. 73
11. Narayan Ghatowar, "Asomot Chah Uddyogor Adi Parba", in *Juhar* (ATTSA Souvenir, 1998).
12. *The Assam Tribune,* 10.3.99.
13. *Prahlad Tasa,* (1991) p. 63.
14. Atmaram Kumar, "Sottor Lakh Seujia Seenyar", in Kachasona, (ATTSA Souvenir, 2000) p. 106,
15. *Abhiram Tasa* (2000) p. 100.
16. Bina Bawri, "Chah Jonojatir Somosya Samadhanot Yubok Yuboti, Chattra Chattrir Bhumika", in *Kachasona* (ATTSA Souvenir, 2000) p.114.
17. D. Saikia, *Bagicha Shram Aain Aru Asom Bidh,* (1996) pp. 7 - 8
18. *Ibid.,* p.73
19. Walter Fernandes, "Compulsory Education : Right or Duty?", in *Assam Tribune,* 2.12.2001.

21

WOMEN AND DEVELOPMENT IN RURAL INDIA

Bhola Nath Ghosh
Utpal Kumar De

Introduction

The analysis of the problems of women and their status in the society has become the focus of attention of several studies at the local as well as global level only a few decades ago. The importance of the gender studies grew with the realisation that development of any society will not take place at the desired pace unless almost the half the population i.e., women remain backward. The female folk must be involved in the developmental process along with their male counterpart to keep the society on the desired path. In most cases the women can not take part in different activities beyond their own confined domain because of the particular social structure which is reflected by their position in the society and attitude of the society towards different aspects of women.

Several authors have studied the status of women in different dimensions. Empirical evidences are there to confirm that improvement of status of women (like literacy, education, occupational structure etc.) help reducing fertility rate, maternal mortality, childhood mortality and promote rapid implementation of family planning programmes which are some of the obstacles of development. A number of demographic factors like low age at marriage, maternal mortality, high fertility, adverse sex ratio, the social factors like crime against women, their relegated position in the family, limited political participation and the economic factor like low female work participation rate are among the major factors, inimical to the improvement of status of women in most of the developing countries. A poor performance in all these fields is reflected in the poor performance of the economy.

India's developmental process is also characterised by great regional disparities and with this background women's status can be explained through inter-state comparisons. Women in India have to face the lack of freedom to do other things for continuous bearing and rearing of child. Reductions in birth rate have often been associated with enhancement of women's status and voice. In this context the most significant factors, those affect fertility are education and labour force participation.

This paper tries to explain the status of women in terms of social economic and demographic situation. This paper also intends to draw a relation between the status of women and the development. We hope that this analysis would provide a lead in understanding the contemporary Indian society in a better perspective.

The status of women is examined through their education, health and family planning, crime against women, economic participation like employment, religious tradition and their participation in the socio-political process. These are analysed with a focus to social development. For the purpose of analysis, data regarding all those aspects have been gathered from various secondary sources.

Majority of Indian women population lives in rural areas. But here we shall concentrate on the status of women in general though the problem of rural women is more severe and hence a special attention is given to that. The problems of rural women can be seen as an integral part of the general socio-economic and political problems of rural India. Their social and economic status is an indicator of gender discrepancy and of level of real development. It is impossible to differentiate women from the social milieu in which they live, for their poverty, illiteracy and ignorance are merely a part of the totality which is characterised by ever rising population, smaller fragmentation of firms increasing landlessness and unemployment.

Although the vast majority of the rural population is under privileged and poor, the condition of women is worst. Most of the rural people are illiterate; the women have relatively higher illiteracy rates than men.

In most of the states in India, the enrolment of boys of age group 6-11 in primary schools has come close to almost 100 per cent, but the percentage is much lower (around 80 per cent) for girls. The drop out rate is also high in their case (Datta, 1994). And the case is more severe in case of rural women. The rural people generally compelled to struggle more for their survival, but the women are often the most resistant.

General Status of Women

In the traditional societies, the role of women has been characterised by inferior social status, suffering deplorable social conditions and dependency. They have encountered systematic discrimination and exploitation at the hands of the male folk. They are largely ignored; their contributions to the family's economy is taken for granted and thus never evaluated truly; their status as mother assured only after the birth of a son. A woman even is not known by her own name, but through her association with husband or son's name, as the mother of Ram, Ramer-Ma, X's wife etc. In all aspects of life, except as *ma/mother* a woman is insignificant and even as a mother (ma) her personality is subdued to being not herself but merely her son's mother or someone's wife.

Women in India have generally enjoyed a lower status compared to their male counterpart. In the rural society the divergence is much more. On the one hand, female forms of deity are ritually worshipped as Durga Lakshmi, etc. Whereas, in reality, women are subjected to various forms of harassment in different fields, either at home, or at working place. According to Jayanti Patnaik, former chairperson of national commission for women, 'in every seven minutes some crimes are committed against women in our country. She states that in every fifty six minutes a women is raped, in every 36 minutes one is molested, in every 33 minutes some cruelty is perpetrated against her and in every two minutes a women is murdered for more dowry (*Indian Express*, October 10, 1994).

Tamil Nadu is a state known for its reported cases of high female infanticide. Collector of Salem district Brij Kishore states that in a sample of 12,000 infants death, 45% of the cases were reported as female infanticide. In Madurai district, a local technique is used to kill the newborn female infant. The new born female infant is choked to death by thrusting paddy husk and cactus milk into its mouth (*Hindusthan Times*, 4 September 1994). In many parts of our country, female infanticides are noticed but the cases go unreported thereby making it difficult to establish the quantum of female infanticide.

Another indication of the worst status of a woman is the order in which food is eaten in the household. The woman eats last, after the husband, parents-in-law and children, which is justified as a superb example of the spirit of self-sacrifice. Not only that the quantity and quality of consumption are the other indications. Normally a mother took the residual of food after the consumption of others in the family and of the inferior quality of low nutritional value. It is in fact merely the outward indication of a woman's relegated position in the family and in the society. She is expendable, by her family as a girl, by her husband as a wife. But her very real contributions to the family's economic well-being are ignored, because she brings in no money, because her labour is unseen, and unpaid, her status is correspondingly the lowest. However recent anthropological literature mentioned that the status of women may rise and fall during her entire life cycle and varies across the societies. In some societies women's status is higher at younger ages while in others it is higher at older ages (Bhat, 1996; Foner, 1984; Vatuk, 1987). The women of Jaintia Hills of Meghalaya do not enjoy equal rights with men in the affairs of secular institutions. Even now, neither they can exercise their voting rights in the election of Dolois and Sardars, nor can they contest for election (Chattopadhyay, 1988).

Now we shall try to analyse the status in terms of several indicators like education, occupational participation, fertility, infant mortality, maternal mortality etc. one after another.

Women in Education

In the modern world education is a key factor of human resource development. It also makes a substantial contribution to a person's status. In recent years, women's educational opportunities have improved a great deal not only due to increasing awareness about the importance of education among parents but also due to the changing educational opportunities provided by the government. However, in terms of literacy rate here is a huge difference between men and women throughout India except in Kerala. Caldwell (1979), Dyson & Moore (1983) also pointed out that female education is a key determinant of contraceptive use, which is also a part of women status for fertility control. They have also shown that the relationship between literacy and employment with that of women status.

As per 1991 census report only 39% of women are educated as against 64% of men at the national level. West Bengal shows high female literacy than the national average whereas the female literacy rate in other eastern states like Bihar and Orissa is very poor. Still here also we notice educational differences among men and women clearly in spite of the fact that education in West Bengal is made very cheap up to a certain level. The bias is very high in all the eastern states as is clear from Table-1. Kerala shows the highest female literacy (86%) among Indian States.

Table 1 : Literacy Rates in India (1991)

States	*Female literacy (percentage)*	*Male literacy (percentage)*
West Bengal	46.6	67.8
Bihar	22.9	52.5
Orissa	34.7	63.1
India	39.2	64.2

Source: Office of the Registrar General, India.

Though, in West Bengal public education is very cheap up to a certain level, still not much progress has been made particularly in case of female education where only 42% of the female children in the age group 6-10 years were attending school (Table-2). The above statement confirms when we compare it with national average and other states. Kerala shows almost no gap between male (91.3%) and female (91.1 %).

Table 2 : Percentage population attending school in the age group 6-10 years (1991)

States	*Female (percentage)*	*Male (percentage)*
West Bengal	42.4	49.2
Bihar	26.1	41.7
Orissa	48.0	60.6
India	45.4	56.6

Source: Office of the Registrar General in India.

Religious Tradition

Traditionally, women are associated with the system of religion and they are expected to participate in rituals. They take a major role in the various religious activities and in many ways they are the repositories of religious traditions even though they have no voice in the all-male congregation.

Customarily, a son has the right to light the funeral pyre of his parents and the daughters have no right to do it. In case of Christians, the women do receive some impetus to move out of her small circle, for male and female are expected to worship together and as members of a religious congregation are treated as being equals. In Buddhism too there is more equality between the sexes. Religious folk tradition keeps women separated and unequal. That tradition of gender discrimination is still there.

The religious traditions, apparently are of great importance to people in the rural areas, serve to constrain and confine women. This is particularly true of the major religion. In Hinduism the women are not somewhat free and only in Christianity women as well as men are encouraged to seek a life of service outside the home often at the cost of social disapprobation.

Economic Participation

Women play an important role in the economic life of rural India. Traditionally, their economic activity was limited within the four walls of the house. But it is yet not recognised if women in the rural areas do not look after the chickens, if they do not take part in horticulture, much of the subsistence level income would be worsened. It is only recently that it has ever been documented that if women stopped their activities in the cultivation and harvesting of rice and other crops the agricultural works in India would never be completed. They took part in planting, weeding and other activities except in plough with their male counterpart. Women are mainly responsible for threshing, and for the numerous household activities including process of foods and maintenance of family. The female work participation rate in India and in eastern region in 1991 is shown in Table-3. The table shows that female work participation rate in the country was 22.25 per cent. The three eastern states were running behind the national average. However, Orissa was in a better position than Bihar and West Bengal. Though Bihar and Orissa are lagging behind West Bengal in literacy rate they are much advanced in reducing gender bias in general work. However, in West Bengal during 1981 to 1991 the proportion of women in primary occupation, specially, the number of female cultivators has increased, while that of male decreased. But still the rate remains much below the national figure. In the urban area also the number of female cultivators has increased by more than their male counterpart. In the rural manufacturing sector of West Bengal, we noticed a negative growth of male workforce whereas the female workforce has increased by around 50 per cent (De, 1994).

Table 3 : Work Participation Rate in India during 1991 (Percentage)

States	*Female*	*Male*	*Total*
West Bengal	11.25	51.40	32.19
Bihar	14.86	47.92	32.16
Orissa	20.79	53.79	37.53
India	22.25	51.55	37.40

Source: Census of India, 1991.

In the rural areas, role of women has been increased with the increasing introduction of multiple crop production for which there has been an increasing demand for labour. The problem is accentuated with the gradual shift of male workforce from primary to secondary and tertiary sectors in search of more wage rate. The increasing agricultural activities are now completed with increasing involvement of female worker. Still, in some part and in some section of population women hesitate to come out of home due to their peculiar social structure. If women are to make any worthwhile contribution to the economic development of the country, they have to come out of the four walls. During the last few years we noticed the women increasingly taking part in most of the economic activity with their male counterpart. In rural India, during 1981-91 period proportionate change in employment of female workers increased by 42.09; 20.13 and 61.41 per cent in primary, secondary and tertiary sector respectively. Whereas the figures for male were only 18.79, 11.50 and 52. 10, which are much lower than that of females, This is shown in Table-4. Compound growth rates of female workforce in those sectors were also higher than that of male. The picture of urban India is also similar to that of rural.

This is clear from the increasing work participation rate of women especially in primary and tertiary sector (Census of India, various issues).

Table 4 :Changes in Sectoral Composition of Workforce in India during 1981-91

Sector	*Rural*						*Urban*					
	Proportionate Change in E ployment			*Compound Growth Rates of the Workforce*			*Proportionate Change in E ployment*			*Compound Growth Rates of the Work-force*		
	Male	*Female*	*Total*	*Male*	*Female*	*Total*	*Male*	*Female*	*Total*	*Male*	*Female*	*Total*
Primary	18.79	42.09	24.33	1.79	3.58	2.29	40.21	48.51	41.92	3.44	4.03	3.56
Secondary	12.5	20.13	13.95	1.18	1.85	1.31	22.68	36.54	24.02	2.06	3.16	2.18
Tertiary	52.1	61.41	53.1	4.28	4.90	4.35	44.04	67.37	46.55	3.72	5.29	3.90

Source: Census Reports of India 1981, 1991.

Still the progress is slow because the total participation of female workers is still not comparable with male (from Table-3). Economically, women are the most underutilised resource in the country.

Employment is also considered to be one of the major status-deciding factors. Safillios-Rothschild (1980) showed that women participation in paid employment is highly related to their status. He also stated education and employment help a woman to understand her own image, own identity and individuality. All this measures can be felt and realised perfectly when a woman earns independently and has the options to live by her own living if situation demands so. Moreover a woman in high collar job enjoys more status than that who is in low category job. It was observed that during 1981-91 period employment of women in tertiary sector or service sector has increased in West Bengal differently in different categories.

Social Traditions, Crimes

Within the house the mother is always at the centre of the home. She rarely moves outside the house and her life thus becomes restricted. As the females are normally unable to move out of her small world they have very little exposure to new ideas. Sometimes they are only exposed to those ideas which are communicated by their male counterpart. But it is too limited and precarious. Thus they generally conceive different ideas through the eyes of their male members. The changes in the outside world are seen often as a threat, for they are unknown and she has no way of coping with them. Their whole life style is to stress the safety of the home from the nameless threat of the outside world. They will thus cling longer to the safe and known traditional ways of life.

Many of the women in our country are also the victims of social crimes in different ways like rape, molestation, oppression within family etc. that one can not ignore. Not only that the rate of crime against women has been increasing over time. The number of rape case in India has been increased from 14846 in 1996 to 15031 in 1998 (National Crime Records Bureau). However, the actual picture is much worst as most of the female victims hesitate to record their sufferings and try to conceal it for fear of losing prestige and other social bindings.

Another important issue is the case of dowry, which has been leading to the sacrifice of life of several wives, in different parts of India. According the National Crime Records Bureau death related to dowry case has been increased from 513 in 1996 to 697 in 1998.

This situation is rendered worse by the fact that few women participate in the educational process. Of the 6 million girls of primary school age, only 2 million enter school and two-thirds of them drop out by the end of class II. Less than one-fifth of those who enter stay on up-to class V. Thus the one acceptable avenue available by which to open up their horizons a little, is not taken by the majority of our women. The census of 1991 revealed that the literacy rate in west Bengal among men was 67.24 per cent, while that for women was only 47.15 per cent. The percentages are higher than those of the country as a whole. But there are states like Kerala where percentage is nearly 100.

The Government of West Bengal sometimes declares particular districts as 'fully' literate. But the Primary Census Report 2001 shows that it is far away from that (Census of India, Provisional Population Totals, 200 1). Adults are brought to literacy camps and are sent out as having passed the literacy tests. There is no arrangement for any follow-up work.

The main reason for the poor literacy rate is failure in the field of primary education particularly for girls. The directive principles of the Constitution required that all children between six and fourteen should be given free elementary education by 1961. We have not reached the constitutional target. In most states, including West Bengal, the enrolment of age group six to eleven in primary schools has come close to 100 per cent, but the percentage is much lower (around 80 percent) for girls. The drop our rate is also high in their case.

It is often held that young girls do not come to school because their mothers keep them at home for help in domestic work. This is only partially true. One of the most important factor is poverty. Another reason is that, heavy dowry is required for marriage of an educated girl with a more educated boy compared to her, which is essential due to our social customs. Many surveys have shown that girls of school going age often do not have the minimum clothing necessary for coming to school. Another important factor is a systematic neglect of girls and parents think that their daughters do not require education at all. Girls are neglected, while all attentions devoted to boys. Boys do not lack the clothes necessary for coming to school

Urban middle class women who on the whole tend to be freer, more literate and do work for wages, move in a dream like world far removed from the reality of the vast majority of an average rural woman. It is also observed from the relatively more literacy rate and work participation rate, especially in tertiary sector of urban women than their rural counterpart. They have themselves overcome many obstacles and may justly be proud in their accomplishments, but their relative freedom helps their rural sister for they will have no more contact with their rural roots than will their middle class husbands. Rare indeed are those educated urban men and women who go to the rural areas with anything more in mind than a visit to old parents and in-laws.

Women and Age at Marriage

Early age at marriage forms the major demographic variable that affects the status of women and perhaps with this background Kerala shows the higher status of women. Javillonar *et al.* (1979) argues that female age at marriage and women labour force participation are the two measurable qualities which holds the women status in developing countries. The reasons behind it is early age at marriage prevents girls from acquiring higher education and thereby perpetuates social backwardness among them. Though it is true that in our rural society where virtually all the girls get married early, it does not depend upon their individual decision. It is rather socioeconomic and cultural pressures and social environment that put a girl to an early marriage with no education or minimum education. Dandekar (1974) showed parents are transferring the burden of feeling their female children to someone else as soon as they possibly can. Census data indicate that mean age at marriage for females are on the rise. The mean age at marriage for females in West Bengal, Orissa and Bihar are 18.4. 18. 7 and 16.9 respectively whereas the national figure is 18.3.

Table 5 : Proportion of married female in the different age group

States	*(10- 14) years*	*(15-19) years*
West Bengal	1.9	33.0
Bihar	7.2	55.3
Orissa	1.3	22.0
India	4.5	35.3

There is no direct evidence of child marriage in these states. The census data show that West Bengal and Orissa show only 1.9 % and 1.3% respectively in the age group (10- 14) years whereas Bihar shows a high value 7.2. National figure stands in between these two divisions

(6-10) years school attending census data in Bihar confirms the early marriage. This indicates that early marriage is very few in West Bengal in comparison to Bihar and national average.

Table 6 : Mean age at marriage of currently married women who married during 1986-91 with educational level

States	*Mean age*	*Illiterate*	*Literate but<middle*	*Middle but <matric*	*Metric but< graduate*	*Graduate and above*
West Bengal	18.4	17.7	18.0	19.0	21.0	23.2
Bihar	16.9	16.8	16.7	17.0	18.1	20.9
Orissa	18.7	18.4	18.6	19.0	20.4	22.6
Kerala	21.0	20.5	20.4	20.3	21.7	23.5
India	18.3	17.6	18.3	18.9	20.3	22.7

Source: Census Report of India (various issues)

Table 7: Mean age at marriage of currently married (1986-91) female by educational level

		Educational Level				
States		*Illiterate*	*Literate but < primary*	*Middle but <metric*	*Metric but <graduate*	*Graduate and above*
West Bengal	Total	17.7	18.0	19.0	21.0	23.2
	Rural	17.6	17.8	18.6	20.5	23.0
	Urban	18.2	18.7	19.7	21.4	23.3
Bihar	Total	16.8	16.7	17.0	18.1	20.9
	Rural	16.7	16.6	16.8	17.6	19.7
	Urban	17.2	17.5	17.7	18.9	21.4
Orissa	Total	18.4	18.6	19.0	20. 4	22.6
	Rural	18.4	18.5	18.9	20.3	22.2
	Urban	18.5	18.8	19.4	20.7	22.9

Source: Census Report of India (various issues).

Women, Fertility and Family Planning

The level of fertility and the status of women are also related to each other. Status of women by itself generally does not affect fertility independently but it interacts with other variables such as education, employment, age at marriage, quality of health etc. All these factors affect and in turn affected by women's perception, knowledge and willingness to limit fertility and to plan births. So here total fertility rates has been selected as one of the factor under the assumption that a high TFR indicates little control by woman over their fertility behaviour, which is an indication of their low status in recent years. Ahmed (1991) showed the relationship of fertility with status. As fertility period normally ranges from 15 years to 44 years in our country, so level of education of that group is considered in the present discussion. Table-8 shows the clear relationship between education and fertility rate and hence the effectiveness of family planning programmes.

Table 8: Relation with education, fertility and family planning

States	*Literacy in the age group 15-44 years*	*Total Fertility Rate*			*Percentage of effective couple protection (1990-91)*
		Total	*Rural*	*Urban*	
West Bengal	48.5	3.2	3.6	2.1	33.7
Bihar	21.1	4.4	4.5	3.5	26.0
Orissa	36.3	3.3	3.4	2.3	41.0
Kerala	92.4	1.8	1.8	1.7	55.0
India	40.1	3.6	3.9	2.7	44.1

Highest fertility and lowest family planning acceptance are the result of literacy is very much clear from Table -8. In this regard Bihar shows an ideal model, lowest literacy (21.1) with high fertility (4.4) and low couple protection rate (26.0). Though West Bengal shows highest literacy but family planning acceptance is not much successful as that of Orissa or national level. Kerala shows an exception in all these respects.

Women Empowerment in Self Government

Two perspectives have emerged in the contemporary discourse on the modalities of gender equity: women's development and women's empowerment. There are social scientists who have studied women's role in economic development, mainly Ester Boserup's pioneering work which popularised women's development perspective (Boserup, 1970). The development perspective, however, has come under severe criticism not only for its failure to deliver its promise but also for working against the interests of women. Consequently, the decade of 1990s has witnessed the rise of women's empowerment perspective, which shot into prominence at Beijing Conference.

To tackle the problem or gender inequalities, there emerged the strategy of women's development. What has the development planning in general done for the women? Has it enabled them to rise above the position of subjugation? The answer is that it has not.

Therefore, an important critique of women's development perspective pointed to its neglect of power dimensions. From the economic point of view women have not been able to bring themselves at par with men. From different studies it has been observed that improvement of women's economic position has yet not taken place sufficiently. Therefore, the key factor, is her say in the decision making process, her participation in the domestic as well as community power structures. Primary concern of women's empowerment is to give them equal control over levels of power both in the domestic structures and in community power structure as well. Accordingly, on the basis of 73rd Amendment of the Constitution, one third of seats have been reserved for women in the self-government bodies like gram panchayat; panchayat samiti and zilla parishad to empower themselves. Though some states have already implemented the provisions and women are increasingly becoming the representatives of the local people, in most cases the decisions are taken by their male counterpart.

Different social scientists have defined women's empowerment differently:

(1) Griffen (1989) defines women's empowerment as "adding to women's power"

(2) Kabcer (1990: 8) interprets it as a radical transformation of power relations between women and men, so that women have greater power over their own lives and men have less power over women's lives'.

(3) Andre Betille (1999:59) The main point behind empowerment is that it seeks to change society through a rearrangement of power.

(4) Gidden views (1984) it as transformative capacity.

The trajectory of women's development perspective has passed through two phases: women in development (WID) and gender and development (GAD). The former has been concerned with the question of neglect and marginalisation of women in development endeavours while the latter has pleaded for gender planning in development. Altogether, the importance of the role played by women's development perspective in injecting gender concern into development planning can not be overemphasised. At the same time, it has had its limitations as an effective strategy of gender justice.

Clearly, women's empowerment perspective is different from women's development perspective is some very important ways. Women's development is primarily an socioeconomic project while women's empowerment is essentially a political project. The former is concerned with the enhancement of women's position in the economic space while the latter is concerned with the improvement of their position in the political position.

REFERENCES

Ahmed, Nilufer R. (1991), "Family size and sex preferences among women in rural Bangladesh", in, Studies in Family Planning, 12 March: 100-109

Bettie, Andre (1999), "Empowerment" in *Economic and Political Weekly*, March 6-13: 589-97.

Bart, P. (1969), "Why Women's Status Changes in Middle Age : The Turn of the social ferries wheel", *Sociological Symposium*, 3:1–18.

Boserup, Ester (1970), *Women's role in economic development*. New York: St Martin's Press.

Caldwell, John C. (1979), Education as a factor in mortality decline: An examination of Nigerian Data", in Population Studies, 33 (November): 395-413.

Census of India, Provisional Population Totals, 2001.

Census of India, various issues (1981,1991).

Chattopadhyay, S.K. *(1988), The Jaintias: Socio-political Institutions of Jaintia Hills*, Cosmo, New Delhi.

Datta Bhabatosh (1994). "Literacy for Women: Miles to Go", in Images Perspectives, Golden Jubilee Commemoration Vol., Nari Seva Sangha, Calcutta, pp. 33-34.

Deutchman, J. (1991), " The politics of empowerment", in Women and Politics, 11(2), pp. 1-18.

De, U K. (1994), Changes in Population Employment and the Pattern of Occupational Distribution in West Bengal (1981-1991), unpublished M.Phil dissertation submitted at the University of Burdwan, chapter-4.

Dyson, Tim and Mick Moore (1983), *Kinship Structure, Female Autonomy and Demographic Behaviour in India*, Prentice-Hall, New Delhi.

Foner, N. (1984) *Age in Conflict : A Cross–cultural Perspective on Inequality between Old and Young*, Columbia Univ. Press, New York.

Ghosh, Bhola Nath (2000). " Women's Participation in Gram Panchayat: Statewise distribution of elected panchayat members in India", in Social Transformation in Rural Sector, ed. S.D. Mukhayapadhya and S. Choudhury, pp. 174-179, Viswa Bharati University, Santiniketan.

Ghosh, Bhola Nath (1997), " The way the Santal Women Live", in Science Courier, 8th year, No.2, pp. 30-32, Kolkata, Vanyajati.

Ghosh, Bhola Nath (2000), "Position of Tribal Women in their Society. A few cases", in Vanyajati, pp. 4-8, Vol. XLVIII, No. 4, October, New Delhi.

Ghosh, Bhola Nath (1999), "Women Leadership in Gram Panchayat: Prospects and Constraints", in, Socialist Perspectives, Vol. 27, No. 1-2, pp. 35-45, June- July, Kolkata

Gidden, A. (1984), *The Constitution of Society*, Cambridge: Polity Press.

Griffen, V., (ed.), (1989), *Women, Development and Empowerment: A Pacific Feminist Perspective*, Kuala Lumpur, Asia and Pacific Development Centre.

Hindustan Times, September 4, 1994.

Javillonan, Gloria, Laurie Zivetz, Susan Thompson and Janet Griffith (1979), *Rural Development, Women's Roles and Fertility in Developing Countries: Review of the Literature*. (Durham, North Carolina): Research Training Institute and Southeast Consortium for International Development

Kabeer, N. (1990). "Gender Development and Training: Raising awareness in development planning", GADDU Newspack No. 14

Patnaik, Jayanti, (1994), Indian Express, October 10, 1994.

Safillios-Rothschild, Constantina (1980), " A class and sex stratification theoretical model and its relevance for fertility trends in the developing world:", in C. Holn and R. Machensen, (ed.), *Determinants of Fertility Trends: Theories Re-Examined*, Harper and Row, New York, pp. 189-202.

Vatuk, S. (1987), "Authority, Power and autonomy in the life cycle of the North India Woman", in Pal Hoekings (ed.), *Dimensions of Social Life*, De Gruyter Press, New York.

22

POVERTY ALLEVIATION AND RURAL DEVELOPMENT IN ASSAM

Prabin Baishya

Introduction

"It is extremely unfortunate that in today's world people die by eating poisonous materials" - lamented Prime Minister Atal Bihari Bajpayee in the 54th year of India's Independence while referring to starvation deaths of 20 persons after eating 'fungus infected' mango kernels and fermented Ragi cereals in the absence of nice or other eatables in the Kashipur Development Block of Roygada district of Orissa in September 2001. And recall the historic promise of India's first Prime Minister Pandit Nehru on the mid night of August 15, 1947, in which he had set the goals of "ending poverty and ignorance and disease and inequality of opportunities". Now have the objectives been achieved after more than half a century of planned economic development in Independent India? Why starvation deaths now?

Let us go through some statistical data on the checkered history of the pangs of poverty suffered by the people of India. In this connection it is worthwhile recalling that poverty is generally measured by three methods, viz. (1) head count ratio or percentage of population below the poverty line (BPL), (2) poverty gap index or depth of poverty among the poverty stricken population as compared with those above the poverty line and (3) squared poverty gap index or severity of poverty sensitive to inequality among the BPL group itself.[1] Poverty may also prevail for a transient period, say, for a particular period after exhaustion of harvested food grains till the harvest of new crops. Poverty may also be chronic for a long time. In our country as well as in other developing countries "food poverty method" is generally used in terms of monthly per capita consumer expenditure (MPCE) or its equivalent income which should rise from year to year along with rise in the consumer price index. We simply cite below the percentages of BPL population for different years as estimated by different authorities.

Indian Poverty Scenario

The poverty line in our country moves in a zigzag way rising and falling in different years from the base year of 1951-52 with a long term tendency to fall, although the real number of BPL population shows an upward trend as given in Table 1.

Table 1: Poverty in India during 1951-52 to 1999-2000

Sl. No.	*Year*	*Rural %*	*Urban %*	*Combined %*	*Real Number*
1.	Aug 1951-Nov 1952	47.37	35.46	45.46	164.11 million
2.	July. '54-Mar '55	64.24	46.19	61.07	-
3.	Sept '61 -Jul '62	47.20	43.55	46.54	177.00 million
4.	Jul '66-Jun '67	64.30	52.24	62.00	-
5.	Jul '70-Jun '71	54.84	44.98	52.88	-
6.	Oct '73-Jun '74	55.72	47.96	54.10	321.30 million
7.	Jul '86-Jun '87	38.81	34.29	37.69	-
8.	Jul '89-Jun '90	34.30	33.40	34.07	-
9.	Jul '93-Jun '94	36.66	30.51	35.04	320.30 million
10.	Jan '97-Dec '97	35.69	29.99	34.40	-
11.	Jul '99-Jun 2000	36.35	28.76	34.42	337.63 million

Source: Sl. No.1 to 10, *World Bank, India: Reducing Poverty, Accelerating Development*, Oxford, 2000.
Sl. No.11, Sundaram K., *EPW*, August 11/2001, Table 10, p. 3049. Real Numbers of 1951-52 and 1999-2000 are calculated by us.

The data in the table show that rural BPL population was 47.37 per cent in 1951-52 which while falling during next few years had risen to 64.24 per cent in 1954-55, then again falling by certain points rose to 64.30 per cent in 1966-67. Hereafter with a certain percentage point falls, again rose to 55.72 per cent in 1973-74 and thereafter with a tendency to fall reached 35.69 per cent in 1997 and again rose to 36.35 per cent in 1999-2000. In urban poverty also almost the same trend is visible, starting with 35.46 per cent in 1951-52 it was gradually rising to reach the highest of 52.24 per cent in 1966-67 from which point it is gradually started falling the step of 28.76 per cent in 1999-2000. The combined poverty data with the starting point of 45.46 per cent in 1951-52 had risen to 61.07 per cent in 1954-55 after some percentage fall, then with a downward trend, took again an upward trend in 1966-67 and reached 62.00 per cent from which it started coming down with minor variations to reach 34.42 per cent in 1999-2000. But as total population of the country was rising every year, the number of poverty stricken population had increased from 153.56 million in 1951-52 to 337.63 million in 1999-2000.

For finding out year wise real BPL number difficulty is non-availability of data. Hence we use the 1951 census population of 361 million 45.46 per cent of which gives the real number of 164.11 million. In 1961-62 the BPL population according to Profs. Dandekar and Rath was 177 million (·135 + 42 million rural and urban).[2] As per estimates of the Expert group on Estimation[3], the real number of poor was 321.30 million in 1973-74 which came down to 320.30 million in 1993-94. For 1999 -2000 poverty data, it is worthwhile to mention that the results of the 55th round of NSS Sample Survey of Monthly Per Capita Consumer Expenditure have been published. Poverty line on the basis of per capita monthly expenditure has been fixed by experts at Rs. 335.46 for rural and at Rs. 451.19 for urban areas. On the basis of this poverty line it has been estimated that 36.35 per cent of rural and 28.76 per cent of urban population lived below the line[4] in 1999-2000. India's population during the year was less than one billion and supposing it to be 980 million with a rural-urban divide[5] of 75: 25, total BPL number stands at 337. 63 million with rural-urban combined percentage of 34.45 . This implies that 173.52 million more poverty stricken population over 164.11 million of 1951-52 were added, in other words, the number of poor has increased by more than 2 times over the last fifty years.

Poverty in Assam

Now we collate some poverty data pertaining to Assam. The data presented in Table 2 reveal that rural poverty in Assam is some times 2 to 3 times higher than urban poverty. It may be noted that poverty in Assam was a little bit less than the national average of 46.54 per cent (Assam 45.9 1) in 1958, but after 1977-78 it started rising above the national average and in 1993-94 while in India 35.04 per cent of the population was below the poverty cut off line, in Assam the percentage was 52.47, i.e. 17.43 points higher than the national average. Likewise in 1999-2000 too Assam's percentage of poverty stricken people was higher by 20.38 points (National 34.42% and Assam 54.80%). This gives a very grim picture of the performance of the Assam government in poverty alleviation programmes, rather Assam is said to be the worst performer.[6] As the data in the table shows, the real BPL number had increased by 4.49 times during 1958 to 1999-2000 from 31.98 to 143.67 lakhs.

Table 2: Assam: Percentage of BPL population and the Real Number

SL No.	Year	Rural	Urban	Combined	Number
1	1958-00	37.32	16.49	32.11	31.98 Lakhs
2	1961-62	47.67	23.37	45.91	49.76 "
3	1970-71	-50.36	19.00	47.59	70.69 "
4	1973-74	52.67	37.16	51.23	81.87 "
5	1977-78	59.82	37.58	57.63	104.25 "
6	1983-00	42.60	26.38	40.86	87.35 "
7	1987-88	39.35	17.34	36.84	85.44 "
8	1993-94	58.25	10.13	52.41	124.25 "
9	1999-2000	61.78	12.45	54.80	143.67 "

Source: Sl. No. 1, Jha, Raghabendra, Sl. No. 2, Dandekar and Rath, Sl. No. 3, Minhas et.al., Sl. No. 4 to 7 Alagh, Sl. No.8 and 9 Sundaram; EPW, different issues. Real Numbers of 1 and 9 calculated by us.

As per a Rural Survey by the Directorate of Rural Development and Panchayat[7] with 1997-98 as reference year 2,028,058 rural families out of 3,412,506 implying 59.43 per cent were below the poverty line at Rs. 280.85 monthly per capita income. In terms of total BPL persons, the real numbers come to 101.40 lakhs @ of 5 persons per household. Had the monthly per capita income been raised to the prices of the reference year, the BPL percentage and number would probably have been higher than the given percentage and number.

The Departmental Survey, however, throws light on the BPL classes of households which is very much relevant in the context of rural development programmes undertaken by the government since the launching of Community Development Projects in Oct. 1952. The Survey shows that among the SC and ST communities 259316 and 428337 families respectively were under the poverty line and they constituted respectively 12.78 per cent and 21.12 per cent of all the BPL families and 7.59 per cent and 12.55 per cent of total rural households. It may be recalled that SC and ST population of the state constitute respectively.around 8 per cent and 13 per cent of the total population. The poverty data show that almost all the SC and ST population were below the poverty line in spite of spending crores of rupees in the name of their development.

Apart from caste and tribe criteria, identification of BPL families on the basis of occupational classes, the worst impact of poverty was found among the small and marginal farmers, rural artisans and agricultural labours. Out of the total BPL families, small and marginal farmers form respectively 18.79 per cent and 30.22 per cent while rural artisans and agricultural labours constitute respectively 8.64 per cent, and 38.05 per cent The data show that marginal farmers and agricultural labours are the worst victims of poverty, their combined (1,384,796 families) ratio of total BPL families comes to 68.28 percentage out of 2,028,58 BPL households or they constitute 40.58 per cent of all the rural households.

As regards distribution of consumer expenditure among the poor or what is called depth of poverty some insight may be had from the NSS 55th Round of 1999-2000 results. Households up to monthly per capita consumer expenditure of Rs. 300 (BPL expenditure need is Rs. 335.46) in rural Assam constitute 17.4 per cent in the year under reference while 8.8 per cent could afford only a monthly per capita expenditure of Rs. 255 which shows the severity of poverty of rural poor households. Likewise among the urban households with monthly per capita expenditure of Rs. 425 (BPL need is Rs. 451.19) constitute 11.7 per cent of the poor and expenditure up to Rs. 350 i.e. the worst effected, the ratio stands at 5.2 of the total urban poor.[8] It is interesting to note that the top 5.1 per cent of rural households could afford to spend Rs. 775 and more per month per head in Assam as against 9.9 per cent of the Indian top rural households. In urban Assam 11.4 per cent of the households could afford a per capita expenditure of Rs. 1500 and more per month as against 14.4 Indian urban households affording the expenditure. The low percentage of both rural and urban rich household as compared with the corresponding Indian rich households are also indicative of comparative low level of living standard on the one side and unequal distribution of income on the other in the country as a whole.

Income Distribution

Anyway, why so many poverty stricken people in the state after more than half a century of Independence with the slogan of *Garibi Hatao*? Let us look at the growth of state domestic product of Assam at current prices *vis-a-vis* growth of population. The SDP of Assam in 1950-51 was Rs. 254.4 crores and it had risen to 25, 333 crores in 1999-2000 or it had increased by more than 100 times; her population in 1951 was 80 lakhs from which it had risen to 260 lakhs in 1999-2000 or by only 3.25 times. Likewise her per capita income had risen from Rs. 318 in 1951 to Rs. 10811 in 1999-2000. Average annual per capita income necessary for poverty level in rural Assam of cultivators, agricultural labours and fishers, is around Rs.4000. Now, where has the excess income over Rs. 4000 (10800-4000) has gone? One part of it has, no doubt, gone outside the state through several channels like company dividends, remittances, interest payments on public loans, deposit mobilization by the financial institutions, import bill etc. and the other part has filled the pockets of the rich through the process of income distribution in the state and the country as a whole. Certainly, "Casting the issues of poverty in terms of stratification leads to regarding poverty as an issue of inequality". And the Nobel Laureate Prof. A. K. Sen hesitatingly accedes that "inequality and poverty are not, of course unrelated".[9]

No doubt, poverty, we assert is related to income distribution, but income distribution itself is dependent on distribution of the means of production. Land as means of production is an important factor for peasant households, particularly for small and marginal farmers and agricultural labours. The civil society while emphasizing the right to private property, overlooks the land problem of these three classes of the population. These classes of people having what is called "own labour entitlement" to exchange labour with nature, lack what Prof. Sen calls "production based entitlement" i.e. to apply their labour power to till the land which is either absent or insufficient for producing their sustenance; the agricultural labour in particular remains underemployed for lack of jobs to hire themselves out. It is also well known that with increasing population pressure and land getting divided and sub-divided and at the same time being alienated by mortgage and sale to meet exigencies, the small and marginal farmers (leave aside the landless agricultural labours and rural artisans) can not be provided with the right to an optimum plot of cultivable land. And this is what is called the proletarianisation process in Marxian terms, that is a section of the population loses the means of production in a civil society boasting of the right to private property. In the situation the only alternative besides land reform measures for land to the tillers, is to provide these classes of people with off-farm occupations either as self-employed or wage employed in the form of modern rural industries, social overhead capital construction as well as modem agricultural farms for creation of additional employment avenues.[10]

Relativity of Poverty Concept

Poverty, besides its calorie intake criterion , has several other aspects like health, life expectancy, sanitation, housing conditions, skill development through education etc. The concept of poverty is also relative to the standard of living of a particular community in a given geo-climatic environment. Needless to emphasise that the advertising media in combination with the demonstration effect have created psychological conditions in communities even in remote areas of the global village for satisfaction of new needs and wants. Failure to fulfill these new needs and wants create a sense of deprivation and poverty as compared with those few who are enjoying those bundles of commodities. In other words "poverty is born of super-abundance itself" even in rich societies; "accumulation of wealth at one pole is accumulation of misery at another pole". "Our wants and pleasures", says Marx, have their origins in society, we therefore measure them in relation to society. No doubt, the pleasures of the common man has increased today to a great extent, but their gratification affordable as compared with the rich, has fallen due, what Adam Smith said, to "wherever there is a great property, there is a great inequality". "For one very rich man, there must be at least five hundred poor and the affluence of a few supposes indigence of the many". Hence poverty alleviation calls for changing the property relations of the civil society so as to equalise the gratifications between the poor and non-poor with a view to establishing a harmonious human society free from egoism, greed and lust for power so that the tendency to regression of man to the level of animal is checked.

REFERENCES

1. (A) Ravallion, M. & Dutta, G., *EPW*, Special Number, Sept. 1996, p. 2479.

   (B) UNDP, *Human Development Report*, 1997, Oxford, p. 13

2. Dandekar, V.M. & Rath, N, *EPW*, Jan 2,1971, pp. 31-32
3. Ninth Five Year Plan, Vol. 1, Govt. of India, Table 1.9, p. 27
4. Sudaram, K., *EPW*, August 11, 2001, Table 11, p. 3048
5. NSS 55th Round, Level and Pattern of Consumer Expenditure in India, 1999-2000, 2001, p. 16.
6. Sundaram, K., op. cit., p. 3048.
7. Directorate of Rural Development and Panchayat, *BPL Survey Abstract 1997*-98 (Memeo).
8. NSSO; *Level and Patern of Consumer Expenditure in India*, 2001, Statement 2R and 2U, pp. 32-33
9. Sen, A.K., *Poverty and Famine*, Oxford, 1999, pp. 14-15
10. Baishya, P., Rural Industrialisation for Poverty Eradication. InSamanta, R.K. (ed.), *Rural Development of North East India*, Uppal Publishing House, Delhi, 1991, p. 43
11. Adam Smith quoted at length in Luico Colletti, *From Rausseau to Lenin*, Monthly Review Press, New York, 1974, p. 171

REFLECTION ON DEVELOPMENT OF NORTH-EASTERN REGION

23

RURAL DEVELOPMENT
Nagaland Experience

Chandrika Singh

Rural development according to the World Bank publication, is a process to improve "living standard of the masses of the low income population residing in rural areas making the rural development process self-sustaining." The rural development policies are generally designed "to improve the condition under which the rural people live and work." The priority of the Indian planners has been to gear up Indian economy through centralised macro-level planning putting greater emphasis on industrial and agricultural development. So far the rural development is concerned there was the policy "to grow more food" which benefited big farmers only. The need and significance to incorporate the poor sections of the people in the process of development was seriously felt from the seventies onwards with the shifting of the approach to the planning from centralised to decentralised and macro to micro. The Panchayati Raj system based on the recommendation of the Mehata Committee was introduced all over the country. The purpose of the decentralised planning, in the word of Kartar Singh, was to adopt "concrete and operational programmes and projects taking into consideration the peculiar characteristics and requirements of the district block concern."[1] This became a movement "which permits the wider involvement of people in the process of planning and implementation and reduces discrepancies."

The launching of the Community Development Programme (CDP) in 1956 and creation of some Block Development Offices were the moves to help the Indian farmers and develop small scale industries, but bureaucratic interference in the affairs of village development and non-commitment of the concerned government official to the rural areas did not allow the CDP to achieve the desired objectives. According to B.B. Mishra, "Those who were expected to act as pioneers in a new venture of nation- building become mere cogs in the traditional bureaucratic machine, loosing all sense of drive and initiative."[2] The Mehta Committee, too, found that the CDP had failed to establish contact with rural people and encourage them to participate in rural development planning and implementation.[3] That is why the committee recommended for three tier Panchayati Raj Institution based on the principle of decentralization of power to play dynamic roles in rural development.[4]

The call of the World Bank for redistribution of income combined with "growth-oriented policies" and realization of the government of Mrs Indira Gandhi that some viable steps must be taken up to improve the vulnerable conditions of the rural people reflected in the Fifth Five Years Plan (1974-79).[5] Mrs Gandhi's government with the slogan of '*Garbi Hatao*' declared 'war on poverty.'[6] The Planning Commission, came forward with new strategies and plans to cope with the policies of the government in relation to the rural development.[7] Thus the rural development was redefined as a "strategy, a design to improve the economic and social life of a specific group of people living in rural areas."[8] The Integrated Rural Development Programme (IRDP) was launched and the Sixth Plan emphasized the IRDP as 'single largest anti-poverty programme covering various aspects of rural life and opening wide scope for people's participation in the development administration. The IRDP covered the rural areas through optimum development and utilization of local resources - physical, biological and human bringing 5 necessary institutional changes by developing a package of service to encompass not only the economic field but also the establishment of the required social infrastructure and services in the areas of health and nutrition etc.[9] The Planning Commission reiterated its commitment for giving "a practical shape to the nation's collective will for using all the latent resource and energies of the nation for an effective attack on poverty, unemployment and inequality."[10]

The District Rural Development Agency (DRDA) was made a special agency capable of managing anti-poverty programmes of the Ministry of Rural Development and also a coordinating agency to effectively relate rural development programmes to the overall efforts of poverty eradication in the district. The IRDP came under the control and supervision of the DRDA with its all components such as National Rural Employment (NREP), Rural Landless Employment Programme (RLEP), Training of Rural Youth for Self-Employment (TRYSEM) etc. Thereafter a new Yojana, namely, the Jawahar Rojgar Yojana (JRY) appeared with the marked objective "to provide fuller employment opportunities to at least one member of each family living below the poverty line who seek unskilled employment," and to "ensure the fuller participation of the people in implementation."[11]

The programmes for rural development launched before the advent of the IRDP such as SFDA, MFAL, DPAP, HADP, TADP, CSRD, FFW etc. launched during the Fourth and Fifth Plans had increased the gap between the rich and the poor. Stating the cause of non-satisfactory performances of the programmes, the Programmes Evaluation Organisation of the Planning Commission said that most of the agencies neither exercised proper care in electing beneficiaries nor in ensuring extension of service or supporting facilities. Agricultural labourers have been almost totally neglected in the matter of credit.[12] Moreover, there was lack of sufficient funds and proper technical skill.[13] But then the IRDP was launched, both the sufficient funds and technical skills were provided. This time special care was taken for the people belonging to the Scheduled castes and the Scheduled Tribes.[14] During the regime of the National Democratic Alliance led by the Bhartiya Janta Party, the Swarnjayanti Gram Swarozgar Yojana (SGSY) was launched in April 1999 which has replaced the earlier self- employment and allied programmes aiming at "establishing a large number of micro-enterprises in the rural areas" offering "perfect balance of credit and subsidy.'[15] Among the Swarozgaris at least 50% must be the scheduled Castes and Scheduled women and 3% disabled. At the same time a new Yojana, namely, Samagra Awas Yojana was launched to "improve the quality of life of people and overall habitat in the rural areas. Another Yojana called as Jawahar Gram Samridhi Yojana, stands for "creation of demand driven community village infrastructure including durable assets at the village level and assets to enable the rural poor to increase the opportunities for employment," and also "generation of supplementary employment for the unemployed poor in the rural area."[16]

The Indira Awas Yojana (IAY) is a beneficiary-oriented programme aimed at providing houses for SC/ST households who are victims of atrocities, households headed by widows/unmarried women or who are below the poverty line. Sufficient amount is provided free of cost from the government to construct new *pucca* houses. All these programmes are centrally sponsored and they are funded on cost- sharing basis between the government of India and the states in the ratio of 75:25.

Under the direction issued by the Central government, Nagaland took up the initiative to launch various rural development programmes. The Department of Rural development set up the DARA and in lieu of the Village Panchayat, the Village Council and the Village Development Board (VDB) were allowed to work for the implementation of programmes sponsored by the centre. The VDB "incorporates the ingredients of traditional wisdom and at the same time is in tune with the needs and requirements of modern societies.[17] There are Common Fund Committee and Village Social Security Trust under the Village Council which used to deal with village development affairs. The Common Fund Committee was later converted into the Village Development Board which has become the core village body having its own Management Committee headed by the Deputy Commissioner or the Additional Deputy Commissioner. The Secretary of the Committee is a literate villager who has been assigned dominant role in handling the case and distribution of loan among the villagers.

Matching Grants released by the Government of Nagaland to the VDB equal to the amount raised by the Common Fund of the villagers and the fund allotted by the central government to implement various centrally sponsored programmes are two main source of income of the VDB. According to the provision the amount is kept in the bank in the form of fixed deposit and it cannot be withdrawn except interests. Power and responsibility of the Secretary has made him more influential. He maintains all records regarding VDB schemes, money drawn, loans issued against fixed deposit security, manners of utilisation of interests amount and other issues. It is he who deals the development matters along with the district authorities related to the rural development. The Deputy Commissioner, the Block Development Officers, members of the District Planning Board and the Rural Development Department of Nagaland are involved in giving practical shape to the policies and programmes of rural development. The planning process begins at the grass-root level where the Gram Sabha plays vital role. The VDB sends the formulated schemes to the BDO who after scrutiny forwards them to the District Planning Board. The Department of the Rural Development lastly approves the schemes and sanctions funds. After obtaining a completion certificate from the BDO the required money is withdrawn from the bank.

The main priority of development works in Nagaland have been to construct community halls, playgrounds, community latrines, waiting shade, village approach road, primary school buildings, running of community buses, dairy, piggery and poultry farms and development of small scale industries. There is provision to grant sufficient loans to the villagers for initiating personal schemes like tea and coffee plantation etc. All the schemes and Yojana for generation of self-employment run in the state. Under the Indira Awas Yojana and Samgra Awas Yojana lakhs of rupees have been sanctioned. The objective of the Matching Grant is not only "the resource that the VDB could mobilize but also the judicious utilisation of resources for gainful purposes."[18] In Nagaland the VDB has assumed the status of Non-Banking Financial Institute and has become "a popular agency to give effect to newly launched multi-dimensional programme like JRY, JGSY, SGSY, IAY, etc. It is true various schemes and programmes of rural development in states of India have provided economic relief to the rural people, but the targets fixed and objectives prescribed have not been achieved so far. The study of rural development progemmes brings the fact to the light that the development benefits have mostly been accrued to the people who are economically better off, socially high-ups and politically advantageous. The Sixth Plan's report reveals the fact that " much of the benefits from infrastructure have accrued largely to the relatively affluent. Scheduled Castes and Tribes have not shared fully the benefit growth."[20] Bribery, malpractice and embezzlement of funds came on the way to block the progress of rural development. Despite the efforts to alleviate poverty it has continued to grow at faster rate because of high concentration of wealth in the hands of corrupt and selfish members of the society. Nagaland economy like other states of India has moved towards polarisation of social fabrics. Only a few affluent Naga families have been lucky enough to enrich themselves because "the income distribution flow of capital, concentration of economic power contains to be in favour of the upper income brackets in the rural and urban areas."[21] The development process in Nagaland has widened the gap between the rich and the poor. The state has developed and the society has changed, no doubt, but real beneficiaries are those who have successfully maneuvered to exploit economic machinery of the state to serve their private ends. The poor sections of the people are yet deprived of even essential daily requirements.

The VDB in Nagaland has lost much of its initial momentum. In the words of R.K. Misra, "the initial emphoria was over, the level of interests and extent of participation by the administration waved."[22] This is all because "BDOs, EACs, SDOs, do not take as much tour of the villages under their preview as expected of them."[23] The Naga villagers lack the spirit of professionalism and they are still ignorant of the real process and procedures of the development. No effort has been made to make them aware of emerging new opportunities of the rural development programmes. Only a few conscious, developed and alert Naga families are real beneficiaries. R.K. Misra who had been the Commissioner and Secretary of Rural Development of Nagaland is of the view that " due mainly to the short circulation of procedures by the Secretary and VDB members, often in collusion with the EBOs' the villagers do not avail chance to participate in scheme formulations and in their implementation.[24] The rural people of Nagaland are "not able to exercise control over the VDB Secretary and other members do not feel themselves accountable to the people."[25] There is some elements of truth in the statement of Hokishe Sema, the Ex-Chief Minister of Nagaland which inter liter alia says that "Nagaland's process of development has stopped. What exists today are dilapidated run-down symbols of the efforts made in the sixties and early seventies."[26]

REFERENCES

1. Kartar Singh, *Rural Development: Principles, Policies and Management* (Sage Publications, New Delhi, 1986, p. 266.
2. B.B. Misra, *Government and Bureaucracy in India, 1947-76*, New Delhi, 1986, pp. 121-351.
3. Seventh Evaluation Report on Community Development and Allied Fields Progression, Planning Commission, Govt. of India, New Delhi, 1960, pp. 121-35.
4. Report of Mehta Committee for the Study of Community Project, National Extension Service, Vol. 1, New, November, 1957, pp. 5-7.
5. See Chenery H., *Redistribution with Growth : Essay in Honor of B.H. Farmer*, Oxford University Press, London, 1974.
6. Ganguli, *Studies in Indian Economic Problems*, Calcutta, 1980, p. 700.
7. *ibid.*
8. B.B. Mathai, "Organisation Design for Rural Development in North-East Region," P.D. Saikia and U. Phukan, (eds), Delhi, 1989, p. 49.

9. G.P. Bhave, "Institutional Finance and Integrated Rural Development," *Kurukhestra*, Vol. XXIX, No.20, July 16-31, 1981, Bombay, p.5.

10. Planning Commission, Government of India, Sixth Five-Year Plan (1980-85), New Delhi, 1981, p. 32.

11. Jawahar Rojgar Yojana: A Manual, Department of Rural Development, Govt. of India, August, 1989, pp. 4-5.

12. Report on Evaluation Study of Small farmers and marginal Farmers and Agricultural Labour Projects (1974-75), New Delhi, 1979, p. 14.

13. Dantwal, Working Group's Report on Block Level Planning, Planning Commission, Govt. of India, 1970, p. 15.

14. Jawahar Rojgar Yojana: a Manual, op. cit. p. 1.

15. Swarnjayanti Gramin Swarojgar Yojana, Ministry of Rural Development, Govt. of India, 1999, p.1

16. *ibid.*

17. B.P. Maithai and A.R. Rizwana, *Decentralised Development*, National Institute of Rural Development, Hyderabad, 1999, p.1.

18. Information furnished by Mr Hello Rengn a, Project Director, Govt. of Nagaland through a Pamphlet, Mokokchung, 2001.

19 C. Sriniwass Shastry, "Structure and Pattern of Panchayati Raj", Indian Journal of Public Administration, Vol, VIII, No 4, October, December, 1962, p. 460.

20. T. Roy, "Some Thought on Community Participation", *Kurukshetra*, Vol. XXXI, May 16-29, 1983, p. 18.

21. R.N. Wali, "Indian Development Process: Parameters of Development in North-East India". In: V.S. Mahajan, (ed), *Emerging Pattern of North-East Economy*, Deep Publications, New Delhi, 1987, pp. 52-53.

22. R.K. Misra, "Accountability Counts in Rural Development", Nagaland Page, Easter Clarion (Dimapur), August 18,1997, p.5.

23. *ibid.*

24. *ibid.*

25. Maithai B.P. and Rizwana A.R., *Decenteralised Development*, op. cit., p. 69.

26. Hokishe Sema, "Reformation at all cost", *Nagaland Page*, August, 18, 1997, p. 5.

24

DEVELOPMENT OF NORTH-EASTERN REGION
Some Issues to Ponder

Kishore S. Rajput

It is often argued that rapid economic development, supported by sound political measures, can solve the problem of socio-political instability of the North-Eastern Region (NER). But, unfortunately, for a long time the north-east (NE) economy has been trapped in the vicious circle of socio-political instability and underdevelopment. These two forces have been acting and reacting in such a manner that they have not allowed the NE economy to get out of this circle. The vicious circle in the NE is just like what Prof. Higgins said, Each of the characteristic has a 'hen and egg' nature that makes it virtually impossible to separate 'causes' from 'effects'."

Application of the Theory of Big Push looks a sound policy to break this cycle. But the million-dollar question is where from that huge investment will come? The private sector is always guided by profit motive. In the present circumstance when the investors are not sure of safety of their money, the flow of private investments, both domestic and foreign, is and will remain low.

Further discourages the investors the poor level of infra-infrastructures that exists in the NER. Therefore, if this massive dose of investment has to come, it has to come from the public sector. The public sector, therefore, shall have to play the role of senior partner in the development process of the NER. But after the launch of the marker friendly Liberalisation-Privatisation-Globalisation (LPG) policy, the government has been citing resources stringency as a convenient reasons for diluting its direct development role and, hence, the public sector's role has narrowed down significantly in the post-1991 period. So public investment has been wantonly cut in the last decade. But as in the period of increasing public investment (1951-1991), the NE economy did not get equal treatment from the centre vis-a-vis other states of India, the discriminatory policy should, therefore, still continue in the period of withdrawal of public sector activities. But the only difference now that should take place is that the public sector now must focus on the backward states for investment while withdrawing its activities from the developed states. However even with the most optimistic level of expectation, the public sector investment will not be that large enough to break this cycle.

So if this cycle has to be broken, then the emphasis should be placed on creation of a congenial environment for investment that can help in the inflow of domestic and foreign investment in the long run. For that we have to focus our attention more and more to those projects that can sufficiently be undertaken with the help of the internal resources of the NER plus addressing some other issues of political and administrative importance. As far as the public sector investment (central) is concerned, they mainly should be channelised for the speedy completion of the much needed infrastructure projects like construction of roadways, railways, bridges, dams, hydel power plants, etc. which are considered as the basic prerequisites for economic development. Along with this, some of the issues that are quite crucial for the long-term development of the NER are as follows:

Social Sector Development

The NE states must have rapid social sector development; especially in the field of education and health as these are two importance indicators of overall welfare of the people plus an educated and healthy society works as a catalyst to speed up the entire development process. Therefore, if the new liberalization policies have to bring result, then the social sector development of the NER is a basic prerequisite. This is the point Nobel .aureate Prof Amartya Sen has been emphasizing again and again. For instance, before the introduction of the economic reforms, China, where liberalization programme has bore fruits, had wiped out illiteracy and assumed minimum level of social security, including health care to its citizens (Mehta, 2001).

Self-Sufficient Agriculture Sector

Like the country's realization of the objective of the self-sufficiency in the production of food grains, the states of the NER as an individual unit, should also try to achieve this goal. This will enable these states to save valuable money for other development projects. In this respect, unfortunately, for more than three decades, the fruits of publicly funded agricultural research were primarily enjoyed by that small percentage of the farming community that was flush with cash and clout (Singh, 2001). Though already late, the NE states should try to reap the benefits of the Green Revolution strategy. For this, along with some other measures, the need of the hour is to give an easy access to the required information to the farmers.

Development of Village and Small-Scale Industries

In any strategy of self-propelled development of the NER, the village and small scale industries will always hold the key. It is in everybody's knowledge that their requirement of low investment and low entrepreneurial ability suits very much the NER. With proper planning, the local latent entrepreneurial taken as well as the indigenous capital, however meagre that may be, can be utilized for the development of these industries. However looking at the poor performance of these industries during the last 30-40 years, it can be said that the development of these industries on a healthy line is not an easy task, especially under the changed liberalised policy framework. However, due to resource stringency, if the government cannot directly participate in the development of these industries. This is far important because the existence of market imperfections in the NER do not and will not allow the forces of demand and supply to take the optimum and desirable decisions in their regard. In this age of global competition, the government, the central as well as the state, has to intervene in the following areas:

(a) First of all, the government must identify the areas of competitive strength on the basis of a comprehensive study of the economy. After that, according to the saying of the Richardian Theory of the International Trade, we shall have to specialize in the production of those commodities in which we have comparative advantage if want to weather the storm of ongoing cut-throat competition. In short, the focus should be on those industries that can survive and thrive in the long run even if the government withdraws its protection umbrella.

(b) The government should also make very sincere attempts to get worthy results from the many Entrepreneurial Development Programmes (EDPs), conducted by different agencies under government auspices. It is important that these agencies are made accountable for poor result, as their result so far has been quite dismal. For example, the overall success rate of the EDP organized in the NER during April 1990 and March 1996 was only 25.2 percent (Mali, 2001) To step up the success rate, institutes like SIDO, NISIET, NEVON, SIDC, and Directorate of Industries have to minimize the number of candidates opting for entrepreneurial career by chance. Every bit of attempt should be made to bring more and more genuine candidates into this profession. Until and unless we have this class of people with proper managerial bent of mind, the resources would remain unitized underutilized or misutilized. No one would deny the fact that the development process in the NER must have an indigenous base. Some projects might be started with outside aid to stimulate the industrialization process but this will not ensure maintenance of development in the long run. As a result the development process will falter in the absence of internal motivation (Lekhi, 1996). Therefore we must have a real class of entrepreneurs who can undertake various industrial projects to make them survive and grow.

Further for the development of SSIs, adequate and timely institutional finance is considered as a basic prerequisite. The general view of the entrepreneurs of the NER is that financial institutions are unhelpful to the small sector. There is every possibility institutions are unhelpful to the small sector. There is every possibility that they would become furthermore unhelpful as the public sector banks themselves are trying to reduce their non-performing assets (NPAs) and survive from the onslaught of the competition. Naturally the banks would look for safety and security of their funds first. Under these circumstances, the government must evolve a sound policy so that, at least, the genuine entrepreneurs are not deprived of the funds. This argument is further strengthened by the fact that the credit deposit percentage of the banks located in the NER is very low. It is just 29.9 percent, according to the Basic statistics of the NER, 2000.

The success story of the Bangladesh Grameen Bank also shows that in our development strategy, developing entrepreneurship among women should get due importance, especially among the tribal women

In 1990, there were 1166 women entrepreneurs in the NER, accounting for 15.5 percent of total entrepreneurs. This needs to be further strengthened.

(c) With the withdrawal of the quantitative restrictions with year and the likely phasing out of the reserve items exclusively meant for the SSIs, these industries have hard time ahead. If these industries have to survive, they have to be at their competitive best-price wise and quality wise. For this, along with the provision of sound infrastructure facilities, another basic prerequisite for the entrepreneurs of this region is to have an easy access to information in areas like prices and sources of raw-materials, prices of various products in the world market, development of new technology and so on. Undoubtedly the "cyber extension' would be the major form of passing these information to the target groups. In other words, the Internet is emerging as a tool with great potential to the rural development (Ghosh, 2001). Especially in the NEF, as many states have 'IT savvy' people with fluency in English, it is a big advantage for the government to disseminate useful information to the target groups. Therefore, IT should be treated like utility and "should reach everyone like electricity" (Karnik, 2001). However the challenge here is not only ti improve the accessibility of information technology but also to improve its relevance to NER economic development. Already some projects in India like the Warna Wired Village Project (Maharashtra) and the Information Village Project (Pondicherry) has successfully used IT for the benefits of the people.

(d) In this stage of liberalization, another threat that is looming large for the SSIs of the whole country is the policy of dumping resorted by many countries, including China the main threat for out industries. Besides many goods are smuggled into the country without paying appropriate vigilant in this regard. Whenever such cases are detected, the NE states must furnish the information to the appropriate authority to impose heavy anti-dumping duties because some of these items are being imported, especially from China, even below the cost of raw materials used in them (Krishna, 2001).

(e) Last but not the least, the seven sisters of the NE should come together to form a joint body to reap benefits in the areas of common interest like marketing the products, exploring the border trade opportunities, setting up R-D facilities for testing the quality of raw-materials and the products, etc.

Favourable Attitudes of the People Towards Development

Socio-cultural rigidities are very much impediments to the economic development of the NER. In the NE India, socio-cultural life is strictly based on caste, colour creed, culture and customs. By nature people are suspicious towards outside investment, however genuine that investment may be. If we are looking for the long-run economic development of the NER, then this type of attitude has to be changed. The desire to maintain socio-cultural identity should not take place at the cost of economic impoverishment. So favourable attitudes towards the movement of outside co-operate like the capital, labour and technology are a must. In the global set-up of economic development, foreign investments have become key co-operate factor in the development process of UDCs. Even a country like, China has benefited immensely from the foreign investments. To quote the Chinese sources, "The establishment of large number of joint ventures and exclusively foreign funded enterprises has brought in capital, advanced equipment and modern management expertise, greatly enhancing the technological and management level of China's industrial enterprises, enabling the production of China's manufactured goods to quickly catch up with or approach the world advanced level and increasing exports by several folds."

Furthermore a sharp desire for material betterment, a willingness to work hard in a regular and punctual manner, an awareness of the future benefits of present sacrifices are a prerequisite of economic development. We need to develop these attitudes sooner than the later. As Rober Garner stated, "Economic development or lack or it is primarily due to differences to people in their attitudes, customs, traditions and consequent differences in their differences in their political, social and religious institutions."

Administration Efficiency

In the absence of the required political will and administrative efficiency, all policy measures become meaningless. Since we are now moving more and more towards the open market economy, it is imperative that the administrative set up also changes its role-from the role of a regulator to a role of facilitator. Instead of providing helping hand to the private initiative, if it tries to put obstacles, then the attempts to have speedy economic development cannot be materialized easily. Of course to bring a supportive administrative system for the private initiative, a strong political will is required.

It is not only the availability of the natural resources that make a society developed. They need to be used properly. So it is the class of people that live in the society make its own destiny. For the development of the NER, the people here need to have the 'Never Say Die Approach' and the will to follow the 'Do by yourself' policy of the Japanese. The Japanese, without having natural resources at their stake, have reached new heights of economic development due to sheer efforts of their stake, have reached new heights of economic development due to sheer efforts of their own. Even after the mass destruction of the Second World War, they have risen like the proverbial Phoenix from the ashes. If the people of the NE can develop that type of mentality and attitude with openness to outside world, there is no reason why this region can not develop rapidly in the coming years. Just we need to bring the missing links of development, i.e., the co-operate factors of capital, technology and the strong desire for rapid economic development.

REFERENCES

Basic statistics, The North Eastern Council, Shillong.

Das, B. (2001), "Meghalaya Blips on Infotech Radar", *The Telegraph*, 2, September 2001.

Ghosh, S. (2001), "Internet and Rural and Agricultural Development: Indian Scenario", *Yojana*, Vol. 45 September 2001.

Krishna, S (2001), "Phasing Out of Important Licensing: Impact on Small scale Industries", *Economic and Political Weekly*, July 7, 2001.

Lekhi, R.K. (1995), *The Economics of Development and Planning*, Kalyani Publishers, New Delhi.

Mali, D.D. (2001), Entrepreneurship Development in North East India (Issues, and Opportunities) Unpublished Work.

Mali, D.D. and Bandopadhyay, R., *Small Industry Development in North East* (*Status and Strategy*), Omsons Publications, New Delhi.

Mehta, V. (2001), "Economic Reforms in China", *The Assam Tribune*, 5 September, 2001.

Raj, A Besant C (2001), "WTO Requirements: The Lurking Dangers", *Chartered Financial Analyst*, 2001.

Singh, S.P. (2001), "Implications of Agriculture Corporation", *The Assam Tribune*, 12, September, 2001.

25

RURAL DEVELOPMENT IN NORTH EAST INDIA: A Note

N.N. Bhattacharyya

The development is normative concept and it is defined and interpreted in different ways. It implies qualitative and quantitative improvement of human life. Generally development is equated wit economic growth measured in terms of GNP of per capita income. The economies of the present days are no more simple. They are very much specialized and complex. The rural development may be defined as a continuous process which aims at extending the benefits of development to those people whose future lies in the pursuit of a livelihood in rural areas.

Covering 2,55,082 sq km area, about 8 per cent of the country, North East India, comprising Assam, Arunachal Pradesh, Meghalaya, Manipur, Nagaland, Tripura and Mizoram is endowed with a long and colourful history. The region is connected with the mainland by a narrow corridor of foothill land in North Bengal and its terrain conditions like tertiary mountains and hills, mountain basis, Archaean plateaus and river valleys Archaean make it an extremely isolated regions. The climate of North East India may be identified as tropical monsoon with local variations. The terrain conditions, soil types, rainfall, humidity and temperature conditions of the region support an altitudinally distributed vegetations which provide habitats and inches for different varieties of animals. North East India is endowed with minerals like petroleum, coal, limestone, sillimanite and a large reservoir of hydel power potential.

The region as a whole with heterogeneous environmental setting supports a total population of 38.50 million with the highest in Assam having 26.64 million or 68.2% of the populations of the region and the lowest in Mizoram with 0.89 million or about 2 per cent of the region's populations. Similarly the region shows variation of density of population from 340 persons per square kilometer in Assam to only 13 per square kilometer in Arunachal Pradesh with an average of 149 for the whole region. This geographical framework of the region has direct bearing on the development scenario of the states of North East India.

The development of North East India is essèntially meant rural development because about 85 per cent of its people in rural areas. But the development scenario in the rural areas of all the states of the region is very much sad. It is now believed that most of the rural development strategies, so far adopted, have only widened of gap between the have and have not pushing down a greater number of rural people to poverty and unemployment. Perhaps there is a lack of empirical knowledge to help policy makers determine how best to use limited development funds to produce most desired result.

Prior to 1947, Indian economy was extremely backward. The nature and characteristics of such economy were predominance of agriculture, low per capita income and extreme poverty, low food consumption, illiteracy and shortage of organizational skill, high population pressure and poor standard of living. For the last 55 years, various efforts have been made to remove the evils of poverty, unemployment, illiteracy etc. and to increase the agricultural and industrial output. But due to populations growth, poor technique of production and other causes, the results and fruits of developments have not made a distinct impact.

In the first two decades of the planed era (1950s and 1960s), Indian planners placed high hopes on the trickle-down mechanism but this mechanism not only failed to eradicate poverty, rather it increased its intensity, the planers adopted four broad types of programmes in stages to eradicate poverty. These programmes were (1) resource and income development programme, (2) special area development programmes (3) employment generation programmes, such as NREP, RLEGP, TRYSEM and food for work programme and (4) the Minimum Needs Programme. All these programmes did not cover the whole country and their operations also overlapped. Therefore a single integrated programme entitled 'Integrated Rural Development Programme' (IRDP) had been introduced since Sixth Plan period. Several shortcomings have been found in this programme and so suitable changes were introduced in the guidelines of the IRDP. These programmes adopted for rural development have started showing results in positive directions in different parts of India. But in North East India their impacts are not felt at desired level.

The study area is bestowed with better environmental and soil climatic conditions favourable for agricultural development but the progress is very slow due to non-availability of agricultural inputs like quality seeds, fertilizers and modem technology. At the end of the Third Plan a New Strategy of Agricultural Development was adopted in 1964-65 which ushered in the era of Green Revolution in India. According to this strategy emphasis has been given to provide packages of new technology, services including high yielding varieties of seeds, pesticides, fertilizers, irrigation facilities etc. to increase agricultural production. In order to introduce this strategy seven districts were selected and these were: West Godavari (Andhra Pradesh), Shahabad (Bihar), Raipur (undivided Madhya Pradesh), Tanjavur (Tamil Nadu), Ludhiana (Punjab), Aligarh (Utter Pradesh) and Pali (Rajasthan). The first four districts were selected for rice, fifth and sixth for wheat and seventh for millet. But not a single district has been selected for this purpose from North East India. Thus the impact of green revolution has not been felt so far in this region.

The scheme for rural development must concern with the development of agriculture and allied activities, revive the village industries on the basis of locality available raw material and labour. An integrated rural development strategy requires that all natural, socio-economic and institutional relationship and their changes over time be combined in such a way so as to extend the benefits of the development to people living in the rural areas.

REFERENCES

Heredero, J.M. (1979), *Rüral Development and Social* Change, New Delhi.

Ministry of Finance, Economic Division *Economic Survey,* 1993-94.

The Hindu, *Survey of India Agriculture,* 1994.

Elsenhands, H. (1991), *Development and Underdevelopment*, Constance University, Germany.

26

RURAL DEVELOPMENT
A Vision that Failed the Mission

B.P. Sahu

Development implies planned institutional changes so as to bring a better fit between the social resources on one hand and the social policy on the other. Development does not mean only economic growth but also equitable distribution of the fruits of economic growth with social Justice. According to Prof. Gangrade, economic development without social development is no development The overall objective of any developmental programme is to ensure better quality of life for its people through better health, education, housing and welfare facilities. It envisages to remove inequality and poverty, increase material and social prosperity, equitable distribution of resources based upon distributive justice, removal of disparities, participation in decision making and enhancement of technology to bring in wide range of services for a better quality of life.

The indicators of development of any country are the level of income of the people, type of technology and level of productivity in terms of industrialisation, level of employment, nutrition, health, housing, literacy and welfare status of the people, and status of women in a country. An alternative measure, the physical quality life index (PQLI) is also used as a measure of development. This takes into account the life expectancy at age one, infant mortality and literacy as major indicators.

Historical Perspectives of Development in India

Development is a long run phenomenon, which requires adequate planning to achieve the short term and long-term goals. Plan is a conscious attempt to achieve the set of objectives that it has set for itself. India after independence decided to opt for a planned course towards development and launched the first five-year plan in the year 1951-56. It was only in the second five-year plan; emphasis was given to establishment of heavy and strong infrastructure like steel plants and power projects. The ultimate aim was to establish such infrastructures, which would help in establishing small-scale industries in future. By late 60's, it was realised that agriculture was lagging behind and that the country faced an acute shortage of food grains. Therefore, the Green Revolution was introduced in the late 60s. However by the end of 70s it became clear that both the strategies have failed to address the problem of the poor. It was then that the concept of a 'direct attack on poverty' was first emphasised. The Integrated Rural Development Programme (IRDP) was brought into being. During the Seventh Plan the major thrust was on "Food", Work and Productivity.

Rural Development

The rural economy and social structure in our country is characterised by widespread poverty, poor health conditions, illiteracy, exploitation, inequitable distribution of land, lack of infrastructure and public facilities like road and communication. The various dimensions of rural life - growth in agriculture and allied activities, rural industrialisation, education, health, public works, poverty alleviation and rural employment programmes all form a part of integrated approach for the problem of rural development.

Rural development takes into account factors other than economic growth i.e. Education, health facilities, social infrastructure facilities, employment generation, increase in productivity, distributive Justice and equalisation of opportunities in rural areas.

Rural development programmes involve a number of rural development projects. It envisaged bringing changes in various facets of rural economic and social life. But the greatest challenge of Rural Development Programmes lies in its implementation aspects, specially so, in India whose rural population is large, widely dispersed and with varied socioeconomic and natural endowments.

Community Development Programme and Rural Development

In order to give a fillip to the integrated approach to the Rural Development programmes, the community development programme was launched in October 1952 with the following objectives -

1. To secure total development of the material and the human resources of rural areas.
2. To develop local leadership and self-governing institution.
3. To raise the living standard of the rural people by means of rapid increase in food and agricultural produce.
4. To ensure a change in mental outlook of the people, instilling in them an ambition for higher standards.

Initially CDP covered 55 projects with a wide range of programmes for developing agriculture, animal husbandry, rural industries, health, education, housing and rural communication. Each project consisted of 3500 villages with total coverage of 1280 sq. km. with 3,00,000 population. In the first five year plan 1060 blocks were covered, by the end of second plan, the coverage was 31 1 0 blocks (368200 villages) and by the end of third plan all the blocks were covered. The CDP was instrumental in laying the foundations for the development of rural economy of India.

In the third five-year plan, Intensive Agricultural Development Programme (IADP, 1961) and Intensive Agricultural Area Programme (IAAP, 1964) was introduced. IAAP was just expansion of IADP. The IADP programme concentrated mainly on three components, viz., high investment in agricultural production, higher prices for agricultural produce, and modern technological inputs. Then there was introduction of HYV Programme, which ultimately led to the 'Green Revolution' in India.

In the fourth five-year plan, under privileged farmers and areas prone to drought were also covered. Special programmes like Drought Prone Areas Programme (1970), Cash Scheme for Rural Employment (1971), Tribal Area Development (1975), Small Farmers Development Agency (SFDA) and Marginal Farmers and Agricultural Labourers Development Agency (NIFALD, 1971) were introduced.

The Minimum Needs Programme (MNP) was initiated in the fifth plan and covered Elementary Education, Adult Education, Rural Health,

Rural Water Supply, Rural Electrification, Rural Roads, Housing Assistance to Rural Landless, Environmental Improvement, Nutrition, Rural Domestic Cooking Energy, Rural Sanitation and Public Distribution System. The components thus focussed on human resource development and infrastructure development at the ground level. The NM was also implemented in the sixth and seventh plan with additional financial outlay.

IRDP was a major programme of poverty alleviation and rural development. Integrated rural development was envisaged to help small and marginal farmers, agricultural labourers and rural artisans. The different agencies implementing various programmes like SFDA, DPAP and DDP were merged and District Rural Development Agency (DRDA) was created to function at the district level as a single agency for the implementation of IRDP, DPAP and DDP etc. IRDP focussed on providing assistance to selected families for income generating assets in order to raise their incomes through self-employment, so that they can move above the poverty line. Development of women and children in rural areas (DWCRA) was a component programme under IRDP. Under EMP, the beneficiaries were provided a package of subsidy and credit. The government provided the subsidy element and banking provided the loan credit

In India, women and youth constitute a significant proportion of the population. For these two significant groups, in the year 1979, a national scheme for training rural youth for self-employment (TRYSEM) was launched. The basic objective of TRYSEM was to provide rural youth from poor families with training, so that skills could be imparted to them to become self-employed. They become eligible for financial assistance from IRDP after they complete the training.

The National Rural Employment Programme (NREP) was launched in 1980 with a view to significantly increase employment opportunities in rural areas as a major step towards poverty alleviation. It replaced the Food for Work Programme in 1981. The DRDA was responsible for implementing NREP. The NREP had the salient feature of paying part of the wages in food grains.

In the year 1983, Rural Landless Employment Guarantee Programme (RLEGP) was launched. The objective was to provide guarantee of employment to at-least one member of every landless household up to 100 days in a year. The programme gave preference in employment to the rural landless labourers and among them, preference was given to women, SC and ST. Greater emphasis was given to labour intensive projects - particularly during the lean agricultural seasons. The important components of RLEGP were Indira Aways Yojana (IAY), Social Forestry and Million Well Scheme.

In the year 1989-90, NREP and RLEGP got merged into Jawahar Rozgar Yojana (JRY). The basic objective of the programme was to generate additional gainful employment in rural areas. The secondary objective consists of creating objective community assets, which would benefit the poor section, thus strengthening the rural infrastructure. In JRY, the Pachayati Raj institutions were directly involved in the implementation procedure.

In order to percolate the benefit of IRDP to the women, a special programme - Development of Women and Children in Rural Areas (DWCRA) was launched. The DWCRA Scheme envisages the formation of groups (15-20 women) and starting activities, which are mutually beneficial. It was launched in 1982-83 and was implemented in 106 districts by the end of 1989-90.

At present under the Swarna Jayanti Gram Swarozgar Yojana, Self-help Groups (SHG) are considered as powerful tool of socioeconomic empowerment of the poor in rural areas. The SHG is a small body formed by the people for meeting their specific objectives, particularly credit. It is managed by the rules and regulations formed by them and functions on democratic principles.

In order to achieve the objective of sustainable human development at the village level, the Pradhan Mantri Gramodava Yojana (PMGY) was launched in 2000-2001. This focuses on the creation of social and economic infrastructure with the objective of improving the quality of life of the people living in rural areas. Primary education, primary health, safe drinking water, rural shelter, nutrition and rural electrification are the six components of PMGY.

Challenges Ahead

In spite of all these programmes, our rural areas where about 120 million rural households residing in about 7 lakh villages still remained backward in terms of the various indicators of development A cursory look at these gives a glance to the developmental status of our country in general and the rural areas in particular.

- Rural illiteracy was 40.79 percent, it is 29.82% among males and among females 53.42% at the national level (census 2001)
- 12 Crore people do not have access to safe drinking water (Narayana -2003)
- Out of the total habitations of 1422664, 17917 were not covered, 147791 were partially covered under any source of drinking water (Annual Report of the Ministry of Rural Development, as on 29.1.2002).
- According to 2001 census, 40.82 % of total households in rural areas are I -room houses.
- 61% of houses in rural areas are *katcha* (Census, 2001)
- Even after 50 years of independence, 40 percent villages still lack connection with the nearest road or railway station.
- Over I 00 million Indians go to bed with hungry stomach (1 995).
- 330 million people are categorised under nutritionally sick and needs Government security. 36 % of women are with chronic energy deficiency (NFHS-2).
- 47% of children are under weight (NFHS-2).
- 52 % of women suffer from anaemia.
- Estimated 200 million people in India are exposed to risk of iodine deficiency.
- The number of BPL families eligible for subsidised food grains stands at 6.52 crores.
- Only 1.3 % households use LPG as a fuel for cooking in rural India.
- 30.54 % rural households in villages are electrified as of 1991 census.
- Only 17.5 % of the rural population are accessible to sanitary latrines (NSS, July 1999).
- India has 200 million households out of which. 60 million are below poverty line. Of these 60 million households, 15 millions are described as poorest of the poor by the government. Rural poverty in India stands at 39% (UNDP Human Development Report, 2002).

- 90 % women in forest and tribal belts earn their livelihood by carrying heavy loads on their heads (UNDP Human Development Report, 2002)
- The male-female literacy gap is 21 % as per 2001 census.
- 3 1 % of 6-1 1 age group of children are out of school as per 52 d round NSS Data (2002).
- In the matter of energy consumption, Fuel-wood worth 180 million tonnes per annum is consumed in rural areas.
- Housing shortage between 1997 and 2002 is estimated at 187.70 lakh houses.
- Out of a labour force of 400 million, the government employs 20 million people, 6 million in the public sector. The number of unemployed, including the underemployed, at the commencement of the tenth five year plan was estimated at 35 million, Approximately one third of those who are considered as employed are below poverty line (TOI - 3.6.03).

Suggestions

All in all, the rural development programmes met with partial success, as the objective of all the rural development programmes were more about meeting targets and creating physical infrastructure. Once stated targets are achieved by a project, it was assumed that developmental objectives have been achieved. Actions by developmental agencies were in terms of meeting physical targets. The emphasis was on physical targets or "objects" and not on "people" who are the real "subjects" for whom development was supposed to take place. In the context of development, Max-Neef (1991) writes, "development is about people and not about objects". For improving the quality of life of the people, it needs an understanding of the human needs first. In the changing paradigm human development is emerging as the ultimate objective in terms of gaining sustainable livelihood, actualisation of human needs and community empowerment.

Secondly, all these rural development programmes were never "owned" by the people. One lesson that must be learnt that if people do not "own" a programme meant for them, such a project/programme has a bleak future. In that case it becomes difficult to sustain the development momentum. It is common experience that when a project withdraws the initiated development momentum collapses. This is because, either the project activities were not really the felt needs of the communities involved or the organisational set up responsible to carry foreword the momentum was either weak or non-existent. There fore reaching the social and human capacity building of any future development programme should be the priority rather than reaching ambitious targets.

Thirdly, another significant factor influencing the development process was recognition of the fact that there are multiple perspectives of the primary stakeholders of development, e.g. the local communities who have different views. Appreciating such multiple perspectives is crucial in determining the priorities and preferences of the primary stakeholders, who are generally excluded in the decision making process and whose voices do not get heard in the mainstream "development circuits" and citadels of decision making. Such villages are based on local experience and knowledge and their recognition is a way of not merely informing the development process but also creating legitimate space for their involvement and enhancing their problem solving abilities for future.

Today the benefits of governmental policies and programmes are being questioned and there is rising awareness that the conventional model of development and growth have worked in favour of the rich and powerful. Therefore the need is "Problem based intervention" rather than "solution based thinking". Needless to say, without pragmatic and innovative policy initiatives, the country cannot face the challenges of rural development efficiently and effectively within a foreseeable future.

In order to over come the weaknesses of the rural development programmes, it is necessary to decentralise the developmental process. This will lead to greater participation of the women and also will increase accountability on the part of authorities.

The problem of poverty, illiteracy and poor health among the women are to be given top priority at the grass root level. Illiteracy creates a situation in which problems are perpetuated. The spread of education can enable the rural poor to ensure distributive Justice and help them in actively participating in rural development programmes. Further the economic and social welfare programmes are to be coordinated to eliminate poverty.

The conventional world of social development has been slow in recognising the significance of indigenous knowledge. Experts have been considerably reluctant in appreciating the vast storehouse of indigenous knowledge systems. Local knowledge retrieval and local knowledge management has been a major omission in our conventional pursuit of development goals and activates. This has resulted in local communities appearing as a bundle of problems, rather than as plethora of opportunities. Therefore, we watch the feverish and obsessive doings of the technocrats who design solutions before having identified where the real problems lie.

In terms of financial implications, for rural development, an investment of 8% of the GDP is required on social infrastructure, which in absolute terms, works out to about Rs. 4500 billion over the next five years. The rural water supply, sanitation, nutrition and social safe nets to vulnerable sections require much larger allocation than the other areas and need a priority based approach.

Lastly research and extension is very important ingredient of rural development. Research enables furthering knowledge which is appropriate to rural cultures and extension ensures that the gains are actually delivered to the target groups.

REFERENCES

Abdul Kalam, A.P.J. and Rajan, Y.S., (2002), *India 2020 - A Vision for the New Millennium,* Penguin Books, New Delhi.

Annual Report of Ministry of Rural Development (2002)

Census of India (1991).

Census of India (2001).

ESCAP (1997).

Mukhejee, N., (2002), *Participatory Learning and Action,* Concept Publishing Company, New Delhi.

Narayana, K.S. (2003), Unending Debate on Rural Development Issues, *Kurursheta,* Vol. 51.

NSS Report (1999).

NSS Report (2002).

Tamil, B.M., (2002), People Centered Development Projects Through PRA, *Kurukshetra,* Vol. 50.

UNDP Human Development Report (2002).

INDEX